Daylight Upon Magic

Daylight Upon Magic

The Royal Tour of Canada — 1939

Tom MacDonnell

*To der
One of the Royals!
Tom MacDonnell*

Macmillan of Canada
A Division of Canada Publishing Corporation
Toronto, Ontario, Canada

All inquiries regarding the motion picture or other dramatic rights for this book should be addressed to the author's representative, MGA Agency Inc., 10 St. Mary Street, Suite 510, Toronto, Ontario M4Y 1R1. Representations as to the disposition of these rights are strictly prohibited without express written consent and will be vigourously pursued to the full extent of the law.

Material by James Reaney, F.R. Scott, and A.M. Klein used with permission.

Every attempt has been made to trace the origins of each photograph used in this book. However, in certain cases it has been impossible to identify the photographer. The author apologizes for any omissions, and would be happy to include the names of anyone he has missed in any subsequent edition of the book.

Canadian Cataloguing in Publication Data

MacDonnell, Tom, date.
   Daylight upon magic: the royal tour of Canada, 1939

ISBN 0-7715-9229-9

1. George VI, King of Great Britain, 1895–1952 — Journeys — Canada.   2. Elizabeth, Queen, consort of George VI, King of Great Britain, 1900- — Journeys — Canada.   3. Visits of state — Canada — 1939.°   4. Canada — History — 1918–1939.°
I. Title.

FC223.R6   1939   M33   1989   971.063'2   C89-094830-5
F1034.M33   1989

Cover design by Helen Mah
Cover photo supplied by Canadian Press

Macmillan of Canada
A Division of Canada Publishing Corporation
Toronto, Ontario, Canada

Printed and bound in Canada by
T.H. Best Printing Company Limited

For my parents

Contents

Acknowledgements

In reconstructing the story of the 1939 Royal Visit to Canada, I have drawn upon diaries, letters, newspaper and radio reports, archival documents, and eye-witness accounts. My intention was not to write a detailed history of the events of the tour, but rather to bring it alive as a "collective memoir". It was not just the royal party, nor the officials, nor the politicians who interested me, but the stories of the hundreds of ordinary men and women who worked long hours to make the Royal Visit a success. Just as important were those millions of Canadians across the country who lined up for hours for a glimpse of the King and Queen — and who, fifty years later, can look back on the 1939 visit with fond, and even tearful, recollection.

Like those who planned the original tour, I have found it impossible to include everything. To describe each welcoming ceremony, to mention every regiment, dignitary, and flower girl present would be to smother the essential story in detail. Instead, I have concentrated on the unusual personalities and more novel moments encountered during the tour while trying, like any good Canadian, to do justice to each part of the country.

It is not possible here to thank publicly every person who helped in the completion of the manuscript, since I spoke to, or received letters from, close to four hundred people in the course of writing this book. Some few, however, must be mentioned.

Heather Bell was responsible for the research into French Canada. Victoria Margaret Wilcox provided much of the background to the relationship between Mackenzie King and Lord Tweedsmuir. Charles Higham kindly allowed me the use of his research material on Sean Russell. Miss Loys Readwin, John and Marjorie Plowright, and Cecile Paquette must be thanked for their scrapbooks, without which my task would have been a great deal more difficult. Arden E. Doak sent me the Addie Gilks account of the royal visit to Doaktown, Ed Villiers provided the story of Granny Villiers, and I have Mary Ellen Will to thank for the memoir of her wonderful uncle, Pallie Pascoe.

Hugh Keenleyside and Frank Delaute not only provided invaluable insights into the workings of the Interdepartmental Committee, but their generous hospitality as well. James A. Gibson and Deane Russell supplied much useful information on the tour arrangements. Also extremely helpful were the Hon. Douglas Campbell, Muriel Carter, Jim Coleman, Janet Craig, Jim Eames, Art Holmes, Bruce Hutchison, Major the Hon. F.W. Hyndman, Elizabeth MacDonnell, the Hon. Ernest Manning, and Arthur Irwin.

The staffs of many archives were helpful, including: CBC Radio Archives (Gail Donald, as always, was a joy to work with); Public Records Office at Kew; Library of the University of Southern California; British Columbia Archives; Vancouver Archives; Calgary Archives; Edmonton Archives; Glenbow Institute; Saskatchewan Archives; Regina Archives; RCMP Centennial Museum Archives; Winnipeg Archives; Manitoba Archives; Quebec City Archives; the Canadian Railway Museum; Les Archives Nationales and Nova Scotia Archives.

A very special thanks to the National Archives of Canada, the Canadian Pacific Archives, the Western Canada Pictorial Index and the Metro Reference Library in Toronto for their help.

Linda McKnight and Stan Colbert provided early encouragement for the book from their perspective as publisher and agent.

Finally, the book could not have been completed without the extraordinary work of five individuals: Sue Girvan, Philippa Campsie, and Eleanor Sinclair from Macmillan, my brother Rob MacDonnell, and, of course, my editor, Kath Richards.

Canada is essentially a country of the larger air where man can still face the old primeval forces of Nature and be braced into vigour, and withal so beautiful that it can readily inspire that romantic patriotism which is one of the most priceless assets of a people.

John Buchan (Lord Tweedsmuir)

CHAPTER ONE

Below Quebec City

May 17, 1939:

THE DAY BEGAN IN WARM SUNSHINE and the bustle of last-minute preparations. The ship's company had been up since first light, and members of the royal party, who only hours before had danced to "Lily of Laguna" and watched from the promenade deck as hundreds of welcoming bonfires blazed up along the shoreline, now busied themselves in their cabins with final packing. Already, white-coated stewards were discreetly wrestling their large steamer trunks along the passageways to the outside deck, ready for disembarkation.

At 0815, the captain of the *Empress of Australia* gave the order to hoist the anchor. Two days lost to the fog and icebergs off Cape Race had not improved his temper, and he was counting on a fifteen-minute start to compensate for any fresh disasters that might descend on them in the final twelve miles before they reached the estuary below Quebec City. This sudden, unannounced departure had caught the four navy escort vessels off-guard and Commander Peter Dawnay, still in pyjamas and with his face covered in shaving-soap, was forced to race to the bridge of the cruiser *Glasgow* and hastily direct the warships into formation.

By the time the King emerged from his cabin to take the morning air, the *Empress* was already steaming upriver past the green Île d'Orléans. The heavily wooded coastline of the Gaspé glimpsed from the liner the day before had at last given way to farmland, and the remains of Quebec's old seigneurial system could now be seen in the narrow, cultivated fields that stretched down to the edge of the St. Lawrence, spotted here and there with the last of the winter snow. From where he stood, smoking his pipe at the ship's rail, the King could look across the water to the large stone farmhouses as they glided past him, each one built after the old Norman style and many of them on this particular morning decked out in Union Jacks and the French tricolour.

He hardly suited the popular notion of a king-emperor — sovereign to a quarter of the world's people — about to embark on a royal tour of his largest dominion. Slim and compact, with a look of perpetual weariness around his eyes, George VI possessed neither his late father's air of authority, nor the easy charm that for a time had made his older brother David, now Duke of Windsor, the most popular man in the world. And, in spite of having spent his entire life in the public eye, he remained ill at ease with the crowds that pressed around him. Nervous in temperament, he smoked constantly, and in moments of stress tugged distractedly at his tie. Speaking before large audiences was particularly trying for the King because of the stammer that had afflicted him since he was a child. It was true that with the help of the Australian speech therapist Lionel Logue he had made great strides; but there remained the humiliating memory of those times when he had stood on platforms looking out on a sea of faces, quite literally speechless.

None of this had persuaded the Cabinet back in London that a royal visit to North America by the newly crowned King and Queen would be in anyone's best interest — least of all their own. Preoccupied by the Nazi threat in Europe for which they were now frantically preparing — too little and too late — the ministers had grumbled about the headaches and risks involved. What could be gained, they wondered aloud, from subjecting the King's already fragile health to an exhausting schedule of whistle-stop receptions and tiresome civic luncheons across the length and breadth of Canada?

And what about the Americans? Roosevelt, of course, was as keen as the Canadians to parade the royal couple about, but how would his fellow countrymen, who were profoundly suspicious of British motives on the international scene, react to the sight of the King and Queen of England sweeping through their former colonies, trailing the inevitable memories of how the powerful British Establishment had ruthlessly pushed Wallis Simpson aside just two years before?

For all this, Neville Chamberlain had one answer. It was written in the pink and white telegrams that lay folded in the worn leather boxes of the Foreign Office. Alarming reports, written in the dry and precise style of the British career diplomat, pointing to an increasing ambiguity among Canadians in their attitude towards the Mother Country, and to the prospects of another war. Something had to be done, Chamberlain reasoned, to prevent the Empire's most strategically important dominion from drifting slowly out of Britain's orbit and into isolationism.

The King himself had needed persuading that a royal tour was a good idea at this time. By the spring of 1939, Europe was once again on the brink of war, and he was balking at the idea of leaving the country during such a grave crisis. Convinced finally that his duty lay in carrying on with the tour, he nevertheless refused to travel on the battleship *Repulse*. At a time like this, he had argued, the Royal Navy could not afford to spare one of its capital ships. Nothing anyone could say about the danger of attack by German raiders would change the King's mind. And so on May 6 he and the Queen had sailed from Portsmouth on the Canadian Pacific's *Empress of Australia*, which had been hastily recalled, repainted, and refurbished for their use.

It turned out to be a wise decision. For the past ten days, while the *Empress* had floated between the Old World and the New, the royal couple had largely been hidden away from the public, able to relax in the sort of luxury undreamed of on a spartan warship. Even the delay in the fog and ice of the North Atlantic had been a blessing in disguise, allowing the King extra time to shake off the tensions of Europe. While politicians and public servants on two continents had agonized over every wireless report of foul weather and navigational delays, he had played patience with the Queen and watched Walt Disney cartoons in the ship's cinema. The sea journey had been a tonic to him, refreshing his mind and body, and lifting the weight of the past six months from his shoulders. And now, as they moved along the St. Lawrence shoreline, where crowds were beginning to gather in numbers at the sight of the stately white liner, he fancied he could already feel the difference it made being on this side of the ocean.

It had been twenty-six years since he had first set eyes on this country, as a diffident young middy on the battleship *Cumberland*, too shy even to ask the dazzled and eager young ladies of Montreal society for an informal turn on the dance floor. But the leisurely pace at which the Royal Navy conducted its tours in that era had allowed the then-Prince Albert (or Mr. Johnson, as he was known on board) plenty of time to soak up impressions. He had visited Halifax, and had seen where his grandfather's grandfather had once supervised the building of the Citadel fortifications; had played cricket on Prince Edward Island; had taken in the view at Niagara Falls; and with his shipmates had stared across the Detroit River at the hustle and bustle of America.

Certainly now, in middle age, his understanding of this "country of the larger air" was better than that of others whose class and upbringing were similar to his own — those Englishmen for whom Canada had always sprawled across the globe in the childhood nursery, reassuringly pink and British like so much of the world. Yet, like them, he could hardly escape knowing the familiar stories: Wolfe at Quebec, buckskin-clad fur traders paddling into the vastness of the northern wilderness, Arctic explorers battling for survival on the polar ice-cap. In the pages of the *Boy's Own Paper* they had become indistinguishable from Clive of India, the relief of Mafeking, or Scott of the Antarctic — part of the enduring romance of the Empire. It must have been uppermost in his mind that afternoon in Buckingham Palace two years before when he and the Queen had tiptoed in unannounced to listen as that fraud Archie Belaney instructed the two enthralled Princesses in the secrets of Grey Owl's woodcraft.

The King finished his pipe and took a final look at the green fields that stretched up from the St. Lawrence to the distant blue Laurentides in the north. Around the final bend in the river would be a huge expectant throng, waiting as these people waited now on the river bank, as other crowds would be waiting in cities and villages and raw frontier settlements strung out along the country's railway lines. More military bands, more stiffly held guards of honour, more beaming politicians, more little girls in frilly dresses nervously fingering their bouquets of flowers. He turned and walked back to his cabin. It was time to get ready.

High above the St. Lawrence that same morning in an elegantly appointed suite on the eleventh floor of the Château Frontenac, the Prime Minister of Canada sat reading his Bible and attempting to maintain an air of outward calm in keeping with his position. Inside, however, William Lyon Mackenzie King bubbled. His expectations, his dreams, his anxieties about the day to come tumbled over and over with thoughts of his mother and father, of Sir Wilfrid and Lady Laurier, and even of the late King — George V — who had come to him in spirit form a few months before during one of those private sessions at "the little table", reassuring him about the intentions of his son and much-loved daughter-in-law. "The visit," the old King had told him, and the Prime Minister had marked it in his diary, "is due to their affection for you."

For months he had fretted over every detail of this tour, neglecting the urgent business of the country to concern himself with the seating-plan for the state banquet in Ottawa, the arrangement of flowers at the Montreal reception, and the colour of the King's official blue dispatch cases, which the Prime Minister had insisted be replaced by Canadian — and Liberal—red. He insisted also that, with the King in the country, there could be little need for the King's representative, and so with the somewhat appalled acquiescence of the Foreign Office in London it was agreed that the Prime Minister would accompany the royal couple all across the country, *and* into the United States, while the Governor General, Lord Tweedsmuir, went fishing in the Gaspé.

Now, as Mackenzie King sat in his hotel room, his Bible open to the Acts of the Apostles, his valet Nicol turned from the window to say that the *Empress of Australia* was in sight, steaming around the bend in the river, accompanied by a flotilla of Canadian and British warships. The Prime Minister hurried to the window to look out for a moment on the scene three hundred feet below them, then called for his limousine.

By the time the official welcoming party arrived at the wharf at Wolfe's Cove at 10:15, the *Empress*, attached by hawsers to an armada of tiny tugboats, was being cradled gently into the jetty. The King and Queen could be seen waving from the upper deck, and acknowledging the steady cheers that rose from the thousands in holiday dress who had been lining the walls of the Old City since early morning. Down on the wharf itself, among the brightly coloured hangings and the potted palms, various dignitaries and their wives strove self-consciously to maintain some decorum—as well perhaps as a little distance from the hoi polloi — although the Prime Minister, fancying that the royal couple were waving to him alone, smiled broadly and waved back.

Promptly at 10:30, in the black wool and gold braid of their Windsor uniforms, each of them carrying a cocked hat under his arm, diminutive Mackenzie King and his towering Quebec lieutenant, Ernest Lapointe, marched stiffly up the *Empress*'s gangplank to be ushered formally into the ship's elevator. When the doors opened on A Deck, they stepped out to find the King, dressed in the old-style frock coat of a British Admiral of the Fleet, standing in the doorway of one of the salons. Beside him stood the Queen, soft, pink-complexioned, and smiling.

George VI stepped forward and put out his hand in greeting. The Prime Minister took it in his own and, bowing from the waist, recited the lines he had rehearsed:

"Welcome, sire, to Your Majesty's realm of Canada."

The Queen then came forward, wearing a dress of lavender crêpe de Chine with a silver-fox fur draped elegantly around her shoulders. The Prime Minister took her hand, again bowed, and looked up, drinking in those large blue dazzling eyes.

"Welcome, ma'am, to Canada," he said.

Lapointe was introduced. Then they had a few moments alone, just the four of them, chatting naturally with each other, as if the crowds waiting patiently throughout the city didn't exist, and there were no schedules to be met, no reporters, and no clutch of equerries hovering anxiously outside the room, timing the conversation down to the second on their watches.

The King spoke of the long sea journey. The Queen remarked on the beauty of the St. Lawrence. The Prime Minister said how sorry he was that Their Majesties would not have much opportunity to see Lord and Lady Tweedsmuir during their visit. Then it was time for the photographer to come in and record the moment, before the two Canadians returned to their places at dockside for the formal welcoming ceremonies. For a few minutes longer everyone on the wharf stood quietly, as if holding their breath until the curtain went up. The CBC commentator spoke in hushed tones. "The first gun will sound," he told his world-wide audience of millions, "as His Majesty's foot first touches Canadian soil . . . or not Canadian soil here, although the symbolism will be there. It will be red-carpeted cement." Flustered now, he struggled to recover himself: "But still, it's *immobile* — and it's *Canada!*"

There was a shrill fanfare of trumpets as the King, now wearing his cocked hat, appeared at the top of the huge liner's gangplank. The men of the Royal 22nd, in brilliant red jackets and tall black bearskins, snapped to attention. Then, His Most Gracious Majesty George VI, by the Grace of God, of Great Britain, Ireland and the British Dominions beyond the Seas, King, Defender of the Faith, Emperor of India, stepped ashore. High overhead, thousands of Quebecers clung to the parapets of the Citadel and cheered, and twenty-one cannons from the old French garrison began to boom out a royal salute across the water.

The sound of the guns and the cheering carried up through the city streets, which were lined along the royal route with Girl Guides, Boy Scouts, Papal Zouaves, and the various Catholic brigades. And, pressed up behind them, the hundreds of thousands who had stood for hours for a glimpse of the royal couple, and who now stirred in anticipation. Church bells all over the city — and all over the country — began to ring out as the radio commentators at dockside reported that the long-awaited royal tour had begun.

The moment was captured forever by the newsreel cameras which showed the Prime Minister at the foot of the gangplank, bowing from the waist, his face split in a wide grin of delight. The Queen followed her husband down the yellow runway, then paused at the last step. Glancing over to Mackenzie King, she gave him a quick, conspiratorial smile before carefully placing her foot down.

"Canadian soil," she said.

CHAPTER TWO

Preparations

"WHEN I INDUCED THEIR MAJESTIES to come out here," wrote
Lord Tweedsmuir, "I didn't realize I was pulling the string of
such a shower-bath." Even from the first days, it was apparent
that the visit of King George VI and Queen Elizabeth in the
late spring of 1939 was an event like no other in Canadian
history. Everywhere the royal couple travelled throughout the
nine provinces of the Dominion the population seemed galva-
nized by their presence, momentary and fleeting as it was.

> When the King and the Queen came to Stratford
> Everyone felt at once
> How heavy the Crown must be.
> The Mayor shook hands with their Majesties
> And everyone presentable was presented
> And those who weren't have resented
> It, and will
> To their dying day.

Starting from Quebec City, the King and Queen and their
entourage criss-crossed the continent: over the prairies to Vancouver Island; back again through southwestern Ontario; then
four memorable days in the United States; up into the Mari-
times; and, finally, after a brief visit to Newfoundland, home
to England. At each stop, the crowds seemed to grow larger
and more enthusiastic, bemused by the strange sight of royalty
waving and smiling in their midst. The mounted dragoons, the
vivid uniforms, shiny helmets, sabres, kilts, feathers, shakos,
and other remnants of an imperial age, were part of the show
— and all of it set down in a dazzled country still out at the
elbows after a decade of hard times.

Everyone had almost a religious experience
When the King and Queen came to visit us
(I wonder what *they* felt!)
And hydrants flowed water in the gutters
All day.
People put quarters on the railroad tracks
So as to get squashed by the Royal Train

For spectacle, it could not compare with the Durbar of 1911 when George V and Queen Mary had been crowned Emperor and Empress of India. There the elaborate ceremonies in which 20,000 brilliantly attired troops paraded before them so affected the King that the Durbar became a formative experience of his reign. But the flavour of a still-powerful Empire clung also to the Canadian tour, whenever Indian tribes raised banners in greeting to the Great White Father, or frail old men, survivors of the Zulu Wars and the Fenian Raids, stepped forward to shake the new King's hand. And, in its own way, the 1939 visit provided an experience for George VI that was similar to his father's — although the lesson he derived was very different. Removed for a time from the stiffness of the decorum-laden London court, he came home with his own sense of the kind of king he wanted to be.

Canadians too discovered who they were in 1939 — what they stood for and where their loyalties lay — whatever the Statute of Westminster might say. For them the royal tour, although bathed in sentiment, was not a backward tug to colonial days. It confirmed their membership in what they fervently believed to be a progressive and forward-looking Empire; it pulled them together (as the Prime Minister hoped it would), and made them prouder than ever to be Canadians. They shared the journey with the King and Queen. Everyone on the royal route could tell a story, not just about the brief moment when the royal limousine came into view, but about how they had travelled down to the city in dusty old colonist cars, stood in crowds for hours, and afterwards laid pennies on the track. Those who didn't see the King and Queen could follow the tour on the radio, in the newspapers, and in the movie newsreels. War-scare stories were driven off the front page as reporters with cheerful irrelevance wrote accounts of the Queen's wardrobe, weeping veterans, orphan flower girls, and the controversy over hot dogs — until eventually they ran out of ways to convey the size of the crowds, the acres of patriotic bunting, and the unaccountable emotion that brimmed about them. "How in hell am I going to write about this?" complained one newsman midway through the tour. "Even if I tell my readers, they won't believe it."

For the tour's chief architect, the lonely bachelor who ran the country, and fussed over every detail of the royal itinerary, it was a journey which, like the rest of his life, was full of signs, omens, dreams, and mystical visitations.

> But although we didn't see them in any way
> (I didn't even catch the glimpse
> The teacher who was taller did
> Of a gracious pink figure)
> I'll remember it to my dying day.

Whatever the Governor General believed, Mackenzie King gave himself the credit for having "induced" Their Majesties to visit Canada. In London to attend the 1937 Coronation, he brushed aside a discreet hint from the King's Secretary and raised the matter directly with the King and Queen at Buckingham Palace. That he got a favourable, if tentative, response was due in part to months of careful groundwork by Canada's High Commissioner. Vincent Massey had adroitly linked the idea of a royal tour with Canada's new status within the Commonwealth, and to the fact that for the first time the monarch would be crowned "King of Canada".

There it had to rest for a time. George VI was too busy coming to terms with kingship to think immediately about overseas visits. It had been barely six months since his elder brother David had made the famous Abdication broadcast, and then swanned off to France to marry Wallis Simpson, leaving behind — or so the new King believed — a monarchy in crisis. And while George set about restoring confidence in the institution, the news abroad was causing war jitters. In those years, Europe lurched from crisis to crisis, and no British prime minister would countenance a tour of the Dominions while the country remained on the brink.

In 1938, Mackenzie King had his own problems to worry about. Canada was still pulling itself painfully out of severe economic depression, the drought continued on the prairies, and the Prime Minister had his hands full with bitter arguments over defence and foreign policy. Mackenzie King was exhausted and preoccupied; the British seemed mesmerized by the dictators; and it was up to the Governor General to keep the idea alive on both sides of the Atlantic.

By the late summer of 1938, the international situation had at last improved sufficiently for Downing Street to give approval to a royal tour. By September, however, Britain and France were again teetering on the edge of war with Germany — this time over Czechoslovakia — and trenches were being dug in Hyde Park. Stepping onto an aeroplane with a basket of fresh fruit for the Führer, Neville Chamberlain flew to Munich and signed the agreement that finally promised a measure of stability in Europe. With the relaxing of tensions, there came a short announcement from Balmoral Castle on the evening of October 8, 1938:

> The King and Queen have graciously consented to accept the suggestion of the Prime Minister of Canada that they should visit Canada next year. Their Majesties hope to arrive early in the summer and to spend about three weeks in the Dominion.

"First time in history that a British Sovereign has been in North America," exulted Mackenzie King, his proper royalist joy ("real delight") mixed with personal satisfaction ("should help to further a sense of unity between all parts of the Dominion") and a political aside ("this adds much to the history of the Liberal Party"). It would of course mean a busy year. Tweedsmuir, triumphant as well, was able to fill him in on what was being said at the Palace. It was really no different from when the Prime Minister first raised the matter himself at the Coronation: the King and Queen had been eager, the Palace officials inclined to see difficulties.

What was certain, though unofficial, at this point was that the tour would also include a short visit to the United States. In early August of 1938, Mackenzie King and Franklin Roosevelt had shared a limousine on their way to open the new international bridge at Ivy Lea, and the Canadian prime minister had told Roosevelt about the plan for Their Majesties to come to Canada the following year. The President immediately wrote in his own hand to the King, inviting the royal couple to make an informal visit to the United States:

> I need not assure you that it would give my wife and me the greatest pleasure to see you, and frankly I think it would be an excellent thing for Anglo-American relations if you could visit the United States.

Like his good friend Mackenzie King, Roosevelt was a self-proclaimed democrat with a fascination for titled Europeans. His idea was that it would be a sort of *personal* visit to the Roosevelt clan; "if you bring either or both of the children with you," he wrote, "I shall try to have one or two Roosevelts of approximately the same age to play with them." It would be a holiday away from the more formal duties in Canada:

> You and I are fully aware of the demands of the Protocol people, but, having had much experience with them, I am inclined to think that you and Her Majesty should do very much as you personally want to do — and I will see to it over here that your decision becomes the right decision.

As the President explained it to Tweedsmuir, "The American people admire the essential democracy of the King and Queen, and it would help if the formal 'functions' could be supplemented by a peaceful and simple American country home" — by which he meant Hyde Park, the Roosevelts' substantial estate on the Hudson River. Among the President's most cherished notions was that he was at heart no more than an ordinary farmer from upstate New York.

There was no question which part of the North American trip excited the British most, once the news had been made public. From his vantage point in the House of Lords, the Earl of Crawford put it as kindly as he could. "The reference in the King's speech to Canada was well received," he wrote his friend Tweedsmuir, "though the sojourn in the United States touched a more novel note, and has struck popular imagination." At the same time, the British Ambassador in Washington, Sir Ronald Lindsay, was reporting that the President was extremely keen that the royal couple were coming, and could shrug off any criticism that the visit was too much of a family affair. The Foreign Office on the other hand *was* concerned that the Roosevelts might keep the King and Queen to themselves, and risk offending the American people — and, even more important, the power-brokers in the U.S. Congress. Something had to be done to make sure this part of the journey was given the proper profile to satisfy both the public and the politicians. Still, Lindsay remained buoyant at the prospect; Washington was "an unusually beautiful town", and the President himself "was in a spirit of such boyish enthusiasm" that already "he was zealously working out the last details as to train and boat journeys."

Canadians for their part would be just as happy to see Their Majesties' visit to the United States kept to a modest level. Vincent Massey was one who pointed out to Lord Tweedsmuir (as for many others, a readier ear than the Prime Minister's) the folly of allowing the American side-trip to turn into a major show. This would overshadow Canada almost entirely in the minds of British officials and the world press — particularly if the royal party suddenly swelled with British advisers as it crossed the border. It was clear that Canadian officials were going to have to keep a careful eye on how the Royal Visit was planned.

This was already being done by the Prime Minister. Even before the official announcement was made, Mackenzie King had moved to set up two committees to oversee the arrangements. The first, which he would preside over himself, was made up of Cabinet members such as Ernest Lapointe, Thomas Crerar, Charles Dunning, Fernand Rinfret, and Ian Mackenzie, and would deal with the broader questions of policy. The actual working out of the details would be left to a second committee, chaired by the steady, reliable Under-Secretary of State, Eph Coleman. This group, to be known as the Interdepartmental Committee, would include O. D. Skelton from External Affairs, as well as the deputy ministers of Transport, National Defence, and Public Works, and Commissioner Stuart Wood from the RCMP. The Governor General's Secretary, Shuldham Redfern, would act as a liaison to both committees. The pivotal job of Secretary of the Interdepartmental Committee would go to one of External's rising stars, Hugh Keenleyside (interrupted at home while making hollandaise sauce by a confidential call from Mackenzie King, offering him the job), who would also act as the Prime Minister's liaison. Backing Keenleyside would be two experienced and resourceful men from the Secretary of State's Office, Howard Measures and Frank Delaute, who would act as Associate Secretaries.

A small army of public servants was available to assist this second committee in the mind-boggling number of details that had to be worked out. And of course Mackenzie King could be depended upon to keep an eye on matters that would range from court etiquette to the familiar politics of the parish pump. Politics was how Lord Tweedsmuir chiefly saw the arrangement. A tour of only four weeks in a country this size could not hope to please everybody:

> There will be a great deal of unpopularity for somebody and I want to see that it does not fall either on Government House or the Prime Minister. So we are having a big committee of Deputy Ministers who will not do any work but who will be nominally responsible and the target for criticism.

Tweedsmuir could not have been more wrong. In fact, it was the Cabinet Committee, once formed, that was never heard from again. Possibly because Mackenzie King insisted on making every major decision (and a great many minor ones) about the tour himself. It was the Interdepartmental Committee, on the other hand, that got down to work on the details — and it was Eph Coleman's ability as chairman to get all the government departments pulling together that got the job done.

What set the 1939 royal tour apart, of course, was its symbolic and constitutional significance: it was the first time a reigning British monarch had set foot in North America. But Canada was no stranger to royalty. Even as the Interdepartmental Committee sat down to its first meeting in November 1938, its members were no doubt aware that, while there were few valuable precedents to guide them, the country at least had substantial experience of the virtues and vices that British royalty embraced.

There had been no problems of ceremony for the first royal visitor. Prince William Henry, the third son of George III, had despised royal etiquette. He first arrived in Halifax in 1786, while serving with the Royal Navy. A bluff and hearty man, he indulged in heavy drinking, brothel-creeping on Water Street, and balls where he took to the floor with every pretty woman, often dancing into the small hours of the morning. Next to come was his younger brother, Prince Edward Augustus (later known as the Duke of Kent), who was preceded by a very different reputation. An army officer, he had become so cruel in his treatment of his soldiers in Europe that in 1791 "owing to his unpopularity he was sent to Canada." He commanded the 7th Regiment at Quebec, where he lived with his mistress, Alphonsine Thérèse Bernardine Julie de Montgenet de St. Laurent. During his years at the garrison, Prince Edward enjoyed an unusual rapport with the French population, though he continued flogging his soldiers with enthusiasm. He did apparently have his moments of princely grace, however. One enduring story tells how, on the Île d'Orléans, he granted the request of a woman of one hundred to dance a short minuet with her. Later, when he took command of the forces in Halifax, he supervised the building of the Citadel walls. In 1800 the Duke of Kent returned to England to marry, and in 1819 he became the father of Princess Victoria. In his honour, Île St. Jean was renamed Prince Edward Island.

Both of these sojourns were, of course, tours of duty rather than grand tours. The first authentic royal visit would have to wait until 1860, when Victoria's son, Albert Edward, Prince of Wales (later Edward VII), made his way through the colonies from Newfoundland to Lower Canada before paying a call on the United States. While in Halifax, he poked about the ruins of the estate near Bedford once owned by his grandfather, and sent his mother back a piece of sweetbrier he found there. In Quebec, he drove in the last spike of the spectacular Victoria tubular bridge, which connected Longueuil and Montreal.

Of course, the presence of the nineteen-year-old heir apparent to the British throne attracted tremendous public attention and a number of eulogies — most of them more respectful than the one composed by the American writer R. J. de Cordova:

And as for the Canadas! Loyalty's run
into madness almost for VICTORIA's son.

They had dined him, and wined him, in manner most royal,
Addressed and harangued him to prove they were loyal.
They have bored him in parks, and they've bored him in halls
Danced him almost to death in no end of balls.

The 1860 tour had features familiar to all royal visits, whatever their era. Among these were the elaborate preparations.
The young Prince Albert travelled much of the time by wood-
burning locomotive, in a car built especially for him. For his
benefit, special rafts loaded with giant Bengal lights illuminated
Niagara Falls. Here he joined the crowds to watch the great
French daredevil Charles Blondin walk above the chasm on a
tightrope (and had to be restrained from accepting Blondin's
offer to repeat the trick with the fun-loving Prince in a wheel-
barrow). While still in the Niagara Peninsula, he met Laura
Secord, and chatted with veterans of the War of 1812. In
Ottawa, he laid the cornerstone for the new Parliament Buildings, and in Toronto he planted trees in Allan Gardens. The
tour was a remarkable success. Prince Albert was mobbed by
the enthusiastic citizenry everywhere and showered with so
many gifts that when he returned home his luggage was
crammed with mounted moose heads, stuffed birds, and home-
made preserves.

In short, they have followed him, hustled and shoved him.
To convince him more fully how dearly they loved him.

The great highlight of the 1860 visit was a grand ball held
for the Prince of Wales in Montreal. A huge pavilion had been
built especially for the occasion between Ste. Catherine and
Sherbrooke streets and was lit by thousands of gas lamps. Jets
of lavender water and eau de cologne perfumed the air of the
dance floor, which held 6,000 perspiring revellers. And to
refresh them as they stopped to catch their breath, spectacular
fountains of champagne, claret cup, and lemonade were provided. The Prince of Wales, whether out of enthusiasm or a
sense of obligation for the extravagant preparations, danced
until 4:30 in the morning.

How he looked when he danced — when he sat at his ease —
When His Highness had sneezed, or was going to sneeze;
Whether he smiled, or whether he laughed;

All recorded, and morning and night telegraphed,
To the end that New York might reliably know
What his dear little Princeship had done or would do
Till, at length, when routine had most thoroughly tired him,
It struck him that Canada no longer required him.

After that, the country received a fairly steady stream of royal visitors, encouraged by Victoria to visit the far corners of her Empire. Princess Alberta Louise was one, coming out with her husband, the Marquis of Lorne, when he was appointed governor general in 1878. She was still living on in London at the age of ninety-two with her memories of the tobogganing, snowshoeing, and skating parties she had hosted at Rideau Hall.

In 1901, the first really elaborate royal tour since the visit of Prince Albert was taken by the Duke and Duchess of Cornwall and York, who travelled from coast to coast on a specially built CPR train ("a stately pageant, a royal progress the likes of which Caesar had never dreamed"). The future George V watched a lacrosse match, received a special silver telephone from Professor Melville Bell (father of the inventor), went duck-hunting in Manitoba, and caught a bad cold reviewing troops on the Plains of Abraham. Everything was done to make the royal couple's visit a successful one; even the Duchess's polite enthusiasm for the fruit of the Niagara Peninsula was enough to send farmers out by lamplight to provide figs and other delicacies for the breakfast table. In many ways it resembled a modern royal visit, down to the little common touches — like lunching on pea soup and pork and beans at a lumber camp in the Ottawa Valley. But as well there was the presence of the hateful press — correspondents and newspaper artists from Britain and the United States who dogged the royal steps as they had those of the Prince of Wales forty-five years before.

More attuned to the modern world and the demands of tour publicity was their son, Edward (or David, as he was known in the family). The handsome Prince of Wales made his first visit to Canada in 1919 during a marathon tour of the Empire, and immediately received a rapturous welcome. Still possessing the charm and radiance of youth, he captivated the country as he had the rest of the world. He gave hundreds of speeches, met thousands of people (severely laming both hands in the process), and was almost pulled from his horse by hysterical crowds during Warriors' Day at the CNE. There were more visits to the Dominion, including unofficial ones when he stayed at his ranch near High River, Alberta. But even when the Prince of Wales's high jinks began to resemble rudeness (particularly on a visit with Prince George), his admirers seemed willing to forgive him anything. "Such puckish pranks!" exclaimed the Ottawa writer Madge Macbeth fondly, as if recalling a young boy's scrapes, instead of the rather sad immaturity of a grown man who would soon become (for a short time) Edward VIII:

> The popular young Prince refused to dance with stuffy dow-agers who had been promised that honour; ignored the hour set for official dinners; and hid from his distracted aides in the homes of friends whose parties he enjoyed, when he should have been boring himself at functions designed to cement the bonds of Empire. Worse! He waved gaily to several friends in the crowd during the solemn ceremony of unveiling Sir Wil-frid Laurier's statue on Parliament Hill.

Edward's younger brother — and successor — Bertie would cause no such problems to the Interdepartmental Committee. Dutiful and shy, George VI would never be found dancing to jazz records with notorious women; he would not have the experience (as Edward did) of having one of his ménage seen running from a bawdy-house without trousers; and there was no likelihood at all of his attempting a tightrope walk across the Niagara River. Yet none of these previous royal tours, however elaborate their preparations, presented anything like the worries of the 1939 visit to North America. This was the head of the world's greatest empire who was coming to call; princely peccadillos were nothing compared to the problems encountered when real power and status were at stake. The general clamour over tour arrangements, the question of who would escort the King here, who would be invited there, who would liaise with whom — all masked the essential question, *who was really running the show?* A difficult problem even at the best of times, but not helpful when there were one sovereign, two kingdoms, three countries, and four political systems involved (counting the creaky imperial one), as well as a number of personality differences, most of which centred on the Canadian prime minister, Mackenzie King.

A blizzard of telegrams, memoranda, confidential letters, and anguished conversations flowed between the Dominions Office, the Foreign Office, Buckingham Palace, External Affairs, Government House, the American Embassy, the State Department, and the British High Commission. It was like a minuet, adapted for multiple partners and then set to square-dance music. The prospect of people getting their toes stepped on was a virtual certainty. Emotions reached a climax a scarce few weeks before the tour began when, "following another and violent outburst" from Mackenzie King, Shuldham Redfern wrote to the Palace to pass on the Governor General's warning that, unless concessions were made, "in his present mood Prime Minister might cause unpleasantness for His Majesty and ultimate consequences might be serious. . . . "

What had brought Mackenzie King to this state? Partly the exasperation of dealing with men in London too obtuse to understand the nuances of Canada's place in the Anglo-American world. Partly it was the vanity of a prime minister who saw the Royal Visit as a chance to promote national unity and, though he would scarcely admit it, saw himself as indispensable to its glory. London underestimated him. They would learn what Mackenzie King's Cabinet colleagues knew only too well: that under the conventional, even cloying, manner of this fussy old bachelor was a ruthlessness from which flowed all his success as a party politician. The first obstacle to his single-minded purpose was the office of the Governor General.

Lord Tweedsmuir and Mackenzie King presented an interesting contrast of character. Both were self-made men. The Prime Minister had performed impressively in many worlds: the university, business (where he had been a highly valued friend and adviser to the Rockefellers), the civil service (the youngest deputy minister of his time), and finally politics, where his talents and understanding of how this complicated country worked would make him the dominant political figure of the century. At sixty-four, he remained unmarried (though with many women friends), showed a strong sentimental streak (particularly where dogs were concerned) and a consciousness of his place in history (grandson of "the Little Rebel", William Lyon Mackenzie), and had a fascination with the spirit world (especially for the connection it provided with his much-loved mother). Tweedsmuir, on the other hand, a Presbyterian minister's son from Scotland, was best known to the world as John Buchan, author of *The Thirty-Nine Steps* and other thrillers. His route up the ladder had included Oxford, law, and the House of Commons; though in all this he had concealed his considerable talent and ambition behind a throw-away aristocratic manner. The pose was convincing; and it became the real thing in 1935 when he was created first Baron Tweedsmuir.

This was also the year he was appointed Governor General of Canada, and began an uneasy professional relationship with his old friend Mackenzie King. Even the physical contrast between the two was striking: Tweedsmuir, a small, spare man, "neat as a pin", with thin lips, a high forehead, and an engaging manner; the Prime Minister, short, pudgy, slightly dishevelled, emotional in manner, and largely unloved among his electorate (unlike Tweedsmuir, who had become very popular in his travels throughout the Dominion). As Shuldham Redfern was to write many years later, what they had in common, "a simple Puritan background and mutual admiration for each other's intellectual capacity", counted for little when compared to their differences:

> Tweedsmuir, for instance, could never reconcile himself to King's flabby sentimentality, his belief in predestination and the mystical influences of an occult world. Tweedsmuir's lucid and antiseptic expression of the English language was in sharp contrast to King's verbose and cliché-ridden exposition of both the written and spoken word.

Given Mackenzie King's temperament, and his deep suspicion of viceroys in particular, it was inevitable that there would be a clash over the preparations for the Royal Visit. The planning had begun well. When the tour was announced in October 1938, the Prime Minister had hurried almost immediately to Rideau Hall for advice, and Tweedsmuir had been happy to provide it. He spoke, and Mackenzie King wrote his words down, as if taking dictation (later using the Governor General's thoughts almost verbatim as a broad outline for the tour's organization). But one vexing question remained between the two men. Who would meet the King and Queen as they stepped ashore in Quebec City—the King's representative, or his First Minister?

Tweedsmuir had raised the matter at the very beginning, suggesting lightly that the honour might fall to himself. Mackenzie King, however much he needed the Governor General's advice on other points, was immediately clear on this matter: he, along with the Dominion Cabinet, would be welcoming Their Majesties next spring when their ship docked at Quebec. There was no firm precedent, but constitutionally he seemed to be on good ground: Tweedsmuir as viceroy had no ceremonial or legal purpose when the King was in the country. For the duration of the royal tour, "the Governor-General withdraws," as Sir Robert Falconer later wrote: "he is functionless; even the brilliant star of the morning fades as the sun rises."

Back in London, the King's Secretary, Alexander Hardinge, saw things differently. As the King's man, the Governor General should be the first to meet the King and Queen. But, as Mackenzie King was quick to point out, that would make it appear that "all Canadians including the Prime Minister are not so much subjects of His Majesty the King as subjects of the Governor General," something that would be seen — always a particular sticking-point with the Liberal leader—as "a reversal to colonial status".

Mackenzie King understood the importance of the precedent that would be set in Quebec City. Although the Statute of Westminster, enacted in 1931, had established Canada once and for all as a self-governing Dominion of the British Commonwealth, that autonomy had yet to be demonstrated in any tangible way. Here then was the perfect symbolic moment. When George VI stepped ashore, it would be as the King of Canada, and he should be greeted not by his ceremonial stand-in, but by his principal advisers. Hardinge's intransigence in the matter only provoked the Canadian prime minister and proved to him that the King was surrounded by people utterly lacking in any understanding of how the Empire had evolved.

Of course, for Mackenzie King, being right wasn't enough. He must evoke once more the memory of his rebel grandfather and his ever-present sense of self-righteousness:

> I feel that through Destiny it has been given to me to round out at the end of one hundred years, the struggle not only for self-Government and responsible Government but for national sovereignty in Canada for which my grandfather stood, fought, and eventually died suffering imprisonment and exile. It is the way in which God vindicates the right in the end.

The Prime Minister's view of things seemed to suit the amiable Tweedsmuir, who had acquiesced immediately, turning to his secretary, Redfern, and saying, "as soon as the King sets foot on Canadian soil, you and I are out of business." He even confided to his friend the Earl of Crawford back in England that he hoped to get away for a month of fishing while the King and Queen were in the country. Despite his own healthy self-regard, and the great hopes he held for the royal tour, the Governor General did not feel driven to be in the public eye at such a moment. This, however, did not save him from getting into hot water with the Prime Minister when, early in December, he happened to let drop the fact that he had cabled Buckingham Palace about the matter. This, in Mackenzie King's mind, was clearly disloyal, the act of a man who had ignored the advice of his First Minister. Reasoned constitutional arguments went out the window, leaving only galloping paranoia and prissy self-justification:

> I have felt all along that he was itching to be in the foreground on the arrival of the King. I have had no such desire, but I have had, before me, the position of Canada as a nation. . . . I can see, however, his own ambition. . . . What a pity it is that men with such fine natures and capacities such as he should be caring a continental for personal prominence.

In Mackenzie King's over-heated imagination, the issue now approached the seriousness of a constitutional crisis, a fact he made clear to the Governor General during their meeting on December 5. Poor Tweedsmuir. He had enough troubles on his plate. The Foreign Office was still bristling over the idea that he had tried to arrange the American tour with Roosevelt on his own — a suspicion which caused the phlegmatic British High Commissioner in Ottawa, Sir Gerald Campbell, to forget himself for a moment and admit he "was slightly perturbed", and, as he thought about it, "more than slightly perturbed". Buckingham Palace had managed to smooth the matter out with the Foreign Office, conveying on the one hand that it was not true (though not quite categorically denied) that Tweedsmuir had overstepped his office, while suggesting by its tone that the Governor General may just have had his wrists lightly slapped for any indiscretion (certainly never confirmed). And now Tweedsmuir was hemmed in on the one side by those same Palace officials, who were determined he should be the one to welcome Their Majesties, and on the other by a dangerously aroused prime minister, who on a cold winter afternoon in Ottawa was insisting on reading aloud to him from speeches on the King/Byng Affair. The G.G. must have wished he was anywhere else. Fishing perhaps.

Eventually, by agreeing repeatedly with what Mackenzie King had to say about the issue, he convinced him of his own good faith. His Excellency had long since learned that the way to get along with the Prime Minister was never to disagree with him. Mackenzie King's suspicions were finally put to rest (although he noted somewhat severely in his diary, "Tweedsmuir has still to see the real significance of the relations of the Crown with its people. Something he should have been the first to see"). The real enemies were obviously the King's advisers — principally Hardinge and his assistant, Alan Lascelles. Before settling accounts with them, however, Mackenzie King became embroiled in a second, even greater, battle over tour arrangements — a battle in which Hardinge and Lascelles also played a part.

The question of who if anyone should accompany the King to the United States as Minister in Attendance was a complicated one. After talking with the Americans, Whitehall had reluctantly agreed that it would be a mistake for the British Foreign Secretary, Lord Halifax, to be seen in Washington at the King's side. American public opinion, strongly isolationist, would be inflamed by any suggestion that the British were using a "friendly visit" to twist arms, and involve the United States in another European war. Everything Roosevelt had accomplished in the past few years to nudge the United States into line against the European fascists could be undone in a matter of hours. Having accepted this, the British went further, arguing that if Lord Halifax was to stay home, then Mackenzie King should not go either; "the presence of any Minister, even a Canadian one would be enough to lend colour to this argument," according to E. J. Harding, the Dominions Secretary.

Harding's view, expressed confidentially to Tweedsmuir, that the Americans might somehow view Mackenzie King as part of an imperial war conspiracy was laughable. It sounded more like sour grapes than anything. But it reflected increasing British irritation with the way the Canadians resisted every attempt to tamper with the tour. However many offices were involved in the various discussions concerning the Royal Visit, it was clear now that both sides saw the matter as a straightforward clash between British and Canadian points of view — with the Scots Governor General coming down in support of his adopted country. When for example the British attempted to rework the tour itinerary to add a stop in Chicago, the proposal was firmly resisted. "Can't see why the Canadians should take upon themselves to oppose a visit to the middle west," one of the panjandrums had scrawled in the margin of a Foreign Office paper. To which someone had scrawled peevishly in reply, "The Canadians are jealous of every hour spent outside their not very interesting country." Into this strained atmosphere dropped Tommy Lascelles like an exploding firecracker.

The King's Assistant Private Secretary, Alan Lascelles (known to everyone as Tommy), arrived in Ottawa at the end of February to meet with the Interdepartmental Committee about the tour preparations, before continuing on to Washington for similar talks with the Americans. A lover of Wagner, Lascelles would have appreciated the operatic storm that broke about him and continued after he was gone. Dining one evening with Mackenzie King in the gloom of Laurier House, he steered the conversation in what he must have supposed was a tactful way to the Prime Minister's role during the tour. They chatted easily about the issue of who should meet Their Majesties at Quebec and accompany them to Washington, and Lascelles once again presented the "Palace" point of view: the difficulties, the strong feeling expressed by the U.S. State Department against *any* minister joining the royal entourage. He was smoothly solicitous about the Prime Minister's health, mentioning how his friends in London had expressed concern that he might be over-taxing himself in trying to accompany the King and Queen all the way across Canada.

"Another Court manoeuvre to euchre me out of this obvious duty," reflected Mackenzie King as he smiled and sparred gently with Lascelles that evening. The tone was amiable, but he believed he could detect the influence of Hardinge, the King's Private Secretary, behind what was being said to him:

> They both made up their minds to reduce my part to as small a one as possible:
> 1. Did not want me to be the first to meet the King and Queen at Quebec;
> 2. Did not wish me to accompany them through my own country;
> 3. Did not wish me to appear with the King and Queen in the United States.

"They will be beaten in all three," he prophesied grimly, "much to the advantage of the King and Queen and British connections."

If one moment could be pinpointed during the dinner at the Prime Minister's residence when the entire rickety structure of Anglo-Canadian relationships collapsed in a shambles, it was in Lascelles' casual remark about the Governor General handing over "his charge" to the King at Quebec City. The comment appalled Mackenzie King. Why didn't he just call the country a "colony" and be done with it? he demanded of Tweedsmuir when they met to discuss Lascelles' visit.

The remark seemed uncharacteristic of Lascelles. He knew Canada well, having travelled across the country with the Prince of Wales during the twenties (when "Fruity" Metcalfe had escaped trouserless from the Winnipeg bawdy-house), and had served as Secretary to the Governor General, Lord Bessborough, from 1931 to 1935. He even provided Bessborough's successor, Lord Tweedsmuir, with a witty and insightful essay on the country. Very tall and spare, and looking younger than his fifty-one years, Tommy Lascelles had made a great many

friends in Ottawa, as he did everywhere he went. It was clear
that he was fond of Canadians, and touched by their devotion
to the Crown:

> They sing "God Save the King" as if it really was a prayer,
> and with their whole hearts in it. Their devotion to the British
> throne is entirely genuine, and almost an article of faith. It
> makes one feel . . . that there must be something worth work-
> ing for in an institution which stirs a fine people so deeply.
> For they *are* a very fine people. . . .

If Lascelles gave offence at all, it would be because of his
unbending code of ethics, or his candour, not his tactlessness,
or his ignorance of Canada. Even Mackenzie King had found
him a "very easy and pleasant" dinner companion; it was only
later, when he went over their conversation in his mind, that it
occurred to the Prime Minister that he had been insulted. He
rushed to Government House to relate this latest outrage to
Tweedsmuir, who (probably from long practice) nodded,
frowned, and clucked in horror at appropriate moments.

Thoroughly aroused now, Mackenzie King was more determined than ever to get his own way in all things — not for
himself, of course, but because of his sense of duty:

> There might be riots. There might be anything. If I had
> allowed the King and Queen to travel without my being there
> to protect them, the country would never forgive me.

But what rankled him most of all was the campaign to prevent his going to Washington, and in his mind the circle of
conspirators now widened to include the British Ambassador,
Sir Ronald Lindsay. It was intolerable, he told Tweedsmuir,
that "the King should cast him aside at the frontier like an old
boot."

His Excellency listened to it all, laying his hand on the Prime
Minister's shoulder from time to time in sympathy. Tweedsmuir
himself had not been well. The strain of the preparations and
the increasing acrimony surrounding the tour had begun to tell
on his health and alarm his friends, "his health being so closely
connected to the sensitive balance of his mind," as Redfern put
it. Aware of this, the Prime Minister ended their conversation
by telling Tweedsmuir how much he appreciated his support,

remembering what Redfern had said: that a few words of encouragement would "do more good at present than the attention of the most skilled physicians."

In spite of his anger, the meeting had been a satisfactory one. The Prime Minister knew what he was doing, knew as he returned to Laurier House that evening that what he had said would — and did — get quickly back to Lascelles, Lindsay, Hardinge, and the Foreign Office. He had some reason for grim satisfaction as he climbed into his bed that night:

> I venture to say that Mr. Lascelles will do a little squirming tonight, and will have a few troubled hours, and that Lindsay will think twice before he butts in again.

The British were bewildered. The Prime Minister clearly "had gone off the deep end" as far as London was concerned. Sir Gerald Campbell, the U.K.'s High Commissioner, showed more compassion. "He is tired," he wrote to Harding at the Dominions Office, "Lascelles came to that conclusion comparing his condition with that of four years ago, and I can see it too — and being tired things probably rankle him. . . . " The prevailing feeling in the Foreign Office was, however, that Lascelles had blundered.

There was one aspect of the Prime Minister's determination to go to Washington they had not recognized. This was Mackenzie King's strongly held belief that he had a special role to play as arbiter between the two great powers of the Anglo-American world. Being shunted to one side at the border would expose this idea as merely *folie de grandeur*. On Friday, March 3, he wrote a personal confidential letter to Roosevelt which was sent by the American diplomatic bag directly to the President. Mackenzie King was adamant that he would preserve Canada's special relationship with the United States, frustrate the schemes of the King's advisers, and "spike the guns of intrigue at the British Legation."

The next day he phoned the White House, and heard the reassuring voice of the President come on to the line to greet his friend "Mackenzie" (only FDR ever called him that). Roosevelt listened to the whole story, not with the sort of nervous attention of Lord Tweedsmuir, but with the confident sympathy of a real friend. "It is the same old game," he told the Prime

Minister. "I am afraid neither you nor I would make good
diplomats. We are too accustomed to dealing straight with each
other." Of course he was welcome in Washington; the previous
invitation still held. And when the King and Queen came to
Hyde Park, he must stay in the house with them all. It was
already arranged. Mackenzie King hung up the phone with a
feeling of real joy.

His mood was very different, however, when he met with
the Governor General a week later to discuss matters. The
irony had not escaped him that because of the squabbling over
precedence, it was essentially the Americans who would be
deciding the make-up of the royal party. The idea put him in
a dangerous mood:

> I said: Do you wonder, in these days, when great trends are
> being considered, for example, as to whether Canada is going
> to find her greatest future within the Empire or in the conti-
> nental relationship, that acts of this kind make a man feel like
> saying: Let them all go to hell so far as Britain is concerned.

It was an extraordinary scene, the "violent outburst" that
sent Redfern fumbling for a cablegram to London. Citing the
examples of South Africa and Ireland, the Prime Minister told
Tweedsmuir, "Do not be surprised if some day you find this
country in a very different position than many people in the
Old Country believe it will be." He went on to talk about the
invitation he had received to attend the World's Fair on July
1, and his tone, as he later recorded it in his diary, was an
ominous one:

> I said I intended to go there and make an important speech.
> What I say will depend a good deal on what happens between
> now and that time. . . . I did not propose to be tramped on
> because I was polite and deferential in matters that were
> important.
>
> I said that when I talked with Hitler, Hitler had said to me
> his reason for building up his armaments was that some
> nations would listen to nothing unless it was backed by force;
> that he needed force and power in order to be listened to. I
> said I am afraid I have come to the same conclusion, and I
> intend to let Britain see whether I have any power or have
> not, when it comes to these matters. . . .

Tweedsmuir pleaded with Mackenzie King not to blame England for what its officials were doing ("Hardinge after all was only the son of a man who had been trained in India . . . "). The Prime Minister took some pleasure in how worried "the Governor" looked, how he addressed him as "Dear Rex", his favourite nickname, and attempted to soothe his miseries; "but the tragic part was that all happiness had been taken out of the whole visit by this kind of thing."

Tommy Lascelles meanwhile was in Washington conferring with the President and the British Ambassador. He was aware by now of the confidential letter to the President, and that Mackenzie King was "making a personal matter of this question". He did not press Roosevelt about it, as he explained huffily to Hardinge back at Buckingham Palace, as "it is, after all, no business of his." There was a bitter tone to his report, as if he realized the battle was lost. But he repeated his assertions that those closest to the President were irritated about the Canadians' tendency to regard the visit as "their show", and he had himself noticed traces of this same sort of feeling in the State Department.

In Ottawa, Mackenzie King kept up the pressure, even sending a very long telegram to Neville Chamberlain setting out his views. Things were going from bad to worse. "The Prime Minister is much upset," Campbell wrote to Harding at the Dominions Office, echoing Redfern's warnings; "he may act in a dangerously foolish manner not only in regard to Their Majesties' visit but also to other questions of importance at this critical juncture." It was the matter of "other questions of importance" that set off warning bells for the British. By the late winter of 1939, they realized a larger game was afoot than merely the injured pride of a Canadian prime minister — namely, the growing Nazi threat in Europe—and so, as far as Ottawa was concerned, they prepared now to bow to the inevitable.

"You have already lost South Africa pretty well out of the Empire," Mackenzie King had told the Governor General; "have lost Ireland out of it; are rapidly losing Canada." The Prime Minister had managed to link his frustrations over the Royal Visit preparations to imperial disintegration. But what he said had a certain nasty ring of truth for those in Whitehall who had watched for years as Canada dragged its feet on issues of imperial defence, and made ambiguous and apparently contradictory statements on matters of neutrality. Growing pro-German sentiment in South Africa, scenes in the cinemas in Dublin where crowds enthusiastically cheered Hitler whenever he made an appearance—and now this spat with the Canadian prime minister gave credence to the British view that the country had come under the spell of " 'highbrows', isolationists, French Canadians, Irish disloyalists . . . and intellectuals."

In fact, the British had been snookered. They had given too much credence to the comments of O. D. Skelton's bright young men in External Affairs who expressed leftish, pacifist sentiments that were honest reactions to both the rise of the fascists abroad and the scarring experience of the Depression at home. Contradicting the Mother Country would be a pleasure to these men, many of whom had gone to war for the Empire only to suffer as much from the habitual condescension of British officers as they did from the misery of the trenches. Their sentiments would have astonished and dismayed the country's English-speaking population, a great many of whom had British parents or British neighbours, felt kinship with the Mother Country, and, in the majority of cases, considered themselves as much British as Canadian.

French Canada was another matter, of course. But here again the Foreign Office read the signals wrong, confusing what the Prime Minister said for domestic consumption with how the country would react to the prospect of Britain at war. Mackenzie King's affection for the Old Country was matched only by his contempt for the bunglers of British foreign policy. He would steer an independent course within the Empire, support the British in wartime—but in the meantime his priorities were to keep the country united. F. R. Scott, a better poet than politician, would later write of the Prime Minister:

We had no shape
Because he never took sides,
And no sides
Because he never allowed them to take shape.

In an honest moment, Mackenzie King would not have disputed this. The Conscription Crisis of 1917, which had nearly

torn the country apart, had shown the peril of taking sides in
Canada. In a country where consensus was never easy, and
often impossible, it was at the very least political suicide to
allow anyone to define the country's shape too precisely. Moreover, Quebec was the anchor for the Liberal Party; its support
had been the single decisive reason that Mackenzie King was
elected party leader. He owed his political career to a part of
the country where he couldn't make himself understood clearly
enough to buy a loaf of bread. So, if he spoke cautiously and
ambiguously about Canada's role in a future war, it was not
because of any ambiguity in his mind. Only his concern for
Quebec. The British employed appeasement in their torturous
search for peace in Europe, haunted by the scenes of slaughter
in Flanders twenty-five years before. Mackenzie King did what
he did because he was similarly visited by memories of Canadian troops marching through their own streets with bayonets
fixed, and mobs in Quebec City carrying axe-handles and
singing the Marseillaise.

So he had continued to dance around suspicious Quebec
nationalists and unrepentant Tory "jingos" — he and that other
well-known song-and-dance man, Ernest Lapointe from Quebec, taking turns leading each other around the floor to a
variety of show tunes: activist — interventionist — neutralist —
isolationist — will fight — won't fight. The definitive statement
of Mackenzie King's position was made on January 16, 1939,
when he stood up in the House of Commons and quoted Laurier, who had faced the same dilemma in 1910, and had eventually been destroyed by it:

> If England is at war we are at war and liable to attack. I do
> not say that we will always be attacked; neither do I say that
> we would take part in all the wars of England. That is a matter
> that must be guided by circumstances, upon which the Cana-
> dian parliament will have to pronounce and will have to decide
> in its own best judgment.

That seemed to wind the matter up in enough wool to provide a dubious kind of comfort to everybody. It was a perfect
statement of its kind: quoting a French Canadian about standing shoulder to shoulder with the British, and yet adding
enough qualifiers and backtracking statements to lose virtually

everybody in the syntax. If the average Canadian even bothered to lift his head and concern himself with this purposeful
confusion, his head would be spinning. But to the British it
spelled serious trouble.

For London, the Royal Visit to North America was now too
important to future good relations with Canada and the United
States to sacrifice to one man's pique, and so they moved
decisively. On March 17, Sir Alexander Hardinge cabled
Rideau Hall to confirm that Mackenzie King would greet the
King and Queen in Quebec City, while Lord Tweedsmuir
would remain in Ottawa. On March 29, Neville Chamberlain
responded courteously to Mackenzie King's telegram, suggesting that a letter from Buckingham Palace would arrive
shortly that would "finally remove all his dissatisfaction and
suspicion" concerning the issue of Minister in Attendance to
the King. It was Tommy Lascelles, however, who spoke for the
private British view. "I do not think it matters a brass farthing
whether M. King comes to the U.S.A. or not," he concluded
sourly. "His presence on the visit will not excite the Americans;
his absence from it will not grieve the Canadians."

Mackenzie King had won, but the strain of the parliamentary session and his constant supervision of tour preparations
had left him tired and complaining of sciatica. Across the country, he was being attacked by political enemies like Mitch
Hepburn of Ontario for neglecting the urgent business of Parliament. Tweedsmuir, who had returned from a tour of the
West, found the criticism coming even from men in the Prime
Minister's own Liberal Party. As he confided to the British
High Commissioner, Sir Gerald Campbell:

> Men like the Lieutenant-Governors of British Columbia and
> Saskatchewan, and the Premier of British Columbia, join with
> Conservatives in ridiculing a Prime Minister who never travels
> west of Toronto in the ordinary course of events but insists,
> even to the possible detriment of his health, in spending every
> moment he can with the King and Queen.

Meanwhile, in Eph Coleman's office in the East Block, far
from the emotional pyrotechnics and the hand-to-hand of diplomatic combat, the Interdepartmental Committee worked
steadily through the winter and spring of 1939 on the mundane

details of the tour itself. The committee's broad mandate was to make it possible for the King and Queen, in comfort and safety, to see and be seen by as many Canadians as possible. "Trying official functions" would be kept to a minimum, and every effort would be made to ensure that the King "will not be maimed with handshaking as the Duke of Windsor was on one of his trips to this Dominion." There would be no honorary degrees, and no visits to educational or charitable institutions, or industrial plants. Special access would be provided for veterans and children. It was almost word for word as Tweedsmuir had suggested it to Mackenzie King in November.

Transportation and accommodation would not be a problem. The country's two railway giants, Canadian National and Canadian Pacific, had both volunteered their services, not only from patriotic motives but with regard for the kind of publicity the tour would attract world-wide. Their transportation and hotel networks were so vast, and their experience in providing for a traveller's every want so extensive, that the tour could not have gone ahead without them. A Royal Train would be assembled from their best rolling stock, with quarters for the King and Queen located in the Governor General's own two luxurious touring carriages. In addition, four special touring cars would be at the disposal of the royal party; they had been specially built in Windsor and Oshawa, and equipped with every convenience, including bullet-proofing, a secret vanity case for the Queen, and sufficient headroom to accommodate the King's plumed hats.

The crucial problem that faced tour organizers, however, was the mapping out of the royal route. News of the Royal Visit had resulted in a flood of invitations and requests from cities, towns, villages, commercial establishments, clubs, individual families, even Sunday schools, all hopeful that the King and Queen might grace their platforms, cut their ribbons, spend a few moments in their communities. Politicians of every stripe had lined up to lobby — each for his own particular bailiwick. But of course in a country as large and fractious as Canada, there was no pleasing everybody. Outrage — loud and predictable — greeted the first public announcement of the planned itinerary. "Not a royal tour but a royal torture," sniffed the *Ottawa Journal*, and one letter to the editor suggested the schedule had been stuffed with too many dull formal events and dull formal officials, and urged that any parts of the itinerary "that minister in the aggrandizement of pushful individuals" be vetoed. "The custom is outmoded of motoring eminent visitors to see the gas works, the tannery, the abattoir . . . but that need not prevent our visitors receiving entertainment that would administer some thrills."

"Not a mile on fresh water," moaned another:

No Great Lakes sail of even limited extent, no sight of St. Clair, Detroit or Soo Rivers, no glimpse of the Grand at Galt, only a fleeting one at Paris from train, no Thousand Islands or the charming highway reach along the St. Lawrence between Brockville and Cornwall, a scant half-hour for the scenic beauties of Thunder Bay region, no stop at Lake Louise about which artists rave — these are a few of the things which our beloved guests are to miss, through being confined for the most part in a stuffy railway train, rushing about after the manner of the ludicrous American tourist abroad. If their Majesties wish to make the trip in order to see and meet Canadians, a thousand miles should have been arranged here and there by motor through the charms of the May-June countryside past cheering sightseers on highways and in villages and towns. . . .

Far from being discouraged, "pushful individuals" from all points of the compass — Truro, Windsor, Brandon, Guelph — had been buttonholing anyone and everyone to press for their rightful place in the royal progress. Thanks to Windsor Mayor David Croll and other area politicians, like Paul Martin, the King and Queen would now see the Detroit River. And Thunder Bay had managed to wrestle more time for itself from the schedule. Other localities were not so lucky.

Little by little, between November 1938 and May 1939, arrangements began to fall into place, difficulties were surmounted. Committee members worked out each detail — often through an exchange of memoranda. On November 12, 1938, Eric Mackenzie, Comptroller of Government House, wrote: "May attention be drawn to the fact that all Officers on the Guard of Honour, regardless of rank, must wear trousers and not overalls as is sometimes done." He then went on to complain about the bad springs in the State Carriage, and the bumps on certain Ottawa streets: "It would be positively dangerous to risk Their Majesties being trotted along Sussex Street with the chance of being nearly, if not quite, thrown out of the carriage."

December 17: From Shuldham Redfern to Hugh Keenleyside on the matter of the Committee vetting in advance the dozens of speeches and illuminated addresses:

> Will anyone be so foolish as to read them—whether typed or illuminated, and in any case there would be no means of stopping the last minute enthusiast from pouring out his illuminated soul.

Citizens came forward in droves to offer their services. The Canadian Amateur Lacrosse Association volunteered a demonstration of Canada's "oldest national game". A ten-year-old piano prodigy was put at the Committee's disposal — as was The Great Lipton ("Magic, Illusions, Mental Phenomena, Mirth and Music, Reliable and Up-to-date, Novel, Moral, Instructive and Varied"), and a pageant spectacle called "Romance of a Nation".

January 13: From Colonel Mackenzie:

> My dear Keenleyside . . . I have replied to Miss H_____'s offer of a table made from the excrescence of a tree.

Still others were asking for themselves. "I do not care about these things myself, but . . . " writes one; while from a mayor in Ontario: "I am very loath to take advantage of my position, but . . . " Some were less circumspect. "Is there anything I could be invited to!" writes one charmingly direct matron from Cambridge, Massachusetts, in a personal letter to the Prime Minister ("Sorry to bother you but you have always been so sweet about doing things"), reminding him how long it's been since she was last in Ottawa ("not since I dropped a vote for you as a delegate at that famous convention").

February 17: From Shuldham Redfern to Hugh Keenleyside on the matter of how local officials should deal with the King and Queen:

> Being a goldfish in a bowl is a terrible strain. Another most exhausting feature on these occasions is the process of being

constantly shown things instead of being allowed just to see them. One's vocabulary of appreciative expression dries up.

The Prime Minister continued to fuss over every detail of the planning, professing to begrudge the time it took him away from the problems of the nation, even as he drove his assistants to distraction with more demands, queries, corrections. Speeches, invitation cards, methods of parking cars — nothing escaped him.

April 26: From Arnold Heeney, the Prime Minister's Principal Secretary (sounding a little weary), to Dr. Coleman:

> The enclosed memorandum of the Prime Minister's speaks for itself. Perhaps a note from you to the effect that those matters are already in hand would relieve Mr. King's mind in this respect.

In particular, Mackenzie King worried that money was being spent on too many lavish and high-falutin entertainments. This ran counter to the Royal Visit's modest theme, that of showing the King among his people. Eph Coleman, back from a reconnaissance in the West (where enthusiasm was great among "people of all classes"), was able to report with satisfaction "that he had been able to forestall certain rather grandiose developments that might have been more difficult to eliminate later." And, as the Prime Minister was quick to realize, too grand a display might also prove offensive when thousands of Canadians were still out of work, and relief camps remained full of restless transients.

The unemployed also concerned RCMP Commissioner Stuart Wood, who had visions of shabbily dressed mobs angrily disrupting the tour and embarrassing government officials with their demands for jobs. In Hamilton, the Transient Unemployed Youth League was already making plans to stage a hunger march by five thousand, while in Winnipeg there was talk of another "On-to-Ottawa" trek to coincide with the Royal Visit. The Prime Minister had himself suggested that the unemployed be hired to clean streets and buildings and even to help control the crowds. But Wood had different ideas. The relief camps, which normally closed at the end of April, should be kept open until June; as well, the provinces would be asked to co-operate "in an aggressive campaign for the strict enforcement of the Railway Act, particularly during the month of April, as this would minimize the transient problem at the time Their Majesties are visiting Canada."

The RCMP was also keeping its eye on a number of other groups, including the "radical Irish element" (primarily based in the United States), a tiny Ukrainian group with ties to Nazi Germany, and the Doukhobors (who had apparently made some threats concerning the Royal Visit). The Communist Party, according to police agents, would likely lie low, anxious that "no untoward incident should occur that would hurt or retard the party's aims." The anarchists, under the direction of Attilio Bortolotti, were considered quite dangerous, however, and the RCMP recommended close surveillance. These measures were not enough for Scotland Yard's Special Branch, who came over for a look themselves in February, examining every foot of railway track and pavement on the royal route.

As a final measure, a confidential handbook on "dangerous or embarrassing persons" was issued by the RCMP, and handed around to various police forces. The individuals it listed, province by province, had histories more sad and pathetic than anything else. The men and women were described typically as "imbecile", "bushed", "mentally deranged", or even "eccentric"; and their actions ranged from "holding imaginary conversations with Premier Aberhart" and "writing poetry to His Majesty" to a one-man welcoming committee who liked "firing a shotgun in the air several times". Police needed to watch for the genuine madman with a weapon, of course, but it was clear that people like Bald-headed Bobby and the Head of the Invisible Chain League of Canada, though they could prove an embarrassment, were not much of a menace to anyone but themselves.

The police had less success in keeping track of the booming business in unofficial souvenirs; and the Dominion government, recognizing the futility of the situation, temporarily waived laws in the Criminal Code which forbade the reproduction of likenesses of the King and Queen. The sole exception was candy-wrappers, "a precaution against having Their Majesties' pictures kicking around the streets". The field was now wide open to any form of advertisement, provided it was not undignified. The list of those cashing in was endless: Eaton's, the Hudson's Bay Company, Seagram's (which introduced Crown Royal rye whiskey in 1939), the CNIB (wicker trays), various manufacturers of china and silver teaspoons, Drewry's (periscopes), Cadbury's (which produced the impressive "Cadbury Medal" for the occasion)—and even the Ontario couple with an imagined resemblance to Their Majesties, who offered to take the place of the King and Queen at receptions so they wouldn't wear themselves out.

The business went beyond the country's borders. British and American manufacturers filled their order-books, too. But even in the shadow of war, Japanese factories were busy turning out Canadian and British flags and cheap novelties for the Royal Visit—a fact deplored by the Oxford (Ontario) *Journal*, which urged merchants to insist on goods made in Canada or at least the Empire rather than those from Japan. "In view of this country's attitude towards the British Empire during recent months and their ruthless savagery in China," the paper stated, "it does not seem probable that right-thinking Canadian people would prefer to buy products of this nation, particularly on such an occasion."

As the date of the tour grew nearer, members of the Committee, particularly Hugh Keenleyside and Frank Delaute, were called upon more and more to act as arbiters of taste and royal etiquette for Canadians who had never been to anything more formal than a church supper. Questions ranged from a precise definition of the "afternoon dress" recommended for royal occasions to the King's taste in wines (a check with Government House revealed that the King had "a preference for a light Sherry and also a taste for Moselle").

April 29: From the Vancouver Welcoming Committee to the Interdepartmental Committee (one of hundreds such received):

> I hereby offer one bar of fancy washing soap for the best answers to the following questions: Do you think someone on your staff or at Government House would fill in the answers in the spaces left for the purpose.
>
> When the Manager of the Hotel receives Their Majesties at the Burrard Street Entrance as They come for Luncheon, will he be introduced? (Yes) If so by whom? The Mayor? (Yes)

He has to precede Them to the elevators, through the lane created by the double line of military. Is he to walk backward, and if so, is there any special technique? It is hardly likely he can steer a decent course without being awkward, that is if he is to completely face them as he walks along. (No. Walk *with* them)

May 1: From Shuldham Redfern to Hugh Keenleyside on the matter of the Queen's being invited to join the Bricklayers, Masons, and Plasterers International Union:

Personally, I see no more reason why the Queen should be made a plasterer because she lays the Foundation Stone of the Supreme Court, than that she should be made a Judge for the same reason.

"I know there is bound to be no end of disappointment," wrote Mackenzie King at one point, "and on this score, politically, the visit may prove to be injurious." He was thinking of the general election he must soon call. Tweedsmuir had told him of how unpopular his government had become, especially in the West, suggesting, however, that a successful royal visit — with Mackenzie King continually seen and photographed at Their Majesties' side — might help. This was music to the Prime Minister's ears. "By the time the campaign comes on," he reflected, "having been the one who has succeeded in bringing Their Majesties to Canada, I should receive a support greater than if Their Majesties had not come."

Meanwhile, in England, final preparations were also under way. A Council of State was appointed from those adult members of the royal family closest in succession to the Throne. It consisted of the King's brothers, the Dukes of Kent and Gloucester; his sister Princess Mary, the Princess Royal; his cousin, Princess Arthur of Connaught; and Queen Elizabeth, who remained of course a nominal member, since she would accompany the King out of the country.

The Queen's reputation as a dowdy dresser had been swept away for good the previous summer, incredibly enough during a successful state visit to fashion-conscious Paris. The genius of that transformation, dress designer Norman Hartnell, had then been summoned to the Palace with a far more formidable task. He was to create a travelling wardrobe for the North American tour, "suitable for every extreme of climate, from the sultry streets of New York in a heat wave, through the damp heat of a garden party at the White House, right up to the icy heights of the Rocky Mountains." This had to include everything from lavish ball gowns, and day outfits with accompanying accessories, to gumboots.

The royal couple would travel with a considerable entourage. There were two Ladies-in-Waiting (Lady Nunburnholme and Lady Katharine Seymour), a Lord-in-Waiting to the King (the Earl of Eldon), the Lord Chamberlain to the Queen (the Earl of Airlie), a medical officer, a press liaison officer, and two equerries. Tommy Lascelles would act as Private Secretary to the King for the duration of the tour. For their comfort, the royal party would be attended to by assorted dressers, maids, valets, footmen, a page, several general servants, and the Queen's hairdresser — sixteen people in all. As well, the King and Queen would each have a senior detective from Special Branch to act as a bodyguard.

Books and films on every aspect of Canadian life had been ordered, as well as maps to cover every foot of the journey. The Queen also took precautions not to be found ignorant of the great parliamentary traditions shared by Britain and Canada. As she had never been in the House of Commons, it was quietly arranged for her to slip into the Speaker's Gallery in March to watch debate over a bill to reintroduce passenger steamers to the Thames.

Then, with only a few weeks until the royal couple were due to sail for Canada, and with Neville Chamberlain proclaiming a "tranquil" outlook in international affairs, Hitler once again provoked the threat of war. Having completed the dismemberment of Czechoslovakia, he now cast his eye on Poland. Demands were made, notes exchanged, and the British and French armies once again mobilized. The Canadian government became quietly resigned to the cancellation of the tour. In the end, however, it was decided to go ahead as planned, and the King was persuaded that he could do far more good at this time by travelling through North America than by sitting dutifully at his desk in Buckingham Palace. He in turn was forceful in suggesting that the battle cruiser *Repulse* (due to carry the royal party across the Atlantic) be left behind. The German fleet had been sighted prowling off the Spanish coast, and with HMS *Renown* and HMS *Hood* both laid up for repairs, the Navy simply could not afford to lose a ship with the speed and firepower of the *Repulse*.

At the end of April, the British Prime Minister announced a change in plans. The Canadian Pacific's *Empress of Australia*, formerly the 21,000-ton German liner *Tirpitz*, confiscated as war reparations, was summoned from Southampton. A thousand men set to work for one frantic week to convert the luxury liner inside and out into the semblance of a proper royal yacht. Specially outfitted suites were constructed amidships, and extra water ballast was added to lessen the roll and pitch. In deference to a secret Admiralty report that concluded that the Germans might try to kidnap the King and Queen on the high seas, the *Repulse* was detailed to escort the liner half-way across the Atlantic (along with HMS *Glasgow* and HMS *Southampton*, which would make the entire voyage). Badgered in the House of Commons about the *Empress*'s German origins (it had been designed as a cruise ship for the Kaiser with a special stateroom for each member of the German Cabinet), Chamberlain blandly replied that "it may be some satisfaction to know that the engines of the ship were built in Glasgow."

On May 6, under bright sunshine and blue skies, the King in Admiral's uniform stood with his wife on the ship's promenade deck to wave goodbye to the hundreds of thousands who had lined the Portsmouth docks to see them off. It was a stirring sight, conjured up in its colour and pageantry by the radio commentators, and sent crackling over the airwaves to the farthest reaches of the Empire. Bands played patriotic tunes, a squadron of RAF fighters screamed overhead, and two grey lines of battleships, led by the *Rodney* and the *Nelson*, formed up to escort the *Empress* into the Channel. In the passageway on A Deck, thirteen-year-old Princess Elizabeth threw her arms around her mother and wept, while little Margaret Rose, who a few moments earlier had refused to look at the official photographer's camera for fear of the flash, now stretched up three times to kiss her papa good-bye.

CHAPTER THREE

Fog and Ice

THE FIRST TWO DAYS OUT, the seas were heavy and the waves high, and by Tuesday, the third day of the voyage, the *Empress*'s speed of eighteen knots had been slowed by gale-force winds that beat on the port side, making the ship pitch and roll in the water. This was the day that the *Repulse*, keeping station to the stern of the liner, was scheduled to leave the convoy. First, however, a cask of letters to the princesses back home had to be dropped over the side of the *Empress*. Sealed in grease and marked by flags, the barrel bobbed over the rising waves to the huge battleship. And even in the turbulence of the North Atlantic, naval tradition must be observed. So with the Queen standing bravely by his side at the pitching rail, the King took the salute as the *Repulse* made her final sail-past. The crew of the battle cruiser stood in two lines on the deck, the second row of sailors holding onto the belts of the men in front of them to prevent their being swept overboard, while the band played the national anthem, followed by "Here's a Health Unto His Majesty". That day, tables on the liner were frequently upset, and by dusk waves were rolling over the deck.

None of this bothered the King. For the first few days he had played deck tennis, swum regularly in the pool, and mulled over the details of the visit. Dressed in a lounge suit and top-coat, and with a white-crowned sailing cap jammed on his head, he made regular patrols of the deck with the Queen, who had adjusted nicely to the roll of the ship. Both could be seen at various times performing the usual royal service of chatting inconsequentially with anyone they happened to meet. It was like being on holiday, and even included the perils of the ordinary traveller. The smell of paint from the hasty redecoration still lingered in the King's bedroom, but the crew had hauled in buckets of water filled with sliced onions and these had helped to soak up some of the odour. Along with their personal staff of ten, the royal couple were the only passengers aboard for the nine-day crossing. Tended to by eighteen domestic servants and an attentive crew of four hundred (the liner had a normal capacity for twelve hundred passengers), they could voyage in luxury. There were even some familiar comforts: at night the King slept in the large silver-plated iron bedstead from the Royal Yacht *Victoria and Albert*.

The huge liner itself had been temporarily designated a royal yacht, and it provided a degree of comfort and isolation that was welcome after the wearing effects of the past six months. What Daladier, the Prime Minister of France, had referred to as a new form of war without battles, a war "of uncertainty, of constantly renewed anxiety and broken hopes", had been waged unceasingly by Benito Mussolini and Adolf Hitler. Their trumpeting of the nationalism of "blood and soil", their threats of a real war unless the "knots" in European politics could be untied, had for years kept the other European powers off-balance. The King longed to do something that would help ease the worsening situation.

Like everyone else of his generation, George VI was haunted by the memory of the Great War, and he had been an enthusiastic supporter of Chamberlain's appeasement policies. Repeatedly he had offered to make his own appeal to Hitler, sharing with his brother the Duke of Windsor the idea that kings and princes still had a meaningful part to play in diplomacy, as if nothing had happened to the map of Europe since 1914 when the continent had been the private domain of royal cousins. The British government, recognizing that Hitler and Mussolini were thoroughly modern Europeans, gently deflected the King each time, sparing him the inevitable and humiliating rebuff.

But now this trip had finally given him something to do. It hardly ranked with Edward VII's visit to France in 1904 — that event had sealed the Entente Cordiale — but the visit to North America might have similarly good effects. George VI might lack his grandfather's effortless bonhomie, but the kingship remained a powerful symbol. The ties of Empire needed to be bound up again, the flag shown, the tarnished monarchy re-enhanced. The world needed to see that the Dominions (and, who knows? possibly even the United States) stood together in matters of peace and freedom. It might even, according to Lord Tweedsmuir, make the Americans forget about the Duke and Duchess of Windsor.

In fact, the Duke and Duchess were not in the mood to be forgotten. On Sunday, May 7, the Duke travelled to Verdun to record his own appeal for international peace for the National Broadcasting Company. It may have been the whim of an ex-king casting about for something to do and, like George VI, thinking that somehow he made a difference; it may have been pique on the Windsors' part that their own visit to America had been cancelled by the British government. In any case, it was seen by the furious Foreign Office and the Palace as an attempt to upstage the Royal Visit. And even the Americans took it coolly. The broadcast was not picked up aboard the *Empress of Australia*, which by this time had other more serious things to worry about.

On Wednesday, the fourth day out, a great storm engulfed the flotilla, and the *Empress* was batted about like a cork in sixty-mile-per-hour winds. One moment the ship rested on a calm sea and the next moment huge towers of water collapsed upon it with such force that it seemed about to be knocked sideways. No one on board could remember waves that high before. In the teeth of the gale, sailors demonstrated their non-chalance by playing darts on the lower deck, but even the Queen was forced to stay in her cabin, and many of the royal retinue were discreetly seasick. Through the night, the sea crashed over the *Empress*'s bridge and flowed back over the ship's gunwales in white cataracts. Speed was cut to fourteen knots.

From the beginning, the Royal Navy and Canadian Pacific had quarrelled over the best route for crossing the Atlantic at that time of year. The King, as Supreme Commander of the Royal Squadron, might have had an opinion, but the Sea Lords in London had seen to it that Vice-Admiral Sir Dudley North was put in effective day-to-day control of the *Empress* and her remaining escorts, and his mere presence aboard the liner menaced the performance of the increasingly harried captain, Archibald Meikle. "At that time of year you had to watch for icebergs," recalled Frank Knight, the royal couple's steward, "and of course the captain was well aware of this":

> But since we had the King and Queen aboard, some old admiral came down to take charge. Our captain suggested that we follow a certain course, but the old admiral said, "No, no, we'll go *this* way," and naturally our captain could do nothing else.

Late Wednesday night the storm began to lose its strength, and by morning the sea had flattened out. But, by then, the *Empress* had sailed into a blanket of fog that separated her from the sight of her two escorts. Three hundred and fifty miles off Cape Race, the more experienced members of the crew felt the tell-tale wave of frigid air and got the first whiff of the dank, penetrating smell of icebergs. Before long, the ice had begun to close in, and growlers and icebergs could be seen floating a few hundred yards from the liner's bow. They slowed to a cautious five knots, and at times the engines were stopped completely. At this point, an enormous stillness settled over the ship, and only the sounds of the slow wash of the water on the ice could be heard, and then the regular bellow of the liner's foghorns with its accompanying echo, followed somewhere in the distance by the reassuring answer from *Southampton* and *Glasgow*. The Queen described the experience in a letter to her mother-in-law, Queen Mary:

> For three and a half days we only moved a few miles. The fog was so thick that it was like a white cloud round the ship, and the foghorn blew incessantly. Its melancholy blasts were echoed back by the icebergs like the twang of a piece of wire. Incredibly eerie, and really very alarming, knowing that we were surrounded by ice and unable to see a foot either way. We very nearly hit a berg the day before yesterday, and the poor Captain was nearly demented because some kind, cheerful people kept on reminding him that it was just about here that *Titanic* was struck, and *just* about the same date!

The worst had happened. Captain Meikle, who "knew the Atlantic like the back of his hand", had been bullied into taking the faster, northerly route, in spite of his fears of late-spring ice that was causing abnormal ice conditions as far south as Louisbourg. Ice that should have melted three or four weeks before bobbed menacingly about them. And, while in London the Admiralty fumed, questions were asked in the House, the press on two continents cried out for heads to roll, and Canadian Pacific blandly referred all inquiries back to the Admiralty, the Captain and his crew groped their way ahead, managing just 172 miles in a little over three days.

"I shouldn't have chosen an ice-field surrounded by dense fog in which to have a holiday," the King told his mother, "but it does seem to be the only place for me to rest nowadays!" Bundled up in heavy wool coats, he and the Queen made a show of their unconcern. They continued walking the decks, stopping to admire and take pictures of the towering icebergs or the low-lying floes that floated by. The Queen's energy and attention to detail remained undiminished, and she went on supervising the daily menus, prowling the ship and talking with everybody. Her incessant curiosity eventually caused some grief to their steward, Frank Knight. At one point during the slow journey, when the escort vessels were visible and able to move freely in the ice, she asked about the large canisters secured to their decks. By way of explaining depth charges, the crew obligingly fired one off. This did no harm to the surrounding ships, but the force of the explosion sent a volley of freezing sea-water rushing up the drains of the *Empress*. The unsuspecting Knight, who was sitting peacefully in the lavatory at that moment, was caught in the sudden flood and soaked. Terrified, he shot out of the room "like a rocket", expecting to hear they had struck an iceberg.

The King and Queen's routine went on as before. Every night, in a private room on the promenade deck, the royal party dined—usually with two guests, selected and summoned in advance by a hand-written note from the equerry. At 8:25, everyone would meet in the lounge for some casual conversation—the men in dinner jackets and black ties, the women in long dresses. After a few minutes, the King and Queen would enter. At dinner they sat opposite each other in the centre of the long table. To compensate for the King's habitual reticence (and his appetite), he would be flanked by the two familiar and undemanding ladies-in-waiting. The Queen, on the other hand, sat between the two guests. While the ship's orchestra played and dinner progressed (for example) through the consommé double Juanita and the rouget sauté épicurienne, she would go to work, chatting amiably with one of those invited, while the other was dutifully engaged by the lady-in-waiting opposite. Then, at about the half-way point in the meal — perhaps while they were consuming the carré de veau rôti with épinards au jus and carottes Vichy—the Queen would skilfully shift to the other guest, leaving the lady-in-waiting opposite to fill in. In this manner, they continued through the mousse à l'ananas, petits-fours, the savoury crêpes Neluskis, the corbeille de fruits, and the demitasse. It worked well. The King could finish his meal without pressure, contributing here and there as he wished, and still appear to be host of the evening.

After dinner, the party went down as a group to the ship's cinema. Here the formalities had been relaxed, so that pursers, cooks, and stokers — by royal command — could group awkwardly around the Sovereign and watch Charlie Chan, Canadian travelogues, and Walt Disney cartoons. When the show was finished, the royal party and their guests for the evening returned to the lounge for a final goodnight before the King and Queen retired.

Isolation from the outside world did not mean complete freedom from state ceremonial. So on Friday, May 12, when the fog lifted briefly, the royal couple, bundled in deck-rugs against the piercing Arctic air, dutifully watched as the two escort vessels celebrated the second anniversary of their coronation by firing off a royal salute into the vast empty expanse of the North Atlantic. In time, however, the novelty of their situation palled and even minor sensations—the First Officer's canary laying an egg, the ship's two doctors launched in a small boat to treat an appendicitis case aboard the *Glasgow*— failed to dispel the growing restlessness everyone felt at the frustrating stoppages and delays.

There was a brief release from the fog on Friday afternoon, a stoppage of engines during the night, and some improvement on Saturday morning until one of the crew sighted "the father of the icebergs", a quarter of a mile off the bow and about the general shape and size of Windsor Castle, according to one of the ladies-in-waiting. Captain Meikle, who by this time must have regretted ever giving up his first job in a bank, prudently reversed the liner's engines, and guided the *Empress* around. Then the fog came down again.

On Sunday, May 14, while the *Empress* and her escorts picked their way through thick pack-ice at a cautious five knots, the Interdepartmental Committee, consisting of whatever members could be rounded up on short notice, held an emergency meeting in Ottawa. The King and Queen could not possibly arrive now before Wednesday morning, which meant that, however painful it might be, two valuable days had to be lopped off the schedule. Unwilling to slight Quebec, particularly in an election year, the organizers had decreed there would be no reduction of the first two days' itinerary. Ottawa's portion of the tour was slashed from four days to two and a half — something that would cause little sorrow in the rest of Canada. Brief stops in Cornwall and Brockville were eliminated with the idea that the Royal Train could slow down as it passed through those communities. Kingston, where Their Majesties were to have spent Sunday, was reduced to a thirty-five-minute tour by limousine. But by Monday morning, when the Royal Train reached Toronto, they would once again be on schedule. It fell to Hugh Keenleyside to contact the mayors of the various communities that were affected by the schedule change. Keenleyside, who in his youth had experienced the earthy language of lumber camps and army barracks, confessed later that he had never heard anything like the vocabulary used by the splenetic civic officials.

There was another reason to spare Quebec. The organizers had for months suffered nightmares about a cold French-Canadian reception for the King and Queen — one that would embarrass the province for years. The responsibility for seeing that this didn't happen was handed over to two Cabinet ministers from the province, Ernest Lapointe and Fernand Rinfret, and they had turned at once for help to the forceful and flamboyant spiritual leader of Quebec's four million Catholics, Jean-Marie Rodrigue, Cardinal Villeneuve.

Villeneuve commanded the resources of an immensely influential church. Authoritarian, paternalistic, hostile to everything the modern world stood for, it had made itself synonymous with the miracle of *survivance* — so successfully that French

Canadians, just 60,000 at the time of the Conquest in 1759, were now four million strong (and, at their present birth rate, poised to become the country's majority group by early in the next century). Lapointe and Rinfret had counted not only on the instinctively conservative temper of the Church, but on Villeneuve's taste for ceremonial and his preference for "the hierarchical, universal, and continuous quality of British institutions . . . over the ephemeral structures of the rambunctious French."

The Cardinal did not disappoint them. In every parish in the province, priests reminded Catholic Quebecers of their duty, as set out in the Pastoral Letter of April 1935, to be loyal to the highest civil authority as represented by the Crown of England. The curés of river-front churches were instructed to ring their bells during the passage of the royal ship, while "all the faithful should obey the wishes of the civil authorities to render to Their Majesties the appropriate honours." Youth associations in particular were urged to turn out and cheer. Even the St-Jean Baptiste Society of Quebec, feeling perhaps a timely archiepiscopal nudge, voted a resolution of welcome to the royal couple.

Quebec's newspapers, especially *Le Soleil*, took up the cause with enthusiasm. In between reminding French Canadians of the King's origins (Norman, like theirs), and of their own unique heritage (Quebecers had always existed under a monarchy in one form or another), they dished out the same stories as the rest of the country about the Queen's dresses, the furnishings on the Royal Train, and the pastimes of the two princesses. The Queen as usual could do no wrong. ("We have watched her grow and grow more and more beautiful until this year, when Queen Elizabeth, certain of her grace both as a woman and *grande dame* has arrived at that almost inexplicable perfection of the ideal woman.")

Sympathy with the Empire and with British foreign policy was another matter. *La Presse* urged its readers to cheer and show that "the loyalty of French Canadians is as enduring as always, that their attachment to the British Crown is as strong as always." But at the same time it sounded a warning note, deploring the rise of "imperialistic propaganda" in the displays everywhere of English flags and decorations:

Why don't we, French Canadians, profit from the occasion to manifest our loyalty and attachment to our sovereigns, certainly, but also to our language, our nationality, our rights, our ethnic character. If we must have inscriptions, let them be worded in French, if we cheer, cheer in French. . . .

So, in one of those strange historical turnabouts, the arrival of the King and Queen became not only a test of the Church's grip on Quebec society, but, for some at least, an assertion of French Canada's national pride.

On Sunday, with the arrival of the *Empress of Australia* now imminent, dense crowds in Montreal took advantage of the warm spring weather to turn out and watch the rehearsals for the royal reception. The custom-built maroon Lincoln limousine that would carry the King and Queen through the city on the second day of the Royal Visit could be seen cruising about, together with a seemingly endless cavalcade of autos, streetcars, and tour buses packed with the curious — all of them eager to trace the processional route. The traffic ("unquestionably the heaviest Montreal has ever seen") brought much of the city to a virtual standstill, particularly in areas like Outremont, Westmount, Côte des Neiges, and Notre Dame de Grâce. In Jarry Park, the eighteen-pound field guns boomed out, and on Park Avenue the children clustered around the Hussars were told to make as much noise as possible to get the horses used to crowds. The Black Watch practised their Inspection March, "The Garb of Old Gaul", for anyone who cared to listen.

In Quebec City, where it was not as warm and where the late snow still clung to sides of the cliffs, there was a special anticipation that quickened with each news story of the liner's peril in the ice floes. Here, there were wild rumours that the *Empress* was really out in the Atlantic dodging German submarines. It seemed reasonable enough. The city itself was under the tightest security in its history, and had over the last few days taken on the appearance of a military camp. The sleepy calm of the Old Capital was now punctured by the roar of police motorcycles careening up and down the slopes of the city in endless rehearsals, escorting the royal limousine as it tested the sharp turns of the centuries-old streets. A dozen undesirables had been picked up by police and told to leave the city, and there were investigations under way at Laval, where posters with the letters "IRA" had been found on the pillars of the university's main entrance.

Elsewhere, priests and nuns rehearsed schoolchildren for the huge rally on the Plains of Abraham. The work-shed near where General Wolfe had landed on a wet, stormy night in 1759 on the eve of the country's most momentous battle (a spot that was now unrecognizable, having been converted to a drab company pier) would soon be dressed up with bright silk hangings and palm trees. A curio shop in the small brown building where Montcalm had died was selling royal memorabilia. An electric crown had been hung on the Legislative Buildings, and the Mayor had bought a shirt with *faux-col* and a tie for each of the city councillors.

By Sunday night, word came that the *Empress* had found its way through the pack ice at last and had reached open sea. It was now reported to be steaming under clear weather at nineteen knots towards Quebec. Celebrations had been postponed for two days, and hotel-keepers threw out mountains of expensive, freshly cut flowers. Monday was business as usual for everybody in Quebec City — everybody except for a church-bell ringer who had been instructed to ring his bell that morning, and obstinately carried on for a full thirty minutes, to the intense annoyance of late-sleepers. Also that morning, in spite of the fact that the Royal Visit had been delayed, thousands of first-day covers dated May 15, 1939 (and bearing new stamp designs of the King and Queen and the two princesses), were cancelled and sent out all over the world by the Royal Train Post Office. Toiling for hours to keep up with the demand was a three-man crew: Postmaster Bill Ross, Lou Gignac, and "Pallie" Pascoe (who had decided to write up his own informal account of the Royal Visit for his family and friends).

Monday aboard the *Empress of Australia* there were blue skies and "a sea with rippling waves kissed by sunshine". The captain, who had kept an almost round-the-clock vigil during the three-and-a-half-day delay, had taken to his bed, exhausted and depressed by the attacks being levelled at him from both sides of the Atlantic, often by people who wouldn't know an iceberg from an ice cube. The first landfall of the New World, the French islands of St. Pierre and Miquelon, were sighted that morning, and seaplanes catapulting off the decks of the warships returned to report that the way ahead was clear. The tension among the royal party, never acknowledged during that anxious week, now broke, and there was much chatter, joking, and laughter as they luxuriated in the warm sunshine and the dry decks.

The King and Queen were on the bridge later that day when the *Empress* and its two escorts skirted the southwestern tip of Newfoundland off Cape Ray, and entered Canadian waters. There they were met by HMCS *Saguenay* and HMCS *Skeena*, two destroyers from the Royal Canadian Navy. The destroyers, decks lined with sailors, swept past the liner in a high-speed salute in Cabot Strait, then took up their positions on the starboard and port sides of the *Empress*'s bow. By Monday evening the flotilla was chugging up the St. Lawrence at a steady nineteen knots.

On Tuesday, the weather was still a little cold in spite of the sun, with a north wind sweeping across the decks. But conditions otherwise were perfect. The ships hugged the south shore all day, moving under the Gaspé cliffs and passing the small farmhouses and shiny church steeples of old Quebec. At Father Point, they were met by the tiny pilot ship *Jalobert* crowded with port officials, RCMP, and sailors. Two tanned faces looked over the rail at reporters craning for a first glimpse of the royal visitors ("Let me tell you, the Queen is radiant, beautiful, surprising beyond all words"). Freighters and tramp steamers heading down the broad river lowered flags and sounded their sirens. At Rimouski, excited crowds had to be held back by the police. As the light faded, the *Empress* moved towards the north shore. Both sides of the river now blazed up with welcoming bonfires. At Rivière-du-Loup, trumpeter Harry Yeo stood on the shoreline and, as he had for every troop train that passed during the Great War, played in salute to the flotilla passing fifteen miles in the distance.

Upriver in Quebec City, where the terraces were now crowded with out-of-town visitors, waves of newsmen moved through the city like marauding armies. Far from being dismayed by the two-day delay ("the first piece of luck" according to *Time* magazine), reporters had had time to set up their unofficial headquarters in the comfort of the cool, dark Terrace Club in the Château Frontenac. There they got deep into the hotel's larder and liquor supply, while dreaming up their leads for Canada's royal welcome ("Decked in bunting, schooled in her curtseys, excited and nervous as a schoolgirl . . . "). Although there were only fifty-six correspondents accredited to the Royal Visit, hundreds were in the city, and hundreds more would be spotted across the country for special coverage. Seventy-three reporters had been assigned to the story by the *Toronto Daily Star* alone. The CBC had ambitious plans to leap-frog its facilities across the Dominion and give a constant coverage of each day's events in both English and French. The job of "pressherd" had been assigned the genial giant Walter Thompson, chief publicity agent for the CNR, who was instructed to give the reporters and cameramen everything they needed for their stories while keeping them gently in line (the Prime Minister being worried that the press might think it was off on some Roman holiday).

Mackenzie King and his Principal Secretary, Arnold Heeney, arrived on a special fast train from Ottawa about eight o'clock Tuesday evening. The Prime Minister's first words as he stepped from the car frowning in anxiety were to ask about the *Empress*'s progress. At the Château Frontenac, he went immediately to the dining-room, where the reporters were having a buffet supper. Not bothering even to take off his overcoat, he seized the opportunity to campaign around the room, greeting every man and woman and shaking their hands. Then it was over to the Citadel to make a quick inspection of the rooms for the King and Queen ("all very simple but very nice"), and then back to the hotel to make some last-minute adjustments to one of the King's speeches, before a final phone call to Laurier House to inquire about his dog Pat.

In spite of the last-minute burst of energy, Mackenzie King was tired. For the past few months he had felt a continuous physical fatigue which had kept him away from the House more than was prudent under the circumstances. The burdens of overseeing the tour preparations and the battles with the British over protocol had sapped his remaining energy. He had even begun to wonder of late whether his political career was over. There were the usual discontents across the country, and the visit itself was already attracting criticism. In the past week alone there had been mutterings about how French Canada had been upstaged by the number of Privy Councillors and others from outside the province who had come to Quebec City. Mackenzie King felt unprepared for all that would be demanded of him in the next four weeks; there had been no time to compose himself. "Can only trust in Providence," he wrote in his diary.

Near midnight, the *Empress*, chipped and bruised, her sides scored by the ice, dropped anchor near St. Jean on the Île d'Orléans. "I have been able to have a good rest," the King wrote to his mother, "and the two extra days will be all to the good for me." A shadow had lifted. From this side of the ocean, Europe and its troubles seemed far away. And yet a small, virtually invisible sign of the coming tragedy had already begun to shadow the progress of the royal tour. Just twenty-four hours earlier, the luxury liner *St. Louis* had slipped its moorings in Hamburg Harbour and headed across the Atlantic to the Caribbean. On board were 937 German Jews, stripped of their property and possessions but each of them clutching in their hands a precious ticket out of the European nightmare — an entrance visa to Cuba.

As for the royal flotilla itself, anyone with a trained eye could see signs of what was coming. The large grey cruisers of the Royal Navy had not been turned out in the customary fashion of a friendly visit. No decorative lights had been strung along the decks, and the ships' brass, which normally glowed from hours of sweaty labour, was now dull and unreflective. These were ships ready for combat. Even more disturbing was the secret cargo stowed below decks in the *Glasgow* and the *Southampton*. Packed securely in their holds and overflowing into the magazines and shell rooms were specially built steel-bound boxes containing 3,550 gold bars from the Bank of England. The British government had used the royal tour as a cover to transport fifty tons of gold to Canada (worth perhaps thirty million pounds in 1939), enough to finance the early stages of a world war. Having come safely through the fog and ice of the Atlantic run, the cargo (the first of billions of dollars in gold and securities transferred to North America) could be discreetly unloaded and stored securely with the Canadian government.

But on the *Empress* that evening there was no evidence of anything but happiness and relief. The dining-room had been hung with balloons and paper streamers, and the ship's orchestra sailed through its repertoire for the benefit of couples dancing on their last night aboard. There were the usual end-of-voyage scenes, with a number of crew members being presented with gifts, including Captain Meikle (now recovering nicely as a Commander of the Royal Victorian Order). The music floated across the water to the shoreline, even at this hour illuminated in the soft glow of hundreds of automobile headlights. The great adventure — two days late — was about to begin.

CHAPTER FOUR

Into the Heart of French Canada

Wednesday, May 17:

THOSE WHO WORRIED about what a cold or even cool reception by French Canada might mean to Quebec's reputation had to be relieved by the sight of the crowds streaming towards the Citadel ramparts to watch as the Royal Yacht *Empress of Australia* steamed upriver to Wolfe's Cove. "Let Us Cheer Their Majesties!" urged *Le Soleil* and other newspapers ("Applause, hands stretched out in a gesture of welcome and above all cheers"), but the first sound from those standing in the drive in front of the Château Frontenac had not been shouts, but a long communal gasp, as if no one could quite believe what was happening — the arrival of George VI and Elizabeth. The church bells of the city, obedient to the instructions of Cardinal Villeneuve, rang out in welcome, and the crowd finally found its voice along with the boats that tooted and whistled up and down the waterfront and the guns that fired out a royal salute.

"Canadian crowds," wrote John MacCormac, "are given to taking their pleasures silently, if not sadly." Like other reporters who stood at the dockside in unfamiliar cutaways and striped trousers, the *New York Times* correspondent was more used to the hoopla with which American political machines surrounded their leaders. "Feeling the eager curiosity and awed reverence with which his people awaited him," MacCormac wrote in wonderment at the King's arrival, "one had to pinch one's self to remember that this was North America and that the year was 1939."

Even Pallie Pascoe, ducking away from his postal chores long enough to catch the great moment, admitted that "you could have heard a pin drop" when the King and Queen stepped ashore ("Every person seemed stunned, but a cordial wave of the King's hand and a warm smile from the Queen broke the spell and from that minute . . . the crowd was madly enthusiastic"). "God Save the King" was played and then the royal couple held court among the palms and potted ferns, meeting Lieutenant-Governor Esiof Patenaude and his wife, members of the Dominion Cabinet, and the other dignitaries. Whatever they were thinking or feeling (and their nerves must have been taut and strained by the occasion), the King and Queen carried off the initial ceremonies well. The Queen in particular chatted brightly, her eyes darting about, missing nothing, while the King inspected the black-busbied and scarlet-coated honour guard of his French-speaking Royal 22nd Regiment.

Ceremonies over, they entered their large open limousine; a Mountie sprang forward to tuck them in with a large blue rug, and they were off, up the winding road to the Legislative Assembly. As the procession moved through the narrow cobbled alleys of the Lower Town, people crowded at the shuttered windows and hung over their balconies for a look. What some had described as a seething hotbed of nationalism looked more like London on Coronation Day. Union Jacks and bunting and portraits of the King hung everywhere. Children sported cheap paper badges with crude, almost unrecognizable, likenesses of Their Majesties. And here again there was a momentary intake of breath as the King and Queen swept by; then everyone cheered so loudly that there was no need of the men who had been placed here and there to stir up the crowd's fervour. As usual, it was the Queen who attracted the most attention. "Her smile matches the sunshine of this glorious spring morning," the CBC's Frank Willis told listeners, "so genuine it is, and so sincerely friendly!"

Cheers from the massive crowds outside echoed around the King and Queen as they entered the Red Chamber of the Legislative Assembly. On all sides, in frock coats, striped trousers, and "a startling array of grey and white spats", stood members of the Empire's only French-speaking assembly (given to such "torrential" emotion, according to one American reporter, that they had "a habit of taking off their shoes and pounding with them on their desks"). Premier Maurice

Duplessis, looking elegant and distinguished, bowed low before Their Majesties and extended a soft hand in greeting.

It was everyone's worst nightmare (particularly those in his own government) that the Premier would show up drunk during the Royal Visit and cause a scandal. This was, after all, the man who in the winter of 1938 strode in unannounced upon the astounded members of the Reform Club, paused to relieve himself on the fire, then without a word walked out to his waiting car. Duplessis's reputation as a bon vivant and a drinker were only rivalled by his truly astonishing recuperative powers. Today he was looking, in his own favourite phrase, "dangerously well", in spite of having been, according to Dr. Coleman, up until five that morning. In a room dominated by a huge crucifix and packed with "grand dames, colorful monsignori and sandaled monks", the *nationaliste* Premier of Quebec officially welcomed Their Majesties, expressing in French "the sentiments of joy, respect, loyalty and affection of the entire Province of Quebec . . . ":

> Always has our province been faithful to the crown of Britain; equally has it been faithful to traditions inherited from our forebears, to the pact of Confederation of 1867, and to that mission which British statesmen in 1791 confided to it — *"to remain altogether French"* [the phrase was spoken in English]. This past we cherish in our hearts and never shall we cease to consider the throne as the bulwark of our democratic institutions and our constitutional liberties.

First in line to greet the royal couple was a smiling Rodrigue Cardinal Villeneuve. Unmindful of the waiting (in some cases, impatiently seething) line-up behind him, the prelate chatted at length with the King, underlining his status as a prince of the Church (and his own significant role in the Royal Visit) with a lingering fatherly pat on the royal hand.

Then, following a brief rest in the Citadel, where the Governor General kept a summer residence, the King met with Roosevelt's man, Daniel Roper, who was officially accepted by the King as Envoy Extraordinary and Minister Plenipotentiary of the United States to Canada. Another ceremonial first for the tour and, significantly, one that involved the United States. Then it was on to the Château Frontenac for the first of the state luncheons.

Assembled in the banquet room among the banks and bowers of roses and delphinium were three hundred distinguished guests, including virtually every living Privy Councillor in the country — men whose careers stretched back to the early days of Laurier. Overhead in the galleries sat wealthy Americans, dense with jewels, who had bought out every available room in the hotel for the right to peer quietly over the wooden railing at the spectacle below. Missing, however, was Premier Duplessis, apparently insulted that he had been seated so far from Their Majesties at the head table. Outside the hotel, soldiers in full-dress uniforms had plunked themselves down unceremoniously on the pavement and were enjoying their box lunches and soda pop. But inside, the lobster tails, grilled breast of chicken, and Grand Marnier soufflé were held up while officials conferred anxiously about what should be done about the missing Premier. The King meanwhile chewed disconsolately on some toast placed in front of him and remarked on the slowness of the service. When the decision was made finally to go ahead with the meal (the Premier never did show up), the King recovered his humour and ate heartily like a schoolboy. He even won affection for his gallantry in disappearing under the table to retrieve the handbag of Madame Lapointe when it fell.

When the plates were cleared away, Their Majesties were toasted in turn with Veuve Cliquot '28, and the King hastily lit up a cigarette as the Prime Minister reminded the guests that "Today, as never before, the throne has become the centre of our national life." Then came the moment the King dreaded. The Queen's face tightened in anxiety as George VI rose to make his first public speech of the Royal Visit. Stammering slightly in English, but with almost no hesitation when he spoke French, he made it through the pleasantries: "two great races . . . the spirit of Quebec . . . vigorous spirit, proudly guarded". The gold microphones carried his words through loudspeakers to the large crowd outside, and to the rest of the country and Empire as well.

Whatever the King's limitations as a performer, the presence of royalty was beginning to work its magic on the country even before the first day of the tour had ended. Even the press was in danger of losing much of its reputation for cynicism. Several reporters had been discovered moist-eyed in the lobby of the

Château cheering along with everyone else as the royal couple left for the ceremonies at Battlefield Park. And already they had begun competing for the patriotic high ground in reports being filed for the late editions:

> A Quebec sun beamed from its bluest heaven. And a mighty river sang softly toward the sea. And a pageantry-proud populace, with flashing eye and tossing bosom and unbreakable grip upon the freedom and the favor that it enjoys, gave spontaneous, stirring "bienvenue" and rose of its own volition to the unmistakable challenge laid squarely on its doorstep. From hearts everywhere — hardened, hearty, lofty and limp — there poured to the brimming over, that respectful, restrained allegiance so deftly won by bayonet and ball of a "thin red line" on Abraham Martin's back acres, 180 years ago.

Almost alone among the three hundred or more journalists in Quebec City who churned out excited copy for their readers that day, Bruce Hutchison had tried to make some larger sense of what was happening around him. No great admirer of monarchical institutions, the bespectacled political correspondent for the *Vancouver Sun* was nevertheless almost literally caught up in the excitement. In the afternoon, he and an American newsman had been carried helplessly along by the good-natured mobs in their Sunday best who surged back and forth through the city, hoping for another glimpse of the royal couple. At one point, the reporters were being swept down the Grande Allée when a government limousine with motorcycle outriders suddenly appeared through the crowd. A door opened and Hutchison's fellow British Columbian, Defence Minister Ian Mackenzie, pulled them inside. At Place d'Armes, young soldiers with fixed bayonets could do little against the hopeless scramble of stalled traffic, so Hutchison and his companion got out of the car and shouldered their way through the flag-waving crowds till they got to the Plains of Abraham.

The old battlefield was flooded by an immense sea of Quebec schoolchildren, forty thousand in all, who had waited for hours under the hot sun for this moment. As the royal limousine drove up to the monuments honouring Wolfe and Montcalm, they screamed and waved their flags and began to sing "God Save the King" as Their Majesties had never heard it before:

Dieu protège le Roi!
En lui nous avons foi,
    Vive le Roi!
Qu'il soit victorieux,
Et que son peuple heureux,
Le comble de ses voeux,
    Vive le Roi!

An old woman was standing near Hutchison as he and the other reporters watched the remarkable scene before them.

> An old woman, in rusty black coat, Irish by her accent, sings lustily in English and as she finishes the last "God Save the King" she turns to us and says as if it were surprising news: "These kids are French, that's French they were singing. They don't know no better."

Three little girls in white net dresses with flowers in their hair, representing the English, Irish, and French populations, advanced on the Queen, curtseyed, and presented a bouquet of English roses, entwined with French lilies of the valley. Then the forty thousand children sang "O Canada" — again in French—unable to keep time together, so that the anthem came out in succeeding waves.

> No Canadian can hear it rolling across the Plains of Abraham from the throats of these dark children without a strange feeling inside. All the history of these hundred years since Champlain's time, the whole story of Wolfe and Montcalm are mixed up somehow in this song.
>
> "That's French they're singing," the old woman tells us again and she seems quite unaware that tears are rolling down her cheek.
>
> It is an unforgettable sight — the French children and long sweep of the battlefield along the cliffs, the towers of Quebec, the walls of the Citadel, the river far below, beyond it the flat rolling countryside of Quebec.

Then it was on to the Lieutenant-Governor's official residence, Spencerwood, for tea *en famille* with the Patenaudes, and a special treat, *sucre à la crème*, made with pure maple syrup tapped from trees on the estate. The Quebec premier had by now bobbed back into view, acting as if nothing had happened. It was his sister, he told Mackenzie King coolly; she had come to town and he had to see her. Then, adding to the Prime Minister's annoyance, he ignored the conventions of light conversation to gossip enthusiastically about politics. The only time Mackenzie King warmed to him was when Duplessis told a rude story about that other great nemesis of the Prime Minister's, Ontario Premier Mitch Hepburn.

In the evening it was Quebec's turn to fête Their Majesties at an official dinner. Now the Premier was able to play the dapper and effusive host, while Mackenzie King was shoved to a remote end of the head table (exactly where Maurice Duplessis had been assigned at luncheon). There would be no grace (which troubled the Prime Minister) and no speeches; but there would be champagne, expensive wines, Russian caviar, rainbow trout, and an orchestra hidden behind the massed blooms in the Château's dining-room that played Scottish airs. More than 2,500 snowbirds had been trapped and slaughtered on the Île d'Orléans for the occasion; the caviar came in crowns carved from solid ice; and there was a great deal of pleasant conversation along the head table. The Cardinal even showed Mackenzie King the large and costly archiepiscopal ring which Duplessis had given to him (and which opened up to reveal the Premier's presentation speech inscribed minutely in gold). But after the long and wearying events of the first day, the royal couple seemed tired. The King dawdled over his food. And the Queen, magnificent in her diamond tiara and necklace, and wearing a crinoline gown of rose satin, played with her gloves until it was time to go. At ten o'clock — none too soon — the distinguished representatives of Church, State, and the Military stood for toasts to Their Majesties, and the banquet was over. There was one last wave to the large crowds braving the drizzle in the square outside the hotel, then it was back to the Citadel to spend the night.

In spite of the exhaustion the royal couple was feeling and could not help showing, the day had been a success — better than many had hoped for. The rest of Canada had been surprised and reassured by the stories of French Canadians in enormous numbers singing, clapping, and cheering the royal party (although the long processional route and city's comparatively small population meant that the crowds thinned out here and there). More interesting, however, was the reaction of Quebecers to Their Majesties. "The thunderstruck spectators cannot utter more than a strangled cry," wrote Jean Dufresne in *La Presse*, and the reporter at *Le Devoir* agreed:

> Strangely, no one was thinking of daring to cry out: "Long live the King! Long live the Queen!" It was more like a huge "aie", that certainly had none of the British dignity.

Typical was Laurent Hardy, a young man of twenty-one, who had gone alone to Côte de la Fabrique that day to be part of Quebec City's "infinitely respectful reception". As he recalled later, the people about him had been friendly and well-behaved, and there was no undue pushing or shoving. Of course, like everyone else, he had heard it said that the war was coming and that the Royal Visit was a sort of prelude. Those *nationalistes* he knew were against the tour, and it was not as if Hardy or anyone around him felt any particular affection for British royalty. But in Quebec there remained "the admiration for authority"; the King and Queen were considered very interesting and powerful — even extraordinary (one of Hardy's neighbours, for instance, could not be convinced that they had come into the world in the same manner as everyone else).

Also, for a population that enjoyed lavish spectacle, there was the sight of the slender, boyish King and his pretty Queen ("charmante" and "chic", people told reporters over and over again, "pictures don't do her justice"). Also long motor processions, society ladies in beautiful dresses, and Privy Councillors who strode about in gold braid and wore cocked hats with soft white silk fringes. The fact that the King had spoken in French impressed everyone. Americans might sniff a little at what they took to be the forelock-tugging of the northern neighbour, and *Time* magazine was quick to point out that the tour had gotten off *literally* on the wrong (i.e. left) foot when both the King and Queen came ashore. But everyone else seemed pleased. "The city was most thoughtfully decorated," concluded RCMP Constable Jim Coughlin, one of the four Mounties selected to travel with the Royal Train. "The people were very enthusiastic and sincere about everything. I believe these French Canadians are good subjects."

Yet there were parts of the French-Canadian experience that would remain completely untouched, even by the most impressive displays of royal pageantry. That night, after the brilliant fireworks display which lit up the sky over Lévis, people tramped home again on the wet streets, tired and happy; and many of them passed by the Franciscan chapel on the Grande Allée. Inside, four figures knelt in the gloom, heads bowed in prayer. All day, while the royal party had passed up and down the street outside, the roar of their motorcycle escorts mingling with the sound of the cheering, the nuns had prayed in never-ending relays before the altar. They had been doing this day and night for fifty years, and they made no sound now except for the soft clicking of their rosary beads.

Thursday, May 18:

Next morning, the King and Queen boarded the blue and silver carriages of the Royal Train, dubbed inevitably by the press the "palace on wheels". Each coach bore the royal cipher and crown and had been elaborately decorated, and each was fitted out with air conditioning, radio, and telephone. There was a barber shop, a switchboard (which could connect them in minutes with the princesses at Buckingham Palace at any stop), and an ingeniously organized system of laundry and food service — including the supplying of pasteurized milk, which was labelled "Royal Train".

The rear two carriages bore the royal coat of arms. These were Cars 1 and 2, the sumptuous living-quarters of the King and Queen. Car 1 contained the two main bedrooms — the King's in blue and white chintz, the Queen's decorated in a blue-grey, with dusty-pink damask chair covers and curtains to match. As well, there was an office for the King panelled in oak, dressing-rooms, private baths, a sitting-room with a radio, and a small library. Two bedrooms were set aside in these carriages for senior staff.

Also on board the twelve-car streamliner were living and working quarters for Mackenzie King, who travelled now as George VI's constitutional adviser. And distributed through the remaining cars was accommodation for about fifty people, including members of the royal entourage, the Prime Minister's staff, members of the Interdepartmental Committee, stenographers, railway workers, maids, and valets. (To the amusement of his fellow-passengers, the somewhat rough and ready RCMP Commissioner had quarters close to the ladies-in-waiting, as well as the Queen's extensive wardrobe.) Up at the front of the train was Canadian Pacific Engine 2850, with its enormous stainless-steel Hudson engine (later to be dubbed *Royal* Hudson), refitted for the occasion. The locomotive had been dressed in royal blue, silver, and gold; and, to add to the impressive effect it would have as it puffed into each station along the route, imperial crowns had been attached to the running-boards and the royal arms were emblazoned over the headlight.

Running a half-hour ahead of the "palace on wheels" was the entirely ordinary-looking pilot train, which housed the radiomen, extra RCMP officers, post office, telegraph, and telephone officials, a special darkroom for the photographers and film crews — and of course the newspaper reporters, who had become uncomfortably aware that they had just bunked down in what was essentially a safety and security precaution for the royal party:

> If a bridge fails, if a freight train gets shunted to the main line, or somebody leaves a bomb on the track it will be 30 minutes before the train bearing King George VI and Queen Elizabeth across Canada this week comes upon the wreckage of its pilot train and the mangled bodies of 56 correspondents and twelve photographers who are covering Their Majesties' trip.

The enormous headaches involved in organizing a tour of this size would have overwhelmed anyone but Canada's two railway giants, who between them commanded the thousands of trainmen, hotel staff, waiters, laundry workers, and servicing crews necessary to keep the passengers on both trains fed, cleaned, clothed — and on time. The CPR routinely scheduled a yearly tour for its president, Sir Edward Beatty, to every part of his empire, so the company's employees were well-practised and confident in what they could provide. It had been agreed that the first part of the tour, west to Vancouver, would be over Canadian Pacific track. The return east would be made largely on CNR track, with Canadian National replacing the Hudson engine with its own locomotive in Vancouver, the ninety-four-foot-long CN 6057, the largest engine in the British Empire. The train itself had been made up of stock from both companies except for the two royal carriages, which were normally for the private use of the Governor General. Understandably, given the enormous effort and expense of the two rivals, each was jealous to claim credit for its own work — so much so that the Interdepartmental Committee had made delicate requests that neither the King nor the Queen make any comment about either railway that might find its way into that company's advertising.

The party set out for Montreal with the royal salute booming out from the 94th Artillery Brigade on the St. Charles River, and the crowd, their inhibitions finally gone, pouring past the station barriers and onto the tracks. At the controls of the train was Eugene Leclerc, a forty-eight-year veteran who had worked as a fireman on the royal train when George VI's father had visited Canada in 1901. They sped through the Quebec countryside past farmhouses where the Union Jacks fluttered prominently and small railway crossings were choked with farm wagons, horse buggies, and cars. Huge crowds were waiting for them at their first stop in Trois-Rivières. This was the city where Maurice Duplessis had been born forty-nine years before, and where he had practised law before beginning his successful political career. The Premier still held the affections of his constituents; and they included him in the ecstatic applause with which they greeted the King and Queen. After the warmth of the welcome in Trois-Rivières, there could no longer be any doubt of the tour's success.

That afternoon as they pulled into Montreal, there was an "air of blissful anticipation", different from Quebec City. People had been pouring in since before dawn, forming up along the curb with picnic lunches, blankets, and steamer rugs against the cold. Reporters and officials estimated that the population of Canada's largest city had doubled overnight to two million. The previous evening, police had cleared Jean Talon Station of those who had come with blankets to spend the night, but by early morning they were back, including one defiant old lady who refused to budge from her spot by the door for the eight hours it took the Royal Train to arrive. Everywhere children could be seen playing and running among the immense throngs with names and addresses pinned to their coats. Two men wandered the streets wearing home-made masks which resembled Hitler and Mussolini. On his back, one of the men wore a sign that read, "Ach Benito, we have been fooled"; to which his companion's sign carried the reply, "Yes — and to think we believed the Empire was crumbling."

As the train shuddered to a stop, Mackenzie King came bustling up the platform — too late — as the troublesome Camillien Houde ("a country uncle with sunflower seeds in his pocket") advanced grinning to introduce himself to the King. Bumptious, cunning, "full of wonderful moods, tricks, imitative talk," as A. M. Klein was to describe him so memorably, the Mayor of Montreal had already caused grief for the Interdepartmental Committee. A political embarrassment because of his right-wing views (only months before, he had declared that Quebecers would support fascist Italy in any war with Great Britain), he had threatened to cancel the civic reception if he couldn't claim pride of place in the the car following the King. The Prime Minister had fumed, but in the end the Committee had given in, concerned about the Mayor's explosive temper and unpredictability, which made him at this moment the most dangerous politician in the country. A loose cannon, they reasoned, and, what was worse, a popular one. (Nevertheless, Houde was interned by the Canadian government in 1940 for advising Quebecers not to register for military service.)

Today, however, for the sake of Madame Houde and his three daughters, all of them thrilled beyond measure by the occasion, the Mayor was on his best behaviour. While the King passed down the ranks of the Black Watch and Les Fusiliers Mont-Royal, Houde chatted pleasantly with the Queen, and showed due courtesy to everyone present, including the somewhat mollified Mackenzie King. The Prime Minister noted, however, that "he took care to take the right of the car when we started off from the station. At first he was inclined to take off his hat to the crowds and when I did not move mine, he gave that up."

More than a million people lined the twenty-three-mile route, the largest turnout of the Canadian tour, and they cheered loudly, with none of the reserve that Quebec City had shown. "It was not the normal Montreal seen on May 18th," admitted *Le Devoir*, sounding almost embarrassed that a city so proud of its cosmopolitan reputation would carry on like this. The sight of the King and Queen in their open limousine, flanked by the horses and the black tunics and gold braid of the 17th Duke of York's Royal Canadian Hussars, "wrenched from normally unemotional breasts clamours that in the eyes of the passing foreigner, could win Montreal a name for abandoning itself unrestrainedly to public demonstrations, especially when they are grandiose."

The hundreds of thousands of dollars the city had spent on its welcome were evident in the lavish decorations seen everywhere along the royal route. Every major department store along Ste. Catherine Street had dressed up its windows with huge portraits and patriotic slogans. The bleachers of Montreal Stadium overflowed with nearly fifty thousand cheering French-Canadian schoolchildren, many of them dressed to form a gigantic human Union Jack. And, in the Canadian way, a different venue, McGill Stadium, was provided for the English-speaking children. In front of St. James Cathedral four hundred priests stood and waved to the big maroon car as it passed. At Lafontaine Park on Sherbrooke Street, where two hundred buckskin-clad Iroquois from the Caughnawaga reservation stood on Lady Raddick's lawn, at Notre Dame, at Place d'Armes by the statue of Maisonneuve, where only a ragged line of Girl Guides held back the crowds, in front of the Royal Victoria Hospital — everywhere people waved that day, "cheering and cheering and cheering".

The day was sunny and clear, although the air was cold. The Queen had refused to bundle up, however, confiding to Mackenzie King with a tug of her dress that she was already wearing her woollies. In any case, the royal pair were too enthralled by their reception to care much about the weather. There were tears among some who watched, and once when the Queen walked close to a group of women in the crowd, every one of them sank down in a curtsey. After one particularly boisterous welcome, the King startled the Prime Minister for a moment by asking if he were deaf — he meant from the shouting.

> The little cubs sounded like a marsh full of frogs in the spring. The crowds in the hollow faces of the big buildings were like a cannonade. I did not see an unpleasant incident all day.

There were, of course, the veterans. At City Hall, where the King wore a pince-nez to write his name in the Livre d'Or, twenty men from the old Montreal Garrison Artillery, veterans of the Riel Rebellion, turned out to greet the royal couple. One Boer War vet had even hired a private ambulance for the day so he could watch them go by. The cheering continued. "You know, Your Majesty," the Mayor ventured puckishly as he and the King stood together on the City Hall balcony overlooking the crowd, "some of these cheers are for you also."

Not everyone cheered. Mathilde Ganzini, eight years old, was the only one in her class to see Their Majesties. In the East End neighbourhood where she lived, such an act was seen as a kind of betrayal — one more reason to look down on her immigrant family with suspicion. Her parents followed the events in Europe on their short-wave radio, but as she remembered it years later, people around them seemed less concerned about Chamberlain or Hitler than by the humiliation they still felt about their defeat at the hands of the British in 1759. "They felt scorned" by English Canadians; this was particularly true of one neighbour of the Ganzinis, a typesetter for *Le Devoir* who vehemently opposed the presence of the King and Queen in Quebec.

In spite of all this, and in spite of her Italian father, who took such things as royal tours with a grain of salt, Mathilde Ganzini travelled to Côte des Neiges across the invisible barrier between the English and the French ("between serfs and seigneurs") to a spot on the processional route by the cemetery. For the young girl, the momentary glimpse of royalty was like an "apparition". It was the same for Bresne La Pierre, a small boy living in Rosemount, who watched with his whole family as the procession passed by Berri near Sherbrooke in the afternoon. Jean-Louis Gouin, only seven, was in front of the Outrement Convent when Their Majesties passed by on the Côte Ste. Catherine. Many in the crowd used the carton telescopes from the "English bakers". "Even if we weren't royalists," he recalled, "I remember that we had a portrait of George VI in the basement. At the time we had a great respect for royalty." In Outremont, the Belangers had guests over for the afternoon to watch from their balcony, and Thérèse Belanger decorated a cake in the form of the Union Jack. For them, as for others, the Queen was inevitably "charmante", the King, less comfortable or demonstrative with the crowds, usually "effacé".

In the afternoon, the royal party drove to the top of Mount Royal and had tea at a chalet perched high above the city. Near where Jacques Cartier had stood four hundred years before, the King and Queen strolled onto the balcony with Mayor Houde and the Prime Minister to look down on the wide expanse of the St. Lawrence, the church spires, and the tall buildings of Canada's capital of business. Then, after the King had unveiled a simple granite block commemorating the visit, the Mayor had a surprise for them. "Debutantes," marvelled Mackenzie King. Houde had arranged for the well-brought-up young ladies who had served the tea and cakes to be presented to Their Majesties. "The King was rather amused; said it was rather a novel idea to have a Court in the middle of a drive — something worth introducing in London."

The fact that the tour was going so well had not stopped the Prime Minister from fidgeting about matters of decorum and protocol. First, it was the order of procession. Stung perhaps by the criticism that he was monopolizing the King's and Queen's attention, he argued with his officials that it was the Lord-in-Waiting and Lady-in-Waiting and not himself who should be walking directly behind Their Majesties. This in spite of the argument, put forward by Keenleyside and others, that it was the Canadians who must be given pride of place on this tour. Then, he arranged to exchange his seat next to the Queen that night with Archbishop Antonio Gauthier, a generous gesture that Houde told him he'd regret. Houde was right.

Tonight, after dressing to go to dinner, I said I thought I should go with the King's party but was told by Heeney, Coleman and Keenleyside that I could do as I did, last night, and take my seat in advance, and let the other party come later. That this had been all agreed. I said repeatedly I thought that was wrong. However, found myself going out alone with two or three members of the public service, hunting around for a car out of doors, and driving around with this group to the Hotel. This was humiliating; then going into the dining-room, was deserted by my own staff and was unable to find a place at the table, my seat not being where it was indicated. Then when it was found I was half way down, at the end of a table with no one at one side of me, and on the other side, Lady Tellier, who cannot speak a word of English, it really put me in a humiliating position. I was kept waiting there without being able to speak to anyone for twenty minutes; waiting for the arrival of the King and Queen. Then the King came in with his suite but I was not a member of it, though Minister in Attendance and Prime Minister of Canada and in the largest Capital of the Dominion. I felt very hurt that I should have been let down in this way, and all against my own repeated statements that I felt we were making a mistake in having me go as I did with members of my staff instead of with the King as Prime Minister as well as Minister in Attendance. . . . I am beginning to find it has been a desire on the part of our own people not to push Canada too far to the fore; they succeeded tonight in pushing Canada out of the picture altogether.

In spite of the Prime Minister's understandable mortification, the formal dinner that night at the Windsor Hotel was one of the memorable successes of the Royal Visit. A crowd of between seventy-five and one hundred thousand in Dominion Square gave the royal couple a great roar of applause as they stepped from their car, the King slim and elegant in evening clothes, his wife wearing a white and silver gown embroidered with crystal beads and diamanté and falling into a graceful train. The air was warm and the honour guard formed by the Maisonneuve Regiment, unable to drink anything, sucked sugar cubes instead to allay their thirst.

The city of Montreal had spared no expense that evening, and the thousand guests accommodated in the Windsor Hotel's two banquet halls sat down to a magnificent feast of spring turtle soup, halibut, squab, Curaçao sherbert and iced strawberries — all at an astounding fifteen dollars a plate. The Mayor of course presided over the evening, but Camillien

Houde, after his effervescent performance in the afternoon, was behaving in an uncharacteristically subdued manner. Someone had obviously made an effort to rein him in before he did something that would embarrass everyone. What happened over the next few hours, however, has passed into the Houde legend — and in a number of variations. The most frequently told version has it that after one particularly long and awkward silence at the head table, Houde made some display of taking a piece of paper from his pocket, then frowned, and spoke aloud to himself.

"Now I have been told that I must not address my King unless he speaks to me first." Naturally, the King reached over for the paper, and Houde was heard to say, not quite ingenuously, "Your Majesty, this is the first time I have ever blushed."

"Did you do this?" The King pointed to something on Houde's list.

"Yes, Your Majesty, I did."

"But you certainly did not do *this.*"

Of course the King ordered him from then on to talk as he pleased, and for the rest of the dinner Houde was his old self, telling little jokes, and making those at the table around him roar with laughter. Journalists who had watched the shy, awkward performance of George VI during his first two days in Canada were amazed to see him suddenly bursting into spontanous laughter, and motioning to the Queen on Houde's left to share in the joke. After platoons of solemn, dignified officials, the royal couple had met the *original* of Canadian politics.

In the meantime, in Dominion Square a mix-up in the announced program had kept the crowd waiting for more than an hour and a half, and their continuous chants for the King and Queen could be heard through the walls of the banqueting-room. Finally, with the Mayor and Mackenzie King, Their Majesties stepped out onto the balcony, and into the glare of a huge spotlight. The cheers thundered about them as they stood silhouetted against the dark stone of the building. First a few quavering voices, and then the whole crowd began to sing "God Save the King". It was a moving, spontaneous moment, and *La Presse* noted how when the royal couple turned to go back to the banqueting-room they did so with moist eyes.

"Never," according to *Le Canada*, "has Montreal known a similar demonstration of loyalty and patriotism." It was to be one of the special moments of the Canadian tour.

When the time came for dessert and coffee, the royal couple moved into the Rose Room to sit with the overflow guests, and the Queen eased Mackenzie King's continuing chagrin somewhat by motioning him to a seat beside her. The Mayor stood then and made a short speech. In somewhat halting English, he welcomed Their Majesties once again to Montreal and said he thanked them from the bottom of his heart for coming. "My wife," he continued, "thanks you from her bottom, too."

Throughout the evening, a quartet had been entertaining those assembled with a selection of French and English folk songs, and Houde now rose to ask them to sing the most famous French-Canadian folk song of all. Everyone in the room took it up except the King, who contented himself with beating time on the table with his spoon. Even the Queen joined in, making the necessary gestures: head, nose, arms. What, she asked the Mayor as the song finally ended, was the status of "Alouette" in Quebec? "If Your Majesty allows me to be frank," replied the beaming Houde, "I'll say it is our national anthem after midnight."

The banquet ended just after ten and the guests spilled out of the hotel and into the cool night air. Frank Delaute and a number of others from the Committee were strolling down the street in their evening dress, feeling a bit grand because of the occasion, until someone in the crowd called out, "Here come the waiters," and they moved on more quickly. At Windsor Station there was just time for the King and Queen to bid farewell to Sir Edward Beatty and the directors of the CPR before the train pulled out. Their Majesties stood on the observation platform waving to the crowds as they left; at Westmount the Queen appeared by herself to wave; and then both again were outside at Montreal West, where at midnight more than five thousand waited for a glimpse of them disappearing down the track. In the distance, from the Dorchester Street Bridge the sound of Montreal's final royal salute could be heard.

After the heat and noise of the banquet hall, Mackenzie King had been revived somewhat by the drive back to the station;

by the time he crawled into his bed at 12:30 that night he had calmed down enough to see things in a more reflective light.

> Had it not been for the humiliating experience of being alone and isolated at the dinner table tonight, I should have enjoyed the evening very much as my mind was clear. . . . I am afraid I am far too sensitive. I shall never forget today, however; scenes of rejoicing, etc. So far as the feeling toward Monarchy is concerned, nothing anywhere could have exceeded the evidence of spontaneous joys, or the day's demonstration. I felt very proud of my country.

Once Ottawa and Toronto were out of the way, he would be able to relax and begin to enjoy the journey. Get to know the members of the party well enough to make a few real friends.

That night, after a short run, the Royal Train pulled off on a quiet siding near Caledonia Springs on the Ontario side of the border. The passengers slept under the clear sky and — unusual for late May — the dancing colours of the Northern Lights.

CHAPTER FIVE

Daylight Upon Magic

Friday, May 19:

"WHAT THEIR MAJESTIES HAD SEEN in the first whirlwind two days was mostly quaint, Arcadian stuff," said *Time* magazine in an article that raised hackles all over Quebec, "a Frenchy people curious, appreciative but not essentially King-loving in the British manner. Beef-eating Ottawa more than made up for this." Things in fact did not begin quite so well for the royal party. Sleet had been seen bouncing on the streets of the capital earlier in the morning; by eleven it had changed to a sullen drizzle that bore down relentlessly as the blue and silver train came chuffing to a halt at the temporary station on Island Park Drive. As the royal couple stepped onto the red-carpeted platform to be welcomed by Lord and Lady Tweedsmuir and other dignitaries, the sun punched through for a few seconds, replaced almost immediately by the rain again. It pelted them mercilessly as they clattered bravely off in the state landau (now refurbished), exposed not only to rain but to the numbing forty-degree temperature.

Ottawa had done its best to shake off its dull image and provide a fitting royal welcome. Ten thousand crown-capped banners fluttered along the royal route. Twenty-five thousand coloured lights hung in Nepean Point Park, set to twinkle that evening from the Outlook to the Château Laurier. Government buildings were floodlit and their lights left on all night as if the old lumber town were suddenly recasting itself as the City of Light. Hotels, boarding-houses, and rooming-houses had all filled up quickly with people flocking to town to see the royal couple. Nervous officials, fearing a crush, asked people not to come downtown, but to watch the royal procession in their own neighbourhoods.

A solid mass of people waited to cheer the royal procession as it moved by the Experimental Farm on its way to downtown Ottawa. At Dow's Lake, a woman watching from a boathouse gave birth to a baby girl, whom she named Margaret Rose. Ten thousand children waited at the Exhibition Grounds in Lansdowne Park as the coach, flanked by a mounted escort of Princess Louise Dragoons, circled the stadium. At Confederation Square, where the RCMP patrolled with long riot clubs and hawkers did a brisk business in periscopes and portable seats, the crowds were enormous. Still, Ottawa had a tough act to follow. "Although the crowd was rather good it was Quiet," noted Constable Coughlin, no doubt recalling the emotional scenes of the day before. From the reassuring warmth of his closed car, Mackenzie King agreed. "The entire route was lined with people; in the centre of the town, there were great crowds, but after Montreal, the number seemed relatively few."

Before an open fire at Rideau Hall, the King shivered off the effects of the eight-mile ride. Ottawa was intended as the ceremonial centrepiece of the tour, and with his stay now shortened by a day and a half, he was expected to begin performing his duties even before the field marshal's uniform he was wearing had dried. There were letters of credence to be accepted from the new United States Ambassador, the American legation to be received, and a group of ambassadors to shake hands and make small talk with — all before lunch.

The day's principal function was the convocation of the two Houses of Parliament to hear the King give royal assent to a series of bills including a United States–Canada trade agreement, a wheat subsidy, and the Dominion budget. Mackenzie King's hopes of proroguing Parliament had come to nothing, but as compensation he would now have a fine display of pomp and ceremony, and later, as a symbolic "Kingly Act", the Great Seal of Canada would be used for the first time.

After a private luncheon with the Governor General, the King and Queen arrived on Parliament Hill about 2:30 for the convocation ceremony. Entering the Senate Chamber in ceremonial robes, they led an impressive procession which included commanders from local militia units, the Earl of Airlie, the Lord Chamberlain, Lords- and Ladies-in-Waiting, and members of the Defence Council. Waiting for them were the Senators, the Speaker of the Commons, the Gentleman Usher of the Black Rod, the Clerk, and the Assistant Clerk. Then came the seven Supreme Court Justices, who bowed as they filed in, and took their places on the large circular woolsack.

Then it was the turn of the Members of the House of Commons, who, respecting tradition, had been waiting in their chamber behind closed doors, all but the CCF members in morning dress. They were now summoned by the Gentleman Usher of the Black Rod, at the request of the Speaker. Also by tradition, backed by historical precedent dating back to the seventeenth-century struggles between Parliament and the Crown, they did not respond to the first, or even the second, knock by the messenger from the Other Place. Only after the third knock were they led into the Senate by their Speaker and the Sergeant-at-Arms, stopping at the Bar, and crowding into the aisle and the back of the Chamber. By now a few of the Honourable Members, who had had enough of the obscure points of parliamentary tradition, so far forgot their dignity as to climb the woodwork for a better look.

This was for Mackenzie King a moment of symbolic triumph, "the full flowering of our nationhood", as he called it later. In a ceremony virtually fallen into disuse (it hadn't been seen in England since 1854), the King sat in the Upper Chamber to give royal assent to nine bills passed by the Parliament of Canada. Seated with the Queen on the red thrones, George VI nodded patiently to each piece of legislation and the deputy clerk droned, "His Majesty doth assent." Some care had been taken not to have among them any Private Members' Bills or Divorce Bills which might spoil the effect of the ceremony.

The pomp and circumstance over for the day, there was just time for a quiet tea at Government House before a special reception for the ladies and gentlemen of the press. It would be hard to over-emphasize what an extraordinary departure this event was for the time. Certainly such a thing was unimaginable back in England, where the newspapers had kept a deferential silence while Edward VIII wooed the American divorcée Mrs. Simpson — all this at a time when Americans were being served up delicious details on a daily basis. Moreover, George VI regarded the press with horror. For him there were still the painful memories of the newspapermen who had dogged his footsteps everywhere he went on his first visit to Canada in 1913. At that time, the prospect of facing them so terrified him that in Montreal he had hired a shipmate to impersonate him, which the young stand-in did with such success that he was able to convince the local press that the young Prince Albert performed his naval duties wearing a bowler hat.

The same fear or mistrust was not shared by Elizabeth, who had in any case from her earliest years learned the tricks of enchanting and pleasing those about her. Newspapers, and the more modern extensions of radio and newsreels, simply provided the opportunity to enlarge her advantages as a woman who, in Tweedsmuir's words, possessed "a genius for the right kind of publicity".

The dangers of press coverage were obvious — had already in fact marred the first days of the royal tour. *Time* and *Life*, writing about the security thrown up around the royal couple in Quebec, reported that they had been conveyed at all times in bullet-proof limousines, but not mentioning that these same cars would be used everywhere on the tour. Nothing could have provoked anger in French Canada more than the heavy contrast drawn between this arrangement and the state landau used in Ottawa ("The only gangsters or gunmen we have," bristled *Le Devoir*, "come to us from the U.S. — from New York or Chicago"). Politicians across Quebec raged at this slight upon their loyalty, and the press took up the cry by making its own comparisons ("We are not yet very civilized," fumed the author of the column "Groucho's Notebook". "It's obvious, since we haven't offered hot dogs or peanut butter sandwiches to our royal visitors, with pickles. . . . That will be for Washington"). The King would be properly sympathetic with these sentiments, having seen firsthand what the press could do. "He is more terrified of the press and their misrepresentation of things than anything else," observed Mackenzie King, adding with some feeling, "What a curse the modern press has become!"

Reporters on the other hand could also be protective of their subjects. Newsmen on the royal tour had for instance been particularly unamused when German newspapers, which had virtually ignored the arrival of the King and Queen, suddenly began running articles that jeered at the event and mocked the "fantastic" security precautions. *Local-Anzeiger* reported that citizens in Quebec City were unable to carry cameras or flowers, appear with arm slings, or even put their hands in their pockets for fear of arrest. Reporters muttered darkly about Nazi agents in their midst, and eventually blamed the reports on "pink-cheeked, 22 year old Bruno Seymours, who had loved to sit around and drink with other correspondents until he suddenly disappeared from the trip at Montreal."

Radio remained an equally subversive medium for the royal family. At the wedding of Prince Albert and Elizabeth Bowes-Lyon in 1923, the Archbishop of Canterbury had forbidden the service to be broadcast, arguing that it was liable to be heard in pubs by men wearing hats. But the power of radio could not be ignored for long. Hitler had already used it to stunning effect on the German people; FDR had put it to better use in his Fireside Chats. And events like the crash of the airship *Hindenburg* a year earlier, or the dramatic rescue efforts at Nova Scotia's Moose River Mine, had showed how radio could reach out to millions. Even George V, who had disapproved of everything since the Flood ("painted fingernails, women who smoked in public, cocktails, frivolous hats, American jazz, and the growing habit of going away for weekends"), had in the end been persuaded to try his hand at speaking in special Christmas broadcasts — a phenomenon for the British public, most of whom had never heard their Sovereign's voice and who in many cases had stood to attention when his voice came crackling over the airwaves. George VI, as conscious of his duty as he was of his humiliating stammer, had bravely reintroduced the tradition that his brother Edward had let lapse.

And of course America *was* Radioland. It might not do back in England for a BBC announcer to appear in anything less than a dinner jacket to read the news, but in the New World, radio was just another word for the wide-open spaces. Aimee Semple McPherson had called to the faithful over the radio waves from California; so now did Father Coughlin, who broadcast his simple, but immensely popular, message of Christianity and anti-Semitism on his program "Golden Hour of the

Little Flower" in Detroit. Broadcasting from the studios of the Prophetic Bible Institute in Calgary, William Aberhart — "Bible Bill" — had sold Depression-weary Albertans on the gospel of Social Credit, and in the process propelled himself into the premier's chair. Sports announcers using sound effects and a bare outline from the wire service could conjure up baseball and hockey games that had no more relation to reality than the contents of Fibber McGee's closet. And it had been just six months since the ultimate demonstration of radio's power, when Orson Welles had stampeded America with his Halloween production of *War of the Worlds*. Radio stirred up, entertained, and intrigued. It was a medium that "created" worlds of its own.

The royal family, which possessed a keen survival sense, was not slow to see that its fate had become entwined with the fortunes of the press, the movie newsreel, and this newest medium of radio. And so at a time when a middle-class Canadian matron in Montreal or Toronto would be properly discomfited to find her name in the newspaper, *for any reason*, the King and Queen had surrendered to the publicity machine. What good was it if they won the affection of millions in North America if the message was not somehow conveyed to the rest of the world? The matter had been put to Tommy Lascelles during his visit to Canada in February, and with the active support of the Governor General, the Palace had agreed. The relationship was now official: the press was to be accommodated, cosseted, humoured, suffered—and now paid attention to.

Thus it was that one hundred and seven men and women from the pilot train, the Parliamentary Press Gallery, and the local newspapers formed a circle in one of Rideau Hall's larger salons to chat politely and with what was for many of them an unaccustomed formality. The press of the day still teetered on the edge of self-parody sometimes with their boozy camaraderie and devotion to a life where the fedora remained firmly jammed on the back of the head. Yet today there was a surprising number of formal dresses, cutaways, and high hats to be seen among them. Even those who earlier in the afternoon had sat with the *Toronto Daily Star*'s Gordon Sinclair in the beverage room of the Château Laurier (standing up on occasion and smashing their empty glasses against the stone wall beside their table) had managed to clean themselves up, squeeze into starched collars, and find their way to Government House to be presented to Their Majesties.

"It will be worth remembering," American newspaper columnist Westbrook Pegler had written, "that they are not coming to visit the American newspapers. . . . There is no obligation on the King or Queen to take any journalists on their laps or invite them to pull up chairs and shoot olive pits with them." Whether they had taken Pegler's words to heart, the reporters —American, British, Canadian—were certainly on their best behaviour when the royal couple entered unannounced that afternoon. One by one, the one hundred men and seven women were presented to Their Majesties by Walter Thompson of the CNR's public relations department, who without notes introduced each newswriter—many of whom he'd just met himself for the first time.

The reception was everything the tour organizers could have hoped for. In the unblushing estimation of the press, tradition had been smashed to smithereens in the Empire on which the sun never sets ("they looked so much like the young couple next door," gushed one reporter, Inez Robb, "that the instant they entered the room I had an impulse to set up the bridge table and go out in the kitchen to investigate ice cube conditions"). While the press was itself dressed to the nines, and bowing and curtseying for all it was worth ("I did a half buck-and-wing . . . getting that old left foot behind the right and flexing the right knee as pretty as if it never had a twinge of rheumatism since last winter"), it was nevertheless the *ordinariness* of the King and Queen that was celebrated. The King had a swell smile, a firm hand-clasp. There was no swank or side about him. As for the Queen, well, what more could be said? Beautiful, charming, gracious, no camera could ever do her justice.

Familiarity made some bold. New York reporter George Dixon ("Dixon of the *Daily News*"), in spite of his Canadian origins, epitomized the jumped-up tough-guy style of the American tabloids. A man who customarily wrote out of the side of his mouth, Dixon filed a lead story (headlined NEWS REPORTER GABS WITH KING) in which he reported the following exchange:

> King: I suppose you have been working pretty hard.
> Me: So have you. But you're certainly in there punching. You sure can take it.
> King: Oh, yes, indeed.

Afterwards, with the press seen on its way, there was time for a short walk around the grounds of Government House with Lord Tweedsmuir before the Prime Minister showed up. Mackenzie King carried with him two of the bills that had received royal assent in the Senate that afternoon. The King signed them, and they were then ratified under the Great Seal of Canada for the first time — another significant step towards recognizing the country's political independence and status within the Commonwealth. Having performed the supreme ceremonial duty of the tour, and rubbed shoulders (metaphorically speaking) with the press — a nod to both the symbolic and the popular ideas of monarchy — the King and Queen finished the day off with a banquet at Government House presided over by Lord and Lady Tweedsmuir.

Saturday, May 20:

This being officially the King's birthday (although George VI had been born December 14, 1895), it had been decided to hold the ceremonial Trooping of the Colour for the first time ever on the green expanse of Parliament Hill. The ceremony was one of considerable pageantry, dating from the time when a knight's standard was paraded before his men so that in the bloody confusion and clamour of battle they could recognize and rally to it. What in London had been done by the Guards Regiments since the seventeenth century was accomplished here by the Governor General's Foot Guards reinforced by the Canadian Grenadier Guards from Montreal in their blue trousers, red coats, and black bearskins.

It was a perfect May morning. The clouds had dispersed, leaving a day lovely and bright. The King stood rigidly at attention on the reviewing-stand in the hot sun. Bands played, orders were shouted out, and the troops wheeled and marched in intricate order among the banners, streamers, and standards on the Hill. The Queen, who appeared from time to time at an open window in the East Block like a mediaeval maiden in distress, was cheered gallantly by the enormous crowd, and when the band swung at last into a stirring rendition of "The British Grenadiers", an ancient and moustached veteran of the Fenian Raids danced a jig on the broad stone steps of the Parliament Buildings.

Next came the laying of the cornerstone of the new Supreme Court Building high on a cliff overlooking the Ottawa River. The Queen, nervous when it came to public speaking, spoke in English and French of the rule of law and the combined traditions in Canada of English common law and the Code Napoléon. Then, spreading the mortar with an ivory-handled gold trowel, she watched as the stone was lowered into place, declaring it well and truly laid. The highlight for the seventy thousand who watched was not the carefully expressed senti-ments on law but the moment when she smiled and joked with a number of Scottish stonemasons and, always alert to the nuance of her performance, spoke with a French-Canadian worker as well. Then the cheers really rang out.

As Dixon of the *Daily News* was to write, "Give the Queen a crowd and she mows them down." Elizabeth herself, behind the façade, was less sure of her success than anyone could have imagined, later confiding to the photographer Cecil Beaton that she found it difficult "to know when not to smile". She paid attention to the newspapers and was pained by what they revealed—a plump, pleasant face, with no hint of the luminous peaches-and-cream complexion or the beautiful blue eyes it contained. "It is so distressing to me," she complained, "that I always photograph so badly." Yet it was clear that she was the driving force of the new, more accessible monarchy. She had the knack of covering her husband's off-moments. For the camera, she had adjusted her hat style — off the face — and had learned to hold bouquets high to allow for good shots. To save her arm from the ache of constant waving, she had devel-oped her own innovation: a particular gesture of waving with the right arm barely raised, the right hand making a half-turn, palm upward. She knew just how to draw people out of Bertie's camera fire. She compensated for his low reserves of energy, his short temper, his lack of confidence, his shyness, and his general tongue-tiedness with her own professional manner (backed by a will of steel), her sense of humour, and her un-equalled ability to make small talk. For the King, people reserved their respect and sympathy, conscious of the troubles that must weigh on him. But for the Queen, the unmistakably dominant member of the marriage, fun-loving and removed from the serious problems of the monarchy, they felt a real love and affection. And nothing could have better characterized her charm and professionalism than her gentle, skilful handling of Mackenzie King, who in her sympathetic presence had become less and less the blustering politico, and more and more the adoring courtier.

After the stone-laying ceremony, while Their Majesties took a quick spin through Hull, the Prime Minister scampered back to Laurier House to see that everything was in readiness for the private luncheon he had arranged for them. It was a small function, cheery and intimate. While they ate (using his Rebel grandfather's forks and knives), the Queen once again per-formed her small miracle of regal intimacy, gossiping with Mackenzie King about various people they knew, and at one point saying how much she would enjoy clapping Lord Beav-erbrook into the Tower.

After lunch he took them through the house — the library, the sunroom (formerly Laurier's library), and his bedroom (where Laurier had died). He proudly showed them his treas-ures: the proclamation in Victoria's name which put a price on the head of his grandfather Mackenzie, the portrait of his mother, and the tiny casket that contained her wedding ring and a lock of her hair. Then he presented the King with a travelling-clock for his birthday and to the Queen he offered his mother's portrait in miniature. The royal couple responded kindly and with interest to everything he did and said, obviously realizing how much it meant to this lonely, complex man to have them there in his house among his dearest pos-sessions. And so they lingered on chatting with him (a half-hour beyond their schedule, as he noted gleefully in his diary that night), even presenting him with a silver inkstand, a replica of the one at 10 Downing Street. As they finally prepared to

Braving the chill air of the North Atlantic, George VI and Queen Elizabeth stand on the deck of the Empress of Australia en route to Canada.

May 17. The King and Queen step ashore at Quebec City to be greeted by Mackenzie King and Ernest Lapointe.

Canadian Government Motion Picture Bureau

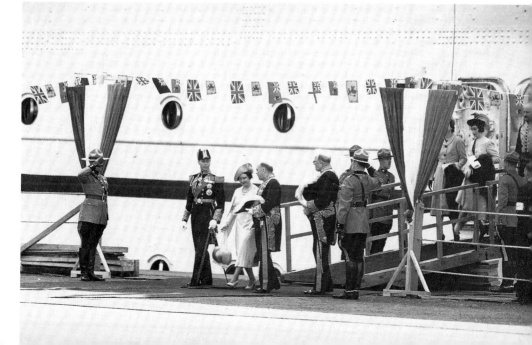

May 17. The royal procession moves through the crowded streets of Quebec City on the first day of the Royal Visit.

May 18. Montreal's colourful mayor, Camillien Houde, looks on as Their Majesties sign Le Livre d'Or at City Hall. Mackenzie King, as always, stands nearby.

May 19. Prime Minister Mackenzie King with Senator Raoul Dandurand in front of the Peace Tower in Ottawa.

Norman E. Carter

May 20. After lunch with Mackenzie King at Laurier House, the King and Queen slip away for a few quiet moments in the countryside outside Ottawa, along with a few members of their entourage. The ever-vigilant Constable Coughlin follows close behind.

National Archives of Canada/C33279

May 20. The cream of Ottawa society reach for pieces of the King's "birthday" cake at the garden party at Rideau Hall.

Western Canada Pictorial Index

May 20. The King and Queen with Prime Minister Mackenzie King at the Parliamentary Dinner, held at the Chateau Laurier in Ottawa.

*May 21. Huge crowds throng Confederation Square in Ottawa for the
dedication of the National War Memorial.*

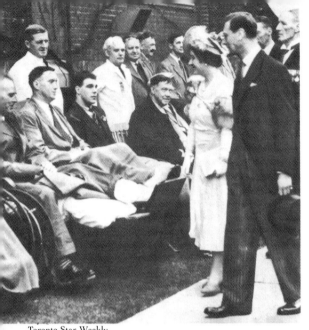

May 22. The royal couple chat with blind and maimed veterans of the Great War at Toronto's Christie Street hospital. The visit was scheduled to last just seven minutes, but the King and Queen stayed three quarters of an hour in order to speak to each man there.

May 23. The Queen accepts a bouquet of flowers at the Indian encampment at Fort William, Ontario.

May 24. Soldiers march along the royal route near Portage and Main on a rain-soaked Empire Day in Winnipeg.

May 24. An old woman sits patiently on Salter Avenue in Winnipeg, waiting for the King and Queen to pass by.

Lethbridge Herald

May 25. Regina's city hall is decorated with wheat sheaves to welcome Their Majesties.

May 26. The King and Queen receive a Wild West welcome at the Indian encampment in Calgary.

make their way down the stairs, Mackenzie King was suddenly overcome by the occasion, informing them

> That I wished I could tell them what their lives and their example meant to the people of all parts of the Empire as in our own country. That there was nothing I could say about the confidence they had given me, and the expression of their regard. That I was prepared to lay my life at their feet in helping to further great causes which they had at heart. What I was saying was quite unpremeditated and words came with very strong and sincere feeling.

"From there to the country in secret," wrote Constable Coughlin of the royal couple's unscheduled drive out to the farmlands near the Aylmer Road. There, with only their RCMP bodyguards near by, they strolled the sweet-smelling fields and, to Coughlin's approving eye, "acted like sweethearts". The Queen stopped to pick wildflowers and the couple struck up a conversation with a boy with a snub-tailed dog who didn't know who they were, and who ran away when he found out.

Back at Rideau Hall that afternoon, the grounds were populated by five thousand of Ottawa's most prominent citizens, come for a Royal Garden Party. "Ottawa people are humorous folk," wrote newswoman Madge Macbeth:

> They groan, "Oh, dear! I've got to go to Government House on the twentieth. Such a bore! I'd rather take a beating!" But if they are not invited . . .

Squirrels hopped about, looking for a royal crumb from the three birthday cakes baked by Morrison Lamothe, but most pieces were carried away for souvenirs. The King wore a grey morning suit, and the Queen was dressed in a long afternoon gown of primrose yellow, with the maple leaf pin her husband had given her. They walked down the cinder paths of Government House under the budding green trees among the crowd, while people discreetly strained and tiptoed for a good view.

In the evening they attended the Parliamentary Dinner in the stately green and gold ballroom of the Château Laurier. This was Canada's Versailles, a palace built with railway money, behind whose doors much of the nation's business — and not a few of its scandals and intrigues — took place. On this night, the Château looked more like a florists' convention than the "third Chamber of Parliament". Lilac-coloured hydrangeas and larkspurs lined the lobby for the royal arrival. In the small reception room where the King met and shook hands with each Senator and Member of Parliament, there were great mounds of hydrangeas and snapdragons, while the dining-room itself was decorated with roses, lilacs, gladioli, and other flowers weaving themselves around the great gold columns of the room.

During the dinner, Canada's gift to their Majesties was presented: a beautiful golden bowl filled with fragrant roses and showing a map of the Dominion and the royal route to be followed (Birks had naturally expected to be called upon to provide the bowl, but the order had gone to Eaton's instead). One hundred and fifteen waiters circulated smoothly among the guests, directed by a series of red and green lights in the ceiling of the room which allowed them to serve and clear the tables simultaneously, as well as negotiate the kitchen's tricky one-way traffic system. It was an impressive feat of organization, and at the end of the dinner, the hotel's reputation — and its dishes — remained intact.

Outside, a crowd of seventy thousand waited with increasing impatience in the cold rain. They chanted for the King, and pushed forward with such insistence that an extra guard line had to be thrown along the curb to relieve the harassed police patrols. Every reinforcement was being thrown into the fray — even Mounties who had just returned from performing the Musical Ride at the New York World's Fair moved in on the crowd with their horses. In the crush, people began to faint, and those in charge became so alarmed that the soldiers present were ordered to fix bayonets in case of any sudden rushes on the hotel. The rain fell in biting gusts for another ninety minutes before the royal couple finally made an appearance.

In the meantime, Arnold Heeney had been discussing the situation with a number of other officials, including Henry Willis-O'Connor, the Governor General's senior Canadian aide. The men left the dinner and went to the hotel balcony for a look; then Heeney pushed the startled Willis-O'Connor forward:

I raised my hand, and the noise ceased and the crowd fell silent. Even the pipe band stopped in the middle of a toot. The spotlight was turned on me and I felt a distinct thrill. In as loud a voice as I could manage, I announced that Their Majesties would come to the balcony in fifteen minutes.

Colonel Willis-O'Connor had no way of knowing if this was true, since he had simply improvised on the spot, but the royal couple did in fact make their way to the hotel balcony in the next quarter-hour. The Queen, looking as a queen should in a white tulle gown, diamond tiara, and necklace, waved off an umbrella, and for ten minutes she and the King stood in the rain to acknowledge the crowd's applause. The noise grew so loud each time they waved that it drowned out the brass band struggling through "God Save the King". People wept with emotion and in the lull between cheers a girl could be heard on one of the nearby rooftops singing "We'll Never Let the Old Flag Fall".

Whatever remained of Ottawa's stuffy reserve had vanished in the past two days. "The sovereigns have, in fact, literally melted the ice of the Ottawa," wrote Lucien Desbiens in *L'Actualité*:

> Whatever it was, this reporter, lost in diverse groups of Anglo-Canadians, saw demonstrations rarely shown in Ottawa: he saw rigid English ladies bring out their handkerchiefs and breathe noisily because they had just realized that they had cried out their admiration at the top of their lungs — just like the Frenchies. One Anglo-Saxon with a monocle said to his neighbour: "As a matter of fact these French Canadians are better than I thought."

Sunday, May 21:

The final event of the Ottawa visit was the unveiling of the National War Memorial to the more than sixty-six thousand Canadians who died in the Great War. The monument consisted of twenty figures of the Canadian Expeditionary Force struggling to haul a gun carriage through an immense Arch of

Sacrifice, which was surmounted by the figures of Peace and Freedom. The size and central location of the memorial gave some indication of the importance Canadians attached to their participation in the war.

That morning six thousand veterans in maroon berets marched into Confederation Square before the service began. As the sun shone warmly, they sang old favourites like "Pack Up Your Troubles" and "Carry Me Back to Dear Old Blighty". The crowd surged around them, taking photographs of flying ace Billy Bishop and the other Victoria Cross winners, and each time the band played "Colonel Bogey", everyone whistled along ("and a nursing sister who knew the Étaples sand dunes the night the Gothas wrote their red, red trail there, unashamedly wiped tears from her eyes over some unforgettable tie-up with that march of marches"). In spite of the jovial goings-on it was apparent that considerable emotion was beginning to build.

Sharp at 10:59, to a fanfare of trumpets, the royal limousine pulled up in front of the veterans, and the brief and simple service began with "O Valiant Hearts" and "The Flowers of the Forest", from the pipes of the Cameron Highlanders, and then twenty-two buglers sounding the Last Post. The King stood at attention, and stared at the veiled memorial:

> And there was a deep hush and a shining silence over the jammed streets, and the figures seemed to stir and whisper from their moulds, and once more—for all old soldiery to catch and to remember — was the dull beat of guns up ahead; and the line of great grey gasbags across the evening sky, and the crumbled ghosts of old towns, and sagging furrows, and from the furrows and the fields the sweetish smell of rotting horses and the human toll.

Then Reveille, the unveiling of the monument, and a brief address from a sombre King: "Not by chance do . . . Peace and Freedom appear side by side. . . . Without freedom there can be no enduring peace, and without peace, no enduring freedom." Afterwards, stepping forward, the King placed a wreath beneath the figures — "from all their places, their worshipped and their unknown places, they are gone to where the newcomers rise golden shining above the dark battle."

The service concluded, the royal couple admired the Memorial, and briefly passed along the ranks of the veterans. Then, in an inspired moment, they turned from the red carpet and waiting car and moved instead towards the cheering men. Almost immediately they were lost to view. Only the Queen's white hat could be seen bobbing here and there among the maroon berets. "It was an amazing sight," Tweedsmuir wrote afterwards, "for we were simply swallowed up. . . . "

> The faces of the Scotland Yard detectives were things I shall never forget! But the veterans made a perfect bodyguard. It was wonderful to see the old fellows weeping, and crying, "Ay, man, if Hitler could see this."

For a solid half-hour the King and Queen moved through the thick crowd, while Tommy Lascelles strode up and down in a dither, helpless to reach them. "My God," exclaimed Willis-O'Connor in the crush, "where in hell is the woman going?" — only to hear the mild voice of the King behind him saying, "Don't ask me." A greying veteran grasped the King's hand with his right, and the Queen's with his left. Others slapped the King on the back, and wrung the Queen's free hand. "You don't need any bullet-proof glass here, Your Majesty!" someone cried in a voice that boomed all the way across the river to Quebec, "God bless you, you're among friends!" There was a confusion of hard hands, neckties awry, rows of medals.

> A blind veteran who last looked on the world at Vimy Ridge, a war nurse, a mother of two sons killed in action, empty sleeves, a typical group, rallied around. The King and Queen met them all, embraced them all, obviously loved it.

"May I suggest that Your Majesty turn back now?" said the Earl of Airlie, who had finally battled his way to the Queen through the crowd. The Queen smiled and continued on. Other than the odd comradely pat on the back, the crowds remained for the most part orderly and respectful. "If any chap had even muttered a word off-colour," asserted one veteran afterwards, "we'd have torn him to bits." The RCMP and Scotland Yard were less sure of the safety of the situation; and, in the end, the entire ceremonial party was bundled off with the aid of quick-thinking officials. Arnold Heeney, according to Mackenzie King, "had to help to lift Lady Nunburnholme and Lady T[weedsmuir] into a car, shoving them in practically."

But as Willis-O'Connor said to Tommy Lascelles afterwards, "You can go home and tell the Old Country that any talk they may hear of Canada being isolationist . . . is just nonsense." Certainly no other event in the entire tour had such an impact on Canadians as a whole or, for that matter, on the King and Queen themselves. From that point on, George's confidence grew with the size and enthusiasm of the crowds that seemed to spring up in larger numbers at each stop. If there was any doubt before that Canada had taken the royal couple to its heart, there could be none now. After Ottawa, the King and Queen took every opportunity to depart from the formal arrangements and get closer to the cheering throngs that surrounded them.

The press co-operated in stressing this new "common touch", particularly as it played upon the larger events of 1939. Over and over again, the implicit comparison could be made between the royal couple — husband and wife — moving freely among their people and the strident displays of the dictators; between the warming sight of old imperial soldiers shuffling forward to meet the King and the cold precision displayed by Axis troops as they performed the goose-step and the passe-romano. A typical cartoon of the time shows Hitler and Mussolini throwing a tantrum while the radio streams forth with news of the royal tour's success — and the continuing popular triumph of the King and Queen.

But in fact there was nothing new in George VI's attempt to reconcile the powerful mystique of the Crown with the human, and even ordinary, qualities of the Sovereign. The source of the contradiction was nearly a hundred years old and had begun with Queen Victoria's husband, the first Prince Albert. It was he who had devised the idea of a modern, *working* monarchy whose members personified the best qualities of the nation. With Albert's death from typhoid in 1861, however, the monarchy went into eclipse as the widowed Queen withdrew almost completely from national life. Republicanism was revived, and Victoria's popularity reached such a low point that she was regularly hissed at during her infrequent public appearances. It was left to the English prime minister, Benjamin Disraeli, to deal with the situation, and it was his influence that led to the re-invention of the monarchy in a form very different from the one Prince Albert had envisaged. The Queen was gradually persuaded to return to her public role by the late 1860s, but this time she came in a new guise, surrounded by the spectacle of mediaeval pageantry and other revived (and sometimes invented) rituals. Albert's concept of royalty survived, especially in the idea of the royal family as a model for the nation. But, in addition, Victoria now loomed as a sort of imperial icon — so impressive that far into the twentieth century North American Indians would refer to her without a trace of irony as The Great White Mother.

The combination had worked spectacularly well for her. But every succeeding King and Queen down to George VI and Elizabeth had to deal with these two opposing ideas about monarchy — how it could be both tribal and modern at the same time. The confusion was shared by their subjects, and it explained why people throughout the 1939 Royal Visit would exclaim over the royal couple's "natural" qualities, yet at the same time describe their encounters with them as if they had been near-religious experiences.

The problem lay in finding the right balance between the images of the sovereign — how to reach out and connect with ordinary experience while not giving away the dignity or mystery of kingship. "Above all things your royalty is to be reverenced," wrote the nineteenth-century political journalist Walter Bagehot, "and if you begin to poke about it, you cannot reverence it." And then he warned, in a phrase that was to become familiar to many of Victoria's descendants, "We must not let in daylight upon magic." Times, however, had changed. When the King and Queen chose to step over the streetcar tracks and stroll among the Ottawa crowds, they dispensed with a little of the magic that made them different from other people. The first royal walkabout (as some later claimed it was) had not been planned. But now that it had happened, and had caused such a sensation, both the King and the Queen were determined to follow it up. It was a way of stamping their own style on the monarchy for the first time.

"Leave Ottawa at 2:30 pm for Kingston," wrote Constable

Coughlin, and, no doubt recalling the earlier mob scenes, added, "glad to get out of here" (and never wrote another line in his diary). Fifty thousand people massed along the Rideau Canal, and sang "Auld Lang Syne" and "Will Ye No' Come Back Again" as the train pulled out on schedule in glorious sunshine. Ottawa had been a tumultuous experience. But now the weary local RCMP could take their boots off at last, having been on duty almost continuously for the past three days. And the first-aid workers, who had dealt with three thousand cases (mainly fainting) in that time, were finally able to pack up and go home.

That afternoon, the Royal Train rolled through Cornwall, Alexandria, Morrisburg, Prescott, Brockville, and finally Kingston. At each town and village, the crowds pressed within feet of the track. Country roads were blocked with processions of cars miles long. At Cornwall and Brockville, where the blue and silver train slowed but did not stop (the Brockville mayor had kept an address of welcome ready just in case), huge crowds cheered the royal couple's appearance on the rear platform and children followed them down the track until they disappeared in the distance.

Norman Rogers, the Minister of Labour, had badgered the Prime Minister incessantly about the dire consequences (not least to his chances of re-election) if an important and historic city like Kingston were left off the itinerary. Mackenzie King in turn told Rogers to be satisfied with the hard-fought compromise of thirty-five minutes, predicting correctly that the visit would in the end "extend as a concertina." The royal procession whizzed through the streets of the Limestone City at fifteen mph, affording the seventy thousand along the seven-mile route little more than a glimpse of a royal wave in the dwindling light. Ten thousand children cheered them at Richardson Memorial Stadium; the Smiths Falls Citizens' Band played "God Save the King"; the Royal Military College received new colours from the Queen; and there was a brief halt at Fort Henry. The visit was almost a blur, but at ninety minutes was still too long for many in the royal party, like Lascelles, who were worried about the heavy schedule in Toronto the next day. At the station, the Queen displayed her familiar presence of mind, stopping the King from diving back into their carriage and persuading him instead to stand a few minutes longer on the observation platform while the darkness below exploded with dozens of flash bulbs. As the train moved down the line, the band played "Annie Laurie".

The Royal Train skirted the Bay of Quinte, steamed through Belleville, where fifteen thousand were waiting at the station, then stopped at a siding near Cobourg. It was the end of another exhausting, exhilarating day. But with the cheers of the huge throngs still ringing in his ears, Mackenzie King began to wonder if the tour might not have some extraordinary power to affect the international situation — perhaps by demonstrating to Hitler and others that there was a strong solidarity among the English-speaking nations. "I feel increasingly certain," he wrote that night, "that this visit of the King and Queen is going to be the dust in the balance which will save a European, and if so a world war."

Monday, May 22

Having already disappointed three thousand people in Cobourg by not stopping, the Royal Train pulled into the North Toronto Station at 10:30 that morning. There to greet them was the Ontario premier, his face as round and ruddy as a McIntosh apple as he stood bobbing up and down to the royal party with the other dignitaries on the platform. By unspoken agreement, Mitch Hepburn and the Prime Minister had called off their blood feud for the moment. The personal dislike the two Liberal leaders felt for each other had soured federal-provincial relations, but it would not do to have it spoil this special day. "I was just as natural with him as if nothing bad had ever taken place," sniffed Mackenzie King, while not failing to note that the Premier was "very dissipated in appearance". The royal party moved off while the train engineers threw pieces of Royal Train coal to the spectators to keep as souvenirs.

It had rained heavily in the night, and skies remained overcast, the breath billowing up in damp mist from people's mouths. The wet streets must have kept some at home, for even here in Tory Toronto the crowds occasionally thinned out over the twenty-eight-mile route. One man, watching from a warehouse overlooking University Avenue, claimed later that "there were more soldiers 'guarding' the route than there were people to guard, and in the stands erected at great cost up and down that thoroughfare one could count the occupants of each on both hands." Ironically, the stories of enormous crowds mobbing the royal couple in other cities seemed to have kept people away. "It seems as though Toronto will never grow up," the man concluded sadly. "It still thinks itself the small town of, say, 1880 and gets easily frightened."

Of course, it depended on where you were. Below College Street, as the royal procession neared City Hall, the turnout was enormous. The city itself claimed to have had a million visitors that day, and people were reported to be paying five dollars apiece to watch from choice spots on the tops of buildings. One dentist invited his patients to watch from his office windows, even providing them with a buffet luncheon. Traffic in the downtown area was so snarled that two planes were kept aloft all day to keep track of the situation.

Certainly thousands had braved the cold and wet the night before to get a good location downtown. Laden down with umbrellas, camp stools, oranges, coffee, milk, and sandwiches, they sang and jollied each other through the long hours, scurrying for shelter only when the rain came down in heavy bursts. When police in one location moved the barriers back a hundred yards, five thousand people, some wheeling baby carriages or lugging infants, abandoned their dignity and raced down the street for a better view. They were like Canadians everywhere who waited for hours for a brief glimpse of the King and Queen — and nothing illustrated their patience and good humour better than the account of "Merlinne". A Toronto housewife married to a veteran of the Great War, she recounted how she arrived from the suburbs at 6:05 a.m. with family, friends, "stools, lunches, umbrellas, flags and what have you" to settle in a good location near Bay Street:

As the crowd gathered and pressed, Friend Husband put his strong arm around me, the years rolled back once again, he was my "steady", his portly figure melted away, and he and all these other bereted men were boys again. I nuzzled my ear and cheek against rough khaki, brass buttons gleamed, there were marching feet, yes, there was war, but to youth the big thing of the moment was that we two belonged to each other.

Five hours after "Merlinne" and her family had found their place, the royal procession came down Yonge Street, stopping at City Hall for a brief ceremony. Their arrival caused pandemonium among the people assembled:

There rose a mighty cheer, the young lover was gone, my none too slight figure was left to the mercy of the throng, Friend Husband threw both arms into the air, shouted till he was hoarse, emotions ran riot — we pushed rudely, every man for himself, tore periscopes from more fortunate neighbours, trod on the lunch, danced on other folks' shins, for the King, the King had arrived. . . .

Unfortunately for "Merlinne", an escort of Royal Canadian Dragoons had also arrived to line the street where she was standing, and her view was immediately reduced to the close-up of a horse's back end ("the coat was groomed to a satin finish, his tail was a beauty, his legs were fine and strong, the rear view would prove undoubtedly that the front of such an animal would be equally fine"). After a short time, allowing for an address of welcome under the City Hall clock, the royal party moved on towards Queen's Park, leaving the crowd behind.

We gathered the lunch remainders and other impediments, only the kidlets had heart and stomach to guzzle bananas as we strode toward the cars, the stools seemed heavy. . . . 'Mid pleasures and palaces, disappointments and obstructed visions — there's no place like home.

"Merlinne" had better luck that afternoon when a friend persuaded her to "put on a face" and come up to St. Clair Avenue. Standing on an old kitchen chair she got the view she had been hoping for. Initiative was important in these situations, as was mobility. Two ancient spinsters, for example, had scampered about the city all day, managing to see the King and Queen on three separate occasions. But the unstable flow of the crowd could also be dangerous. In two separate incidents on University Avenue, men were able to break through the security cordons to run alongside the royal car and throw in notes. This of course caused enormous concern among the security people, although the two men detained by police had intended nothing more than to present private petitions to the King (who, in one case at least, that of a returned soldier without a job, intervened to have the man released). Fortunately, others in Toronto found less alarming ways to celebrate the Royal Visit. On Elizabeth Street in the city's Chinatown, sputtering firecrackers in long strings were lowered from windows or tossed into the street, and the sound of Chinese orchestras could be heard that day, coming from clubrooms and halls. The bars did not echo with loyal sentiment, however, their owners being under orders to sell nothing stronger than soft drinks until five o'clock. Somewhere in the city a band played "How Dry I Am".

While the royal couple attended the official welcoming ceremonies in the Ontario Legislature, the most eagerly anticipated event of the day awaited them upstairs in the music room of the Lieutenant-Governor's suite. This was the presentation of the Dionne Quintuplets — arguably the only people on the tour who were even better known than the King and Queen. In fact the world-wide fame of the five little girls from Callander, Ontario (and the million-dollar deals that surrounded them), gave their encounter with royalty the aura of a summit meeting. Like the King and Queen, they had arrived in Toronto on their own train, the Quintland Special, attended by an entourage of security guards, nurses, a priest, reporters, and of course Dr. Alan Dafoe, who taken charge of the Quints' upbringing since their birth in 1934.

Their presence, which was *not* on the official itinerary, had come about only after a long battle of wills, largely conducted through the pages of the newspapers. The Interdepartmental Committee, probably wary of the commercial endorsements that seemed a part of every breath the Quints took, had declined an invitation for the royal couple to visit them in Callander. If the Quints wanted to be presented, they would have to come to Sudbury — a plan Dr. Dafoe objected to on the grounds of their health.

There the matter stood until March, when the Hepburn

government, always suspected of mischief where Ottawa was concerned, stepped in and extended its own invitation for Oliva Dionne to bring his wife and children to Toronto. A train was to be put at their disposal, with special private carriages, and bodyguards assigned to prevent kidnappings. Everything would be laid on, down to the refrigerator full of milk and snacks at Queen's Park. After some delay, Dafoe and the Dionnes accepted. The Quints, now approaching five years old, had never travelled farther than across the road, where they had been taken as newborns from the Dionne house to their new home in the Dafoe Hospital. The Hepburn administration, which had already prevented the girls from going to world fairs in Chicago and New York, now proposed an unofficial meeting with the King and Queen in Toronto. The Interdepartmental Committee had little choice in the matter, given Mackenzie King's reluctance to be seen quarrelling with premiers at this time. So they shrugged and accepted the arrangement.

As the time drew near for the visit, the Quints could be seen in movie newsreels and newspapers rehearsing their curtseys (Marie and Emilie bowed so low they toppled over). The design of their dresses for the Big Day, like the wedding-gown of a royal bride, remained a closely guarded secret. The menu to be followed on the train was, however, released to the press. For breakfast: orange juice, soft-boiled eggs, bacon, brown bread, toast, and milk. At 10 a.m.: milk. For lunch: broiled steak, peas and carrots, baked potatoes, orange bavarian cream, and biscuits. At 3:30: more milk. Dinner: cereal, brown buttered bread, applesauce, lettuce and tomatoes, cottage cheese, and milk. Two gallons of Callander water and eight quarts of Callander milk were put on the train for their use.

The Quintland Special, freshly painted in crimson and gold, was quietly boarded at Trout Lake, a subterfuge that disappointed the thousands who had come to see them off in Callander. Along with their luggage and five cots, the Quints were accompanied by their parents, six of the seven other Dionne children, a detachment of police, railway officials, their business manager, Dr. Dafoe, their priest, and reporters from three countries. Oliva Dionne, the press reported, wore a natty new grey suit for the 220-mile journey, while Mrs. Dionne sported a gay flower-topped hat. The T. and N.O. Railway Band played for them when they arrived in North Bay.

Once in Toronto, the Quints were brought by automobile directly to Queen's Park, where they changed into their new ankle-length court dresses of white organdy, made especially for the presentation, with high necklines, cape collars trimmed with small ruffles, and each with a wide taffeta sash that hung down the back. Their costume was completed by white poke bonnets, patent leather slippers, and old-fashioned lace mittens that reached their elbows. Two rosebuds were entwined in each little girl's silky chestnut-brown hair.

This was to be a private meeting between the Dionnes and Their Majesties. Walter Thompson, who had tried to explain that to reporters the night before, had obviously not expressed himself clearly on the point, as the police were forced to confiscate a number of cameras from reporters in the vicinity. The event itself went off very well, in spite of the hoopla surrounding it (the Quints could tell their Royal Guardians a thing or two about invasion of privacy). The King and the Queen, who by now were dearly missing their own daughters, were noticeably taken with any youngsters they saw, and the little Dionnes, with their brown hair, brown eyes, and apple-red cheeks, were certainly appealing children.

The little girls were presented (each one curtseyed wrongways, right foot behind left) and then in turn presented their bouquets: Annette with a green nosegay, Cécile with blue, Yvonne with mauve, Emilie with rose, and finally Marie, who proffered a posy of yellow pansies. Then—perhaps rehearsed as well—they rushed over to the royal couple. The King bent low to show Cecile the buttons on his Admiral's uniform, at which point she put her arms around his neck and kissed him. This was a signal for the others to do the same with both the King and the Queen. All five then exploded in chatter for the next twenty minutes—to the delight of the royal pair.

The Prime Minister was as smitten as everyone else when Hepburn took him over to meet them ("I enjoyed this part of the trip almost as much, if not more, than any, excepting, of course" — catching himself in time — "the great events"). Afterwards, the little girls, like the troupers they were, made their exit through the Legislative Chamber, blowing kisses to the soberly attired Members while the galleries rocked with laughter. Then it was back to the "shiny train" for the long ride home. The next day, seventeen thousand people lined up under the hot sun to tour the rooms where the royal party and the Dionnes had stayed so briefly.

After this momentous meeting, the royal party moved on to Hart House at the University of Toronto where the Queen presented colours to the Toronto Scottish. A few minutes earlier, Mrs. Ralph Day, the mayor's wife, who had injured her foot (it turned out to be broken), was helped to the location of the ceremony by a motorcycle policeman. News of the royal couple's unconventional behaviour had clearly made an impact on Toronto, for when a stylishly attired woman riding in a sidecar appeared on the driveway of Queen's Park, the soldiers snapped to attention, the royal standard was unfurled, the band launched into "God Save the King", and the crowds cheered madly. After a moment or two the mistake was discovered, and the actual ceremony was later carried off flawlessly. But it said something about the expectations of the spectators, and the nerves of the people involved with arrangements.

Luncheon was in the Great Hall of Hart House with five hundred guests, including the actor Raymond Massey, brother of the Canadian High Commissioner to London, who had left his Broadway show to be there. Like every other luncheon and dinner on the tour, this one had been months in preparation. The King ate sparingly, waving aside the assorted hors d'oeuvres, sweet potato, asparagus, and ice cream, and selecting from the menu only a breast of chicken and coffee. The Queen on the other hand ate heartily, even nibbling on her favourite cream cheese, which the royal waiters declined to identify for curious reporters.

In the afternoon, en route to Woodbine for the running of the King's Plate, the royal couple made a quick tour of Riverdale Park. They stood in their open limousine as it bounced over the ground so they could be seen by the twenty-five thousand children assembled there. As the car swung up and down the rows of children, a group of band members suddenly dropped their instruments, ran to a row of little stretchers, picked them up, and ran across open ground with them to the edge of the parade route. Lying on the stretchers were desperately sick children, many of them wearing Wolf Cub caps and Girl Guide hats for the occasion. They received special waves as the limousine passed.

The royal party arrived at Woodbine late, about 3:35 p.m., to a crowd slightly reduced by the poor weather ("Get your souvenir programs here," shouted an enterprising hawker, "you can't tell the King and Queen without a program"). The Dragoons came prancing in, eight abreast, in front of the landau, which moved into the backstretch, "the King's black silk hat moving up and down at a diamond sculls stroke". The 48th Highlanders played, the Royal Regiment paraded in brilliant colours, ladies in fine dresses and hats swanned about with men in silk toppers — but when the band played "I Love a Lassie", the rest of the crowd, more Harry Lauder than High Society, sang along. The King smoked, chatted, and handicapped the race, but "even after the barrier went up, fully half of the crowd continued to gaze up in honest open admiration" at the royal box. "That's the first time I ever knew a crowd to turn its back on a horse race," one reporter muttered.

"And now," said the CBC commentator at Woodbine, "here is the answer to something that all Canadian women, all American women, must be wondering — what is the Queen wearing?"

"Ladies, she's *gorgeous!*" said the fashion reporter, letting the last word stretch out as long as it could. "You've no idea. You can't imagine unless you see her. She's dressed all in blue, that beautiful soft shade of blue that looks so grand! It's a long gown, slim-fitting, with a loose cape falling from the shoulders and making a very regal figure. . . . " And on and on.

For the crowd in the stands, there was more than royalty to gawk at. Mackenzie King and Mitch Hepburn had been thrust into each other's company all day, and people watched their slightest gesture towards each other, some claiming afterwards that neither man had spoken a word to the other, or looked once in the other's direction. In fact, it was Alphonse and Gaston all day long. Hepburn had dragged the Prime Minister over to meet the Dionne Quints, and Mackenzie King had fawned over a nervous and diffident Mrs. Hepburn at luncheon, arranging later for the Hepburn children to meet the King and Queen. Differences between the two men were not mentioned once. At Woodbine, the Prime Minister even gave up his own seat so that the Premier could sit beside the King.

Their very public feud had become a private joke between them. As they went up the steps to the races, the two leaders bantered lightly about giving people a real show by going about together. Mackenzie King even showed respect for the qualities that made Mitch Hepburn such a successful politician. "He has a bright cheerful manner, rather fascinating; that is a hail fellow, well met with everyone; does not care about precedence. Makes friends by breaking the rules, and is good to his own friends." In short, just about everything the Prime Minister was not.

For those who came to watch a horse race, a colt named Ackworth, picked up from the start by the King's keen eye, burst out of the paddocks, ran away from the rest of the horses, and coasted in, an easy ten lengths ahead of Sea General and Skyrunner. Her owner, the handsome and hard-driving *Globe and Mail* publisher George McCullagh, had hurried from the bedside of his gravely ill mother — at her insistence it was said — to see his horse win. He arrived in the winner's circle to collect his fifty guineas hatless, and wearing not the customary frock coat but a grey business suit.

Mackenzie King's political antennae stirred immediately, as did his customary paranoia. It was the *Globe* that had been attacking him so unsparingly for his decision to accompany the royal tour. "I confess when I heard it was McCullagh's horse that had won the King's plate," he wrote later, "I could not help feeling financial circumstances had accounted for it. Both Arnold [Heeney] and I had a feeling as though something had been done to insure McCullagh winning." There were other things the Prime Minister had noticed as well. Just that morning in the Legislature, he had seen Tommy Lascelles in deep conversation with George Drew, leader of the Ontario Conservatives. That was enough for him to conclude that the two men were behind the *Globe*'s attacks — part of a larger plot, perhaps, to put Drew into power in Ottawa ("McCullagh is lending himself to all the Tory blandishments possible"). The settling of differences, however (including those with Hepburn), would wait for another day.

The royal guineas dispensed, the King and Queen drove back to Queen's Park for tea, and then moved on to Christie Street Hospital, where two hundred and fifty disabled veterans had been brought out to sit in chairs, or lay on stretchers on the green lawn. The King and Queen chatted with them all, Elizabeth perhaps remembering the days when her ancestral home, Glamis Castle, had served as a hospital for seriously wounded soldiers, and George, as always, devoting himself to the task, as if paying off a personal debt for what these men had suffered, and doubtless thinking of "the bloody horrors of Ypres and the Somme, the mud and slither of La Bassee and the foot torture and sweat of 20 kms. in full marching order on sun-baked cobble-stones." The seven-minute stop stretched to forty-five minutes.

By the time the royal party reached the Exhibition grounds, more than an hour behind schedule, the thousands of children there had spent more than three hours waiting in the lakeside chill. With them were hundreds of blind people who had come as well, each with a sighted companion to describe the occasion; and an "international brigade" made up of soldiers who had fought against each other in the Great War. The dense fog that hid the grandstand from view lifted ten minutes before the royal party arrived. Periscopes and glasses came up and cheering exploded on all sides. For every child disappointed by the absence of crowns and gowns, there were others reassured by the friendly down-to-earth quality of the King and Queen. "If you put both your arms around her neck to hug her," one little girl solemnly informed a reporter, "she would not mind if your hands were slightly grubby."

It was dusk by the time they reached the train, which waited now at Union Station on the Esplanade. Someone called out "Three cheers for Bonnie Scotland" and the crowd took it up. The King inspected the Queen's Own Rifles, and met the last few dignitaries of the day, then everyone limped off to their carriages. The Royal Train pulled out of the station at 7:45 that evening.

Running more than an hour behind schedule, they passed swiftly through dozens of small villages and towns. In each one, the people had gathered at the station, packing both sides of the track, and even sitting on rooftops and in trees. The local band showed up, ready to play if the Royal Train should happen to stop, or even slow down. When the great Hudson engine finally came into view, veterans came to attention and men doffed their caps. People felt that with such a crowd the train must surely stop. Alas, there were only so many hours in a day when the King and Queen could appear on the platform to wave and smile. The train, steamed through — a blow, as a letter-writer from Alliston was to relate:

> Disappointment is too insignificant a word to describe our feeling as a hush fell over us all, for we realized we had missed that, which for days had buoyed us up and made work easy. Our eager hopes lay in ashes at our feet. The many miles between us and home seemed a dreary stretch, belated suppers were tasteless, unwashed dishes and chores still to be done spelt drudgery.

"One feels almost heartless to rush by some localities without a word," wrote Mackenzie King:

> But it would be physically impossible to do more than the King and Queen have been doing. As a matter of fact they have had really hard physical work which they have performed with wonderful charm and readiness, patience and cheerfulness. . . . At all events, it is helping them to forget Europe. . . .

Sitting back and sipping a Scotch as the train trundled north, the Prime Minister could muse on his own successes that day. "Billy King", people had called out, and "Rex" and "Mackenzie" ("without raising a hand to start a thing of the kind, and scarcely raising a hand in acknowledgment of it"). Tweedsmuir was right. He did need to get out among the people more. Best of all, his elaborate courtesies to Hepburn had gone down well, and there had been no acrimonious moments. At last he could relax. The main ceremonial duties of the tour were over, and from here on, the provincial premiers — even Aberhart — would be friendly.

Later that night, five huge piles of stumps were set ablaze on Carley Hill where the Royal Train stopped to take on water. Six thousand people cheered when the King and Queen came out on the rear platform to greet them, their faces illuminated in the glow of the pitch-pine fire.

CHAPTER SIX

Where the West Begins

Tuesday, May 23:

PULLING INTO WHITE RIVER, the engineer had a clear view of the backwoodsmen, Indians, and townspeople standing expectantly on the station platform, and time enough to press the buzzer to alert the royal carriages. This was the system devised to let the King know whenever a sizeable crowd was waiting. A few moments later, he and the Queen stepped down from the train, and those on the platform were suddenly informed by tour officials that the royal couple wished to meet their mayor. White River being at the time unincorporated, one of their number, George Freethy, was elected on the spot. Then, while the train was being serviced, Freethy showed them briefly around the settlement, which consisted chiefly of muddy and unpaved streets, and had a reputation as the coldest spot on earth. The Queen, as usual, was in her element, graciously accepting a birchbark canoe filled with trailing arbutus, which one of the Indians had made for her. Her presence, said one of the onlookers, made him "run all hot and cold".

From the train window, the Prime Minister watched the King and Queen talk with some Indians on a nearby verandah. Mackenzie King had chosen not to join the others who stretched their legs on the snow-sprinkled platform, preferring instead to meditate on the mistakes of the past few days which he blamed on his "ultra-sensitiveness" and fatigue. Half an hour later, everyone climbed aboard and the Royal Train steamed out of White River, leaving the excited residents to look forward to "the church supper and the barn dance at Spadoni's Hall".

That day the train travelled north and west through Ontario's lake country. People stood and waved at every crossing as the big Hudson engine sped through the Ontario Highlands, past Heron Bay and along the Lake Superior shore, where the sight of moose and red deer sent the King scrambling for his movie camera. Mackenzie King, still tired but with his humour now restored, chatted with Lord Airlie about his Christian Science beliefs. Airlie impressed him with the story of how George V had brushed off the pain of his final suffering with the remark, "Never say you are ill until you are dead."

> I need very much that additional strength at this time . . . having been used to others watching out for me. I now find I have to make a [point of] continually watching out for what the King himself wishes to know, and forget entirely about my own end. It is quite a little strain being in attendance in this way.

Back in the last two carriages — which had become known as the "Married Quarters" — the royal couple spent their time together, reading, chatting, listening to radio programs, and playing the occasional game of patience as the train clacked its way through the Northern Ontario bush. While the King worked at his papers from the black leather dispatch boxes that went with him everywhere, the Queen spent her time arranging the masses of flowers that filled the car, or clipped pictures of her daughters from the newspapers.

Everything had been done to make things as comfortable as possible. The King had only to lift the receiver of his gold telephone to have his hair cut, his trousers pressed, or a meal served from the small, fully equipped kitchen in their suite. The dinner plates came from Ottawa, white Limoges with narrow bands of maroon and gold surmounted by an embossed crown. In the small sitting-room, with its green chairs and apricot-coloured upholstery, a large map of Canada could be rolled down and the royal progress marked. The King's bedroom had been simply decorated: a closely printed chintz in a small blue and pink pattern for the drapes, and a red bed covering for the bed. The adjacent bath was tiled in a pale blue-grey. For the Queen, a soft peach colouring in the brocaded satin drapes and bed covering, and the woodwork finished in blue-grey. In her tiny lavender bathroom, a large egg-shaped cake of yellow soap sat in a dish by the small tub. Works by Canadian artists had been hung prominently throughout the carriages.

Their reading had not been neglected. Bookshelves had been dutifully stocked with works by Canadian authors: Marius Barbeau, Mazo de la Roche, Bliss Carman, Duncan Campbell Scott, Pauline Johnson, Stephen Leacock, and F. R. Scott. As well, they could choose from popular writers like Pearl Buck, Anne Morrow Lindbergh, and Dorothy Parker — and, of course, the Governor General was represented by *The Thirty-Nine Steps*. There was even a translation of *Mein Kampf* to leaf through.

They had done what they could to make themselves at home. Family pictures were everywhere. Mementoes were scattered through the sitting-room, including the tiny canoe, which stayed on the mantel for the rest of the journey. The Queen had her favourite soft boudoir pillows on her bed, and on the night table her *Book of Common Prayer*, along with the stack of ghost stories she loved to read before retiring. In the King's bedroom were field glasses, cameras, and a shelf stacked with white gloves.

The Royal Train's journey across Canada was itself a convenient symbol for national unity. Half the history of the country had been squeezed onto the steel rails that carried the King and Queen from coast to coast. Work trains, colonist cars, harvest specials, silk trains, troop trains. The country dangled from a steel ribbon, communities rising or withering away depending on which turning the railway took. South of the border, America seemed to have spread as if a high wave of population had simply flooded across the land, the railroad hard-pressed to keep up. But in Canada the expansion seemed almost grudging, less manifest destiny than a confederation of diasporas, held together by track. Track floated over the muskeg, punched through the mountains — built to keep the Americans out, to keep British Columbia and the West in. The rails now ran to the shores of three oceans; the country was the dream of tycoons, politicians, and construction engineers. The Limoges china rattled slightly as the train curved unseeing past mosquito swamps, rotten timbers, bits of old blasting caps, empty whisky bottles, and unmarked graves.

Up ahead the pilot train also forged on. The hundred or so reporters, radio men, and other staffers hung their socks on makeshift clotheslines, and the smell of dubbin was strong in the Mounties' quarters. Particularly since the press reception in Ottawa there had been a sense that everyone on both trains was now in the enterprise together, a delicate cohabitation, interrupted only at times like this when there were no major stops. Faced with running one continuous half-hour ahead of the world's best human-interest story, the newsmen looked up sourly from their card games at the endless bogs, lakes, and scrub forest of Northern Ontario — in the words of *The Globe and Mail*'s Doug Oliver, "through a country where nature has attempted to say something and has stuttered for miles and miles" — and contemplated their eventual reunion in near-coital terms:

> Wide-winged gulls follow closely in our train wake, furnishing the first aerial escort of any sort since the long ice-bound *Australia* . . . met Canada's Air Force — or most of it — in the Gulf. . . . We are some thirty minutes ahead of the Royal Train and the observation platform on which Their Majesties like to sit (we're told) studying the countryside with which (they say) they are unalterably in love. As we twist around these sweeping bay waters of Superior — to circumnavigate depressions too deep and difficult to bridge — we are so close to Their Majesties at times . . . that from the rear car of our train we can almost spot the smoke of theirs. . . . And at night, in all these roadside stops with which their crowded itinerary is punctuated, our sleeping cars rest next to theirs, as close communion under the circumstances, as a sometimes humpbacked fourth estate can maintain with Royalty.

The Railways Minister, C. D. Howe, had been through Schreiber on an advance train, making last-minute checks on matters of etiquette and proper dress. The gentlemen on the Schreiber platform protested when it was pointed out that they did not have the required gloves. The glove rule, they said, was just for the east; here, only the women were wearing gloves. "I guess I'm wrong," said C. D., "this must be where the West begins."

That afternoon, the King received word that his mother had

been hurt in an auto collision. The accident was not as serious as it seemed at first. Queen Mary had been returning in her ancient Daimler from a visit to the Royal Horticultural Society when the car was struck broadside by a truck loaded with steel. The Daimler skittered sideways, struck the curb, and overturned. The Queen Mother tumbled about with her companions among the cushions and flowers, but soon climbed out on a ladder supplied by a passing house-painter. She was said to have smiled bravely, and murmured, "Oh dear!" before disappearing into a nearby house where a good hot cup of tea was waiting. She had suffered minor bruises and a bumped eye, and had been comforted by the scores of bouquets that were delivered to her—including a modest bunch of irises and narcissi from the anxious lorry driver.

At Port Arthur and Fort William, terrible rain and high winds from the day before had scattered the festive decorations, and plunged local organizers into deep despair. But the crowds were immense and enthusiastic, and the day was bright if not exactly warm. Estimates of the numbers present ranged as high as 100,000 (double the Twin Cities' normal population), swelled by people from the lumber camps, the outlying mining and fishing communities around the shore of Lake Superior, and a fifty-car procession up from Minnesota. The dense fog that had enveloped Mackenzie King earlier in the tour seemed also to have dissipated as, newly buoyant, he leapt from the train at Port Arthur to introduce the waiting dignitaries.

Waiting there as well were the radiomen from the CBC. Commentators on the royal tour differed widely in their broadcast styles, and they were never named, though astute listeners might recognize the voices of Frank Willis and Elwood Glover among them. The first announcer that day had clearly assumed (correctly perhaps) that he was part of an on-going national soap opera ("All roads lead to Romance. And as the Royal Cavalcade moves ever Westward, we . . . will see Royal Romance re-enacted. . . . "). His colleague at the station, however, chose to describe the sensations of the people as they watched the King making his inspection of the guard of honour:

The band has stopped and the crowd is all standing on tiptoe now . . . saying very little, waving the odd flag. This is just the little breathless hush . . . it happens in waves like that. And it's very interesting, the crowd psychology. They're all watching with their lungs and their eyes and their ears. Watching with everything, so there's no time to shout or cheer or anything like that. . . .

For an hour and a half the royal party toured the Lakehead cities, took in the fine view from Port Arthur Park near C. D. Howe's old home, listened to the Duluth Symphony Orchestra, and visited twenty-five Ojibway Indians at an improvised camp of painted birch-bark tepees by the river. There they met seventy-seven-year-old Chief Sault, who had been the Prince of Wales's guide on an earlier tour, and watched a noisy and spirited war dance.

The Prime Minister was at last becoming used to his role as a slightly harried head waiter, rushing about, making introductions, dropping discreetly into the background to let local Cabinet ministers and dignitaries shine, then smoothly taking charge once again. His energies were gradually returning. He had at last grasped the *pace* of the tour after the stiffness and tensions of the first few days, and no longer felt he was being swept along by events. Things were manageable now.

At Raith, the small crowd sang "God Save the King" without accompaniment while the train was stopped for servicing. When they steamed through Kenora at 2 a.m., five thousand people stood silently by the tracks, so as not to disturb the royal sleep.

Wednesday, May 24:

Before waking that morning, Mackenzie King dreamt that arrangements were being made "for a banquet to myself with 2 plans proposed; one in which all members of Parliament including Hepburn would be present." Rain skidded down the windows of the train, and the prairies at last came into view as they steamed the last miles towards Winnipeg.

Like every other community on the royal route, Winnipeg had been busy making itself presentable. "Little things we despaired of ever seeing done have been done," marvelled the *Free Press*, "waves and dips, and holes in the streets are being repaired, so that there may be no switch-backing as the cars bearing Their Majesties roll along the Royal route." Hydrants were painted, bunting and fireworks purchased, a bouquet picked out. Thousands of people had allowed themselves to be conscripted by the various welcoming committees. Often, they worked for long hours at thankless tasks just to fulfil the organizers' dream that each minute of the visit might flow seamlessly into the next.

The Mayor was not so enthusiastic at the beginning. John Queen (who had been jailed twenty years earlier for his part in the Winnipeg Strike) had declared publicly he would "not dress up or wear a silk hat" for the occasion. His comments eventually reached the ears of the Mayor of Toronto, Ralph Day, and in due course a magnificent silk topper arrived at Winnipeg's City Hall. Asked by reporters what he would do now, Queen replied, "People will just have to wait and see."

The flurry of preparation that preceded the Royal Visit did not go unnoticed by the general public. In large numbers, they wrote to the various officials, offering advice, volunteering their help, or hoping just to push themselves forward a little.

In January, in answer to a *Free Press* article suggesting that the King and Queen visit the home of an ordinary workingman ("average size, two children"), a man wrote in protest:

> Would you call that a real Canadien home[?] No! Don't you think the King and Queen would be more interested in visiting a real Canadien family of (14) fourteen children all living. A swell bunch of kids, healthy and happy. . . . They would certainly get a great [kick] out of it. So much they would never forget Winnipeg.

In April, a storekeeper from Sclater, Manitoba, wrote that his daughter wished to present Their Majesties with a house plant called "Orleander", then in bloom ("about seven feet high and very broad"), offering to send a snapshot, and asking to know by return mail "if there is any use in doing so and do you think they would like it or not and if you wouldn't mind to take charge of it to help me to hand it to them." A woman, one of dozens across the country with real or imagined connections to royalty, wrote to request a meeting, "having played with Her Majesty the Queen in Hertfordshire when she was a child." A letter from the editor of *The New Canadian* sought "names, racial origins, length of residence in Winnipeg, occupation, etc." of those from ethnic groups on the various committees co-ordinating the visit. "Are any new Canadians to be presented to Their Majesties?" he asked. "Are there to be any distinctively new Canadian events in the program? Any statements of loyalty?"

From a senior RCMP officer: "I find the Indians have been placed on my doorstep." The Welcome Week Parade Committee was looking for help in assigning places in Polo Park, Assiniboine Park, and Kildonan Park to native groups travelling to the city to see the King and Queen. One Indian agent was more specific, asking for "a place where there will be no danger of the crowd milling around them, mauling and ruining their expensive and valuable costumes," and adding that "many of these Indians fought overseas and I think it only fitting, after they have come all this way without remuneration, that they be given some such recognition."

"In view of the forthcoming visit of our beloved King and Queen," wrote a woman on Ingersoll Crescent, "I would like you to see a magnificent fern I have." The plant was being offered for ceremonial decoration ("It stretches half way across my living room . . ."). From Selkirk, a woman in obvious mental distress wrote to ask for the King's help:

> It is terrible the way Andrews & Andrews and the Germans have done to take land that I had near 40 years. and then my Father years before me. we paid hundreds of dollars in taxes alone, I paid $22.00 taxes on the same land last fall. then they destroyed my house. fill my well with stones. took my railway crossing cut — my Fence down with a axe. . . . please help me . . . .

Credentials and the Grand Manner were considered by some to be the best method of pushing forward. "I must ask to be excused for trespassing upon your valuable time at this most anxious period of your office," wrote one correspondent to the Lieutenant-Governor, hoping that "there might be space for me somewhere in the great massed crowd" for the visit of the King and Queen.

His Majesty would no doubt know the Premier Baronet Sir Hickman Beckett Bacon whose Son in law the late Mr Ralph Creyke of Rawcliffe Hall Selby Yorkshire was Chairman of my Goole Bench and who was High Sheriff of Yorkshire and who gave me a letter of introduction to the Marquess of Aberdeen, upon my advent in Canada many years ago. . . .

The Lieutenant-Governor himself was besieging Ottawa for advice on everything from the design of menu cards and the serving of cocktails ("the only information I can give you," wrote Keenleyside, "is that Their Majesties are not fond of cocktails") to the introduction of luncheon guests (Lascelles advised that "the husband should precede the wife, since in that way Their Majesties can be certain that they identify the lady with her husband . . . ").

The excitement quickened as the train neared the Manitoba border. It was reliably reported that 250,000 Americans were prepared to descend on Winnipeg from the border states of Minnesota, Wisconsin, Illinois, and North Dakota. A dozen special trains travelling on three different railroads were scheduled from Minneapolis alone. Great Northern planned to dispatch the "Victoria Day Special" (two Scottish pipers, a menu of mutton broth, prime ribs, Yorkshire pudding, a combination London grill and Berkshire bacon, plus a "liquid cargo" of a "decided Scottish flavor"). More than a dozen high school bands were expected, including the National Champion drum and bugle corps of American Legion Post No. 8 from St. Paul with "that peculiarly American phenomenon, a high-stepping, baton-twirling girl band leader". American troops were to be given the honour of guarding one of the city's bridges.

And the city was not lacking in entrepreneurs; some had built sections of tiered seats on the parade route. Fast-food stands mushroomed along Portage Avenue and up North Main. A group of actors, including Mercer McLeod and Tommy Tweed, also hoped to cash in on the occasion; they had rented the Dominion Theatre to stage a production of *The Queen's Husband*, a play whose only connection with the royal tour was its title:

Everything came off fine except the hordes didn't come. The seats were empty. The food was unsold and the play was called off after one performance because it was thought that 3 did not constitute a quorum. . . . The two lead actors rented a small shack on the riverbank near Headingly and hid out until winter.

On Wednesday morning, the expected dignitaries were at the CPR station on North Main — Lieutenant-Governor William Johnston Tupper (son of Charles), Premier John Bracken, and John Queen (who in the end had given in gracefully, and was dressed in a frock coat and sporting his new silk topper). There were last-minute warnings not to shake the King's hand too heartily as he had caught it painfully in the carriage door the night before.

It was still raining hard ("a POURING WET day" was how one member of the honour guard remembered it); nevertheless, the Queen had ordered the limousine's top to be taken down. She put up her umbrella, the King made do with an overcoat, and they set off along the city's wide avenues with a detachment of Lord Strathcona Horse clattering along in escort. The honour guard was in for a busy day of it too, rushing ahead to six or seven more places ("By then, the greatcoats were literally DRIPPING, SOBBING WET!"), turning up so often in the downpour to accept the Queen's sympathetic smile that the men felt she was getting to know them individually.

This was, in any event, not a part of the country where rain was supposed to be bad news. The steadiest rainfall in years, it had come when the farmers needed it most. Certainly it had little effect on the crowds, which were as large here as anywhere. And, it was pointed out, the reception was just as enthusiastic among the large numbers of "ethnic" Canadians represented (most of whom had come — or whose parents had come — from Central and Eastern Europe). No one illustrated the day's predominant sentiment better than the family of five-year-old Larry Zolf, standing together at the corner of Magnus and Main:

My father, devout Jewish nationalist and fanatical monarchist, had outfitted me in full Union Jack regalia. Instead of a skullcap I wore a Union Jack beanie; instead of a prayer shawl, a Union Jack shirt; instead of a *kopota* (the traditional long grey coat of Orthodox Jews) my torso and legs flaunted an exquisite Union Jack-decorated set of short pants. And as I watched my father desperately and in vain try to break through the police cordon to thank Their Majesties personally for providing him with a sanctuary and home in Canada, I was neither embarrassed nor surprised. I knew my father was doing right, and I was proud of him.

The only unpleasantness of any sort that day occurred when onlookers noticed the swastika flying from the German Consulate on Main Street. There was booing, and cries of "Tear the thing to pieces!" but attention quickly shifted when the royal procession came into view on its way to the reception at Winnipeg's gingerbread City Hall.

Their arrival in fact became the occasion for a local radio announcer to perform the finest tongue-twisting moment of the tour — the rough transcript of which appeared the next day in *The Globe and Mail*:

> The King, the Queen and Mr. King have now arrived at the city hall and Mr. Queen is on the steps to meet them. . . . The King is now shaking hands with Mr. Queen and now the Queen is shaking hands with Mr. Queen, and now Mr. King is shaking hands with Mr. Queen. . . . And now the King and Mr. Queen and the Queen and Mr. King are moving into the reception hall. . . . And now the King and Mr. Quing, I mean Mr. Keen and the Quing, I'm sorry, I mean, oh sh--.

Unfortunately, the rain by now had seeped through the red canopy over the welcoming stand, and was collecting in large puddles at the King and Queen's feet, so City Council members and others had to execute an agile "duck-skedaddle" as they bowed and curtseyed.

An even more awkward court manoeuvre was avoided by the King's presence of mind during their visit to the Manitoba Legislature. As he and the Queen were about to mount the steep steps to the throne in the Legislative Chamber, the King realized the impossibility of anyone's being able to climb and curtsey at the same time, and made the wise decision to stand and shake hands with people at the base of the steps. An organizational mix-up led to the visit's one embarrassing gaffe, when Minnesota Governor Harold Stassen and his wife, standing among the invited guests in the Chamber, were *not* presented to the King and Queen. Everything else went smoothly, the brief ceremony so memorable for some of those presented that afterwards they took turns placing their feet exactly on the spot where the King and Queen had stood a moment or two before.

Next came the moment the King was dreading. This being Empire or Victoria Day, he was scheduled to broadcast from Government House the longest radio speech of his life so far — 800 words — to be sent out not only to the Empire, but to the United States and France as well. Public speaking was terrifying enough with a row of faces looking up at him but, as the King confided to the Prime Minister, it was infinitely more trying to be addressing his words to an invisible audience. In any case, the speech seemed to go off very well in spite of a bad case of nerves. The King, seated in the Lieutenant-Governor's drawing-room with the Queen beside him, took as his theme the unity among diverse cultures, and between the Old World and the New.

> For a long period in history it was the mind of Europe which led the march and fixed the aims of progress in the world. But that tide of inspiration is no longer running as it did in time gone by. The Christian civilization in Europe is now profoundly troubled and challenged from within. We are striving to restore its standards; though the task is long and hard. Asia, too, is changing fast, and its mind is deeply disturbed. Is not this a moment when the Old World in its turn might look for hope and guidance to the achievements of the new?

When he had finished, the global broadcast continued. There were voices from Canada and the Empire: a Nova Scotia fisherman, a "French Canadian" in Montreal, an elevator boy in Toronto, a Saskatchewan farmer's wife, an Alberta bush pilot, a Vancouver dockworker, two South African engine drivers (one Afrikaaner, one English), a doctor and a fourteen-year-old girl from Australia, a Maori university student, from India the poet Rabindranath Tagore who read a poem ("Come raise up the banner of the invincible faith, build bridges with your life across the gaping earth, blasted by hatred, and march forward"), a Scotsman who talked of getting apples from Windsor, Ontario, a linen worker from Northern Ireland, a Welsh miner from the Rhondda Valley, an English naval cadet, a tobacco planter in Rhodesia. Then "Land of Hope and Glory" and the broadcast was over.

After luncheon with the Lieutenant-Governor, his wife, and a hundred guests (catered by the Fort Garry Hotel at five dollars a plate — including cooks and waiters), the royal party drove across the river to St. Boniface. Among the cheering and flag-waving crowd along Provencher Avenue were the children of Honoré Riel, a surviving nephew of the Métis leader Louis Riel. Honoré and his family still lived in the old Riel home on the Red River that now contained not only a coloured picture of the King and Queen, but also the plain wooden box that had carried Riel's body back from Regina.

Speaking for the 60,000 French-speaking Canadians of Western Canada, the Mayor of St. Boniface referred to his city as "the cradle of Christian civilization on these immense plains", presuming that the King had come to honour "the valiant heroes of the French race — missionaries, explorers and voyageurs — who were the first to bring the 'good news' to the savage people who inhabited them. You also desired, I am sure, to honour the mixed French nation that played such a great part in that civilization work and aided in conserving this country for the British Crown."

Back across the river, the royal party assembled at the Old Fort Garry Gateway, where the King received "two elkes and two Black beavers", the ancient rent exacted by Charles II in 1670 when he granted his Charter to the Governor and Company of Adventurers of England Trading into Hudson's Bay, "whensoever and as often as Wee our heires and successors shall happen to enter into the said Countryes and Territoryes". "Of nothing are the British fonder than a carefully cultivated anachronism," observed an American journalist present, as four buglers of the Royal Winnipeg Rifles ("the little black devils" of the '85 Rebellion) blew a fanfare, and Governor Patrick Ashley Cooper knelt to offer the tribute. The King was not going to be a stickler for detail; instead of "a ton of meat on the hoof and a pair of rambunctious rodents", he was willing to accept in token the two magnificently antlered mounted heads and a pair of the choicest beaver pelts acquired from the HBC's English auction rooms.

While the royal party moved about the city that day, Pallie Pascoe and his fellow workers had been working feverishly in the post office, having scarcely had time to poke their heads out of the mail car since Quebec City. People at every stop showed up with stacks of letters — all of which were sent out with the special commemorative stamps (the popular cover featured the two princesses), and all bearing the cancellation mark "Royal Train — Canada". On one day alone, they had handled a quarter of a million letters. Pallie had seen little of Montreal, Ottawa, or Toronto; but in Winnipeg, he put on his postal uniform and caught a ride with the mail courier ("He had a big sticker on his car, 'Royal Visit — Royal Mail' and it was fine having the streets opened for us and people gazing at my brass hat. I even got a salute from a soldier boy"). After a fast meal with some friends, he was back with Bill Ross and Lou Gignac in the mail car, which was parked for the day over the Main Street Subway, just west of the Royal Alexandra Hotel:

> The King and Queen were due to pass through the subway at 5 o'clock. . . . Well Sir, it started to rain at 3.00 P.M. and the street was simply packed, but not a soul left, and, unfortunately the parade was late and did not arrive until six something. It takes more than idle curiosity to keep people standing in a downpour for four or five hours.

The only people disappointed with the Winnipeg visit were the fast-buck artists who had counted on an enormous turnout to boost their profits. Bleacher entrepreneurs had taken an awful beating (in one case, selling just two of six thousand available seats). "The Royal Visit here is a 'bust'," lamented one businessman to a friend in Vancouver:

> For some unknown reason only half the visitors expected came to Winnipeg. Merchants are loaded up and made no sales. Restaurants are also holding the bag with stiff prices and no customers. Word got round in the States that the city would be jammed and confusion would prevail and no accommodation be available.

There was an emotional farewell scene at the station, and then the Royal Train was running out on the prairies, lush with the recent rain, and looking as it had in its best years. Young corn was shooting up, the sloughs were full of water, and cattle could be seen fattening on the spring grass ("wonderful to get a glimpse of the prairies," wrote Mackenzie King, "particularly to see a beautiful sunset—all so restful"). At each station stood the familiar crowds. Ten thousand children waited by the white wooden houses and green fields of Portage la Prairie, another large crowd at Carberry, and the biggest one of all—in Brandon—as the train pulled in late that night.

The responsibility for seeing that everything was fitting and correct had caused some sleepless nights for the city's Welcoming Committee. Only twelve days before, they had written Lieutenant-Governor Tupper, apologetic about their arrangements, which were "only now shaping up with some definiteness". Advice was needed on a wide-ranging number of questions, including the plan of presentation—which sounded something like the "March of the Wooden Soldiers":

> It is planned for the gentlemen elected for presentation accompanied by their wives, to mount the platform by the West end steps and in the order listed parade before Their Majesties turning and stepping forward as each pair arrives, the gentleman bowing and the lady curtseying whilst the Mayor announces their names. The pair thereupon steps backward two or three paces and turning to the right leaves the platform by the East steps, the next pair having taken their places before Their Majesties.

Tupper's secretary, tart and condescending, advised that, since it would be after "six o'clock p.m." when the King and Queen arrived in Brandon, "full evening dress would be suitable" for those being presented, and dictated the use of grey or white gloves, "the right glove in the left hand if it is seen that hands are shaken". And adding, "as the sun will have set by the time Their Majesties arrive in Brandon, it may not be considered necessary to lay a *new* carpet on the platform steps."

The organizers needn't have worried. Brandon provided one of the most spontaneous displays of affection in this suddenly fizzing, royalty-crazed country. The city's population of 17,000 had swelled by two or three times its usual numbers; some said there were 50,000 there that night when the train slid into the glow of the floodlights and coloured lamps, for a twenty-four-minute stop. There were farmers, babes in arms, grandmothers, and a choir of ten thousand schoolchildren from 145 prairie schools who sang "O Canada". People stood on the high banks beside the station, and crowded along the track for a good half-mile, shouting and cheering. There had been nothing to match it anywhere on the tour so far. "Nothing more stirring or moving," wrote Mackenzie King, "the gathering of children there was the finest scene on the entire trip. . . . The King and Queen were immensely delighted with it."

At every major stop, it was Mackenzie King's habit to leap from the train with his silk hat and cane to welcome Their Majesties anew, and then to introduce the local mayor and others. At Brandon, however, the train was still moving when he stepped off, and it was only the action of a quick-thinking Mountie that saved the Prime Minister from propelling himself into a ditch. Righting himself immediately, he walked to the platform to perform his duties.

As the last couple in evening dress bowed and curtseyed and retreated down the steps of the welcoming platform, the King and Queen themselves descended into the crowd. For a short time they strolled about at their ease, talking with nursing sisters, returned soldiers, and farm families from some of the worst-hit drought lands of the province. Here and there, some stepped forward and, in a gesture of prairie informality, shyly hugged and kissed the royal couple. "Here it was nearly midnight," wrote Mackenzie King, "and His Majesty there in the midst of the great throng, talking to everyone":

> They moved about freely, walking among the troops, even without police nearby. At one stage, the Queen was by herself the length of a car, without any other person, police or attendant, the King remaining behind talking to some others. Wonderful cheering. A long bridge overhead crowded with people . . . an unforgettable scene. The finest of the trip thus far.

The Queen later described it as "the biggest thrill of the tour". When she returned to the train at last, she could be heard murmuring, "Isn't it wonderful?", and her eyes were moist and glittering.

Thursday, May 25:

Three miles west of Broadview that morning, the train stopped to let the royal party off for a little exercise. The King, an enthusiastic walker, strode off immediately, leaving everyone else behind. The rest of the entourage fell in behind the Queen, strolling along the right of way and enjoying the pleasures of a Saskatchewan spring morning. The train meanwhile chuffed along behind at a respectful distance, like a worried equerry. After twenty minutes or so, the engineer rang his bell, and the train moved forward to pick up the walkers. At this point, the Queen led her party in an enthusiastic foot-race to overtake her husband. When they finally regained the train, several of the courtiers were puffing hard and mopping their brows. Elizabeth, however, was in fine spirits from the exercise. "She is full of life and charm," waxed Mackenzie King, who had watched from the comfort of his compartment.

In Regina, they were welcomed into the heart of the grain-growing country by the Lieutenant-Governor, Archibald ("Archie") McNab, and Jimmy Gardiner, the federal Agriculture Minister. The Mayor, A. C. Ellison, was there as well — daringly got up in a simple business suit and a grey felt hat, the first mayor to dispense with formal wear when meeting the royal couple. The Queen was once again wearing her favourite colour, an aquamarine blue ensemble with the sleeves trimmed in grey fox fur. The King, dressed as an Admiral of the Fleet, shook hands gingerly, still protecting his injured fingers. By that point, someone (likely an idle news reporter) had estimated that he had shaken three thousand hands, and had fifteen to twenty thousand more to go before the end of the tour.

"Pile o' Bones" was what they had first called the settlement when the last of the buffalo herds were just bones stacked for fertilizer along the railway line. Then it had acquired the genteel name of George VI's great-grandmother, Victoria Regina, when the city seemed destined to become the capital of a new British West. And just recently, in the winter of 1939, there had been a rumour that Regina might become the home of the royal family and the seat of the British government if war broke out—having "plenty of sunshine, lots of open spaces and good duckhunting". The stories were untrue, but they caused some diversion in a city almost totally dependent on a farm economy that had been sucked nearly dry in the past decade by wind, drought, grasshoppers, and Russian thistle. In spite of its troubles, the city had still managed to dust itself off for the royal arrival. Wheat sheaves, the symbol of the good years, competed with flags and patriotic bunting on street lights, and picked out the initials "G" and "E" in gold on City Hall.

The air that day was cool, and it was raining — again! — but once again this was good news in an area of the country where the soil still drifted high against the fences and whole families got by on boiled wheat. For one day at least, economic troubles could be forgotten by the families who arrived that morning by trains, trucks, autos, horse-drawn buggies, and rattling flivvers. Schools within a two-hundred-mile radius of Regina had scraped together nickels and dimes from concerts, dances, and bazaars to send in thousands of their schoolchildren in overalls and homemade dresses. The city's population had swollen overnight to fifty thousand. People stood on the wide streets, tortured by the smell of frying hamburgers from the food stands, and cheered and yelled as the King and Queen came down the street in their limousine — top down — with their RCMP escort. So excited was the crowd near the station that, as the royal party crossed South Railway Street, they broke through police lines and ran pell-mell after the procession.

Twenty-five thousand children, as well as a number of groups in ethnic costume, waited at the Exhibition Grounds while the King and Queen attended brief receptions at the Legislature and the City Hall. A replica of Fort Saskatchewan had been erected, and 3,000 Indians from four tribes demonstrated traditional dances to the beat of tom-toms. When the royal party entered the grounds, the Indians gave a special whoop, and raised their tomahawks in greeting. The Queen had the composure to smile and wave back, but onlookers noticed the fleeting look of astonishment on her face.

Then it was time for tea at the RCMP Barracks, with the Commissioner, Stuart Wood (seen for the first time on the tour in his scarlet uniform), his senior officers, and their wives. This was followed by a tour of the buildings, including the little chapel, which dated from the early days of the Royal North-West Mounted Police, and which stood a few feet from the unmarked spot where the Métis leader Louis Riel had kicked and dangled in his last moments a mere fifty-four years before.

Accompanying them everywhere that afternoon was the chunky figure of the Lieutenant-Governor, another charming *original* like Camillien Houde ("Call me Archie," he once told Lord Tweedsmuir. "I've been called damned near everything but that's the name I like the best"). Those who looked to the office of viceroy as an example of decorum and dignity had been dismayed by the appointment of Archie McNab. Never one for putting on airs, he seldom used his limousine and chauffeur, preferring instead to toot around town in his green coupé, or even take the streetcar. His cheerful air of informality had once led someone to mistake him for the janitor at Government House. McNab had denied it, asserting, "They're trying to teach me to be the butler." He had never forgotten his pioneer roots; whether playing gin rummy with the staff, showing up to cheer at baseball games, or (at the age of seventy-five) snaring gophers with small boys behind Government House, Archie McNab had brought a rough and refreshing egalitarianism to his office at a time when Saskatchewan needed it most.

Of course, royal tours called for an entirely different sort of behaviour. Archie, however, had been his usual self. When the King remarked on the crowd at the station, Archie replied, "If you'd brought the kids, there'd have been twice as many." At least three times that day he had to be reminded to take off his hat while "God Save the King" was being played and Mackenzie King, who regarded him with a sort of affectionate exasperation, reported that "during part of the procession, [McNab] kept waving one hand out of the car window, and the other toward the crowd on the other side to get them cheering."

In the evening, while the businessmen of Regina entertained the press at the Hotel Saskatchewan, the royal party dined at Government House as guests of the Lieutenant-Governor. The imposing two-storey residence had been built in some opulence fifty years before as a suitable home for a viceroy whose empire before 1905 stretched west to the Rockies and north to the Arctic. But, in spite of its ornate ballroom, panelled walls, and sunken bathtub (which the Prince of Wales had fallen into one night while drunk), Government House had not intimidated the McNabs. Archie's wife had the same down-to-earth style as her husband, whether gossiping over tea with "the girls" (as they called the maids) or bundling them into bed with hot toddies when they were sick. Nor did royalty pose any problem. When the Duke of Kent (who, in 1927, was misbehaving his way across Canada with his brother, the Prince of Wales) had shoes that needed shining, she told him bluntly, "In Canada we do everything ourselves. I'm afraid you'll have to do it." And the young prince did.

So that evening, while there may have been glass fingerbowls sprinkled with geranium leaves, and the delicate cream and regina blue walls glowed in candlelight, the hard truths of the Dirty Thirties meant that the silver and the dinnerware had been borrowed from Birks and McKenzie Jewellers, and Mrs. McNab had been forced to ask the Bessborough Hotel to send over kitchen staff to help out. This last arrangement was not a happy one. While Chef Zeppo worked his magic on the hors-d'oeuvre Muscovite and breast of Saskatchewan chicken, the "girls" fumed, accusing the Bessborough staff of drinking on the job and very nearly ruining the meal with their behaviour. And then Mrs. McNab had come through the door and nearly thrown a fit when she saw the small slices of chicken being cut off, and the carcasses thrown away. In Saskatchewan in 1939, waste like that was offensive.

In the dining-room, while the orchestra played selections from *The Mikado*, Archie McNab was performing as host for the evening. "Don't bother to pick it up," he advised the King, who was fumbling with the cutlery, "we've got lots of spoons." The Queen had asked about how the caragana bushes had survived the drought so well (the King seemed to think they were talking about spinach), and Archie saw to it that they had a package of seeds to take back with them. At the end of the evening, he had barged into the cloakroom, saying, "Where in hell is the King's coat? The bugger wants to go to bed," unaware that the King was following on his heels. "A dear old man," said the Queen.

In fact, the royal party still had one more function before bed. The Royal Train delivered them to Moose Jaw late that evening for a final late-night stop. Waiting for them there was

Pallie Pascoe, who had stayed behind in Brandon to clear up the overflow of mail and then skipped ahead by freight to his home-town to spend a few hours with his wife ("Ada met me at the station and had the car all dressed up like a Christmas tree. I wondered if the Royal auto had broken down and they had asked Ada to drive . . . but when I found out she had dressed it up for me, I decided to keep her and to return home after the Tour").

Moose Jaw, in the heart of the Dust Bowl, had not seen a decent crop in years. But, even without money, the town still retained that capacity — legendary in certain prairie communities — to organize events. The churches, the Moose Jaw Curling Club, the Women's Art Association, the Oconot Club — everyone pitched in to make the visit a success. Restrooms, first-aid stations, and other facilities were set up to handle the crowds, which, hours before the Royal Train was due to arrive, had more than doubled Moose Jaw's normal population of 20,000. "The home show may not have been the biggest," wrote Pallie afterward, "but I think it was the prettiest. Main Street was a picture. It will be many a day before we local lads will see the home town dressed up like it was that night." Not that he had time to do much more than kiss his wife goodbye and leap onto the pilot train, where more sacks of mail were waiting for him ("I was really too busy trying to account to Ada about how I spent my time when off duty — that would be between 1.30 a.m. and 7.00 a.m. I told her I slept and I believe she believed me").

The problem for communities like Moose Jaw was how to entertain the huge crowds and keep them happy until the King and Queen finally arrived (the visit itself would only take thirty minutes). The town couldn't afford the popular attractions of the day — like Calgary's elaborate stage show (the Yodeling Cowboy, the Vest Pocket Acrobat, the Hong Kong Pigeon Mystery), or Edmonton's Automobile Thrill Day ("Moondips, broad jumping autos, T-bone crash, and clowns"), or Regina's Flash Williams Thrill Show, or Winnipeg's elaborate entertainments, including an ethnic pageant and a ballet called "Kilowatt Magic". Instead, as their Royal Visit Programme shows, Moose Jaw overwhelmed its visitors with popular diversions — a rural schools' softball tournament, a swimming regatta, an outdoor organ recital (on Main Street outside Eaton's), a ladies' softball tournament, community singing, and a grand parade featuring bands, schoolchildren, and "Colourfully Costumed National Groups". And, if that wasn't enough, organizers also threw in horseshoes, billiards, bowling, oceanbathing at the natatorium, and flying stunts.

There was also last-minute advice to the throngs who wandered up and down its streets. "Listen to the Loud Speaker Cars. . . . No persons allowed on roofs. . . . Beware of pickpockets, confidence men, subscription takers, and too friendly strangers generally. . . . Have a good meal before coming down to the royal procession. . . . " And finally: "Be happy, though a bit uncomfortable at times. . . . Forget yourself and think of the other person. . . . JOIN IN THE COMMUNITY SINGING. HAVE FUN! CHEER YOUR KING AND QUEEN!"

Moose Jaw was a long blaze of coloured light from Main Street to Caribou when the Royal Train pulled in late that night. Mayor W. P. Johnson stood in nervous splendour on the platform to greet the King and Queen. He had, to the delight of his electors, made good on his promise to appear in a top hat, evening dress, and patent-leather shoes, and as well he carried a gold-tipped cane and wore a gardenia in his buttonhole. Again the rain had preceded the royal party, the first in weeks. It was as if the Royal Visit were also making good — quite literally — on its billing as a celebration of the end of the Dirty Thirties. The King was now referred to by the farmers as "George the Rainmaker".

In that spirit, the King ordered the top of the royal auto to be once again lowered, and the Queen, now in a blue gown and feathered hat, waved off her umbrella. They toured Moose Jaw's muddy streets, with its elevators, stockyards, and oil refinery, and waved cheerfully to the pandemonium. At Fairford Street, a small, pinched-looking woman picked up her small son and pushed to the front of the crowd. "There they are! See them! See them!" she cried. A woman on the opposite corner fainted. "The sight of the streets lighted at night, despite the rain was very beautiful," wrote Mackenzie King. "Foreigners like Ukrainians, Chinese and others were dressed in their best native costumes. . . . " Eleven-year-old Winnie from the Children's Shelter took in the scene from the back of the

IODE Truck for Sick and Crippled Children, and then summed up the Queen's remarkable charm as well as anyone ever has. "Sweetest face. Grand hands. She made you feel as if you had known her all your life."

Back at the station there were the veterans, and the patients carried down from the hospital. And with them a nine-year-old boy suffering gangrene poisoning who had been given only a few days more to live. Caught up like everyone in the excitement of the Royal Visit, he had been brought in the thirty-seven miles from Parkbeg in the back of an open truck. Mackenzie King followed the King and Queen to his cot ("the little lad first smiled very pleasingly at me, and then later at the King and Queen. Waved his little flag. It was quite a touching affair").

By the end of the thirty minutes, the King's face had begun to show the exhaustion he was feeling from the long day; the Queen, however, remained radiant, and continued to wave. Back on the observation platform, and out of sight of the main crowd, and still waving to those on the south side of the tracks behind the barrier, she was finally taken in hand by the King, who propelled her firmly into the carriage. The fireworks fizzled in the damp weather, and the train was forced to pull out of town in a modest anticlimax. But then, with the lights of the royal carriage disappearing down the track, Moose Jaw went on "the biggest binge in its history".

The Midway opened for business on High Street West; people flocked to the giant street dance, "Old Time Dance from River to High, Jitterbug Jamboree from Fairford to Ominica". Returned soldiers paused to consider their choices—the dance at Temple Gardens, a rally at the Canadian Legion, or another rally at "The Old Dugout" ("Castle Hall behind the sandbags"). At 11 p.m., professional boxing was scheduled ("five big bouts"), and at midnight a community singsong. Organizers promised bravely that the Midway would go on until dawn if necessary, while the Jitterbug Jamboree was guaranteed to continue "as long as addicts are willing".

"The way in which these communities help each other to share things is one of the most pleasing of all features," wrote Mackenzie King in his diary that night. "One thinks in terms of a Happy Land when one witnesses these scenes." Meanwhile, in front of him lay the latest Foreign Office cables from London:

> A German has been shot by a Pole in Danzig. Alliance with Russia about to be concluded. Japanese warning that it will mean Japan definitely siding with Germany and Italy. I am not without hope that this visit may help to let the peoples of Europe see how firmly the democracies are standing together.

Friday, May 26:

No one was up at six to see the twelve thousand people who gathered at the Swift Current station. Though the band played, and the mayor led the singing, the shuttered train moved through without acknowledgement.

At Medicine Hat, where they spent twenty minutes, the Prime Minister again leapt from the train while it was still moving (this time without incident), and joined Mayor Hector Lang, who was wearing a top hat and tails. The King for his part had embraced western informality, and emerged bare-headed into the sunshine in a lounge suit; the Queen wore a beige outfit with a hat in the now familiar off-the-face style. The bands played (including a girls' band up from Big Sandy, Montana) and the King shook hands with the veterans (including some from the South African and Zulu wars). Boy Scouts stuck their hats on staves and twirled them over their heads. Mere fireworks would not do in a town that boasted Medicine Hat's reserves of natural gas (Rudyard Kipling called it a town with "all hell for a basement"), so, as the Royal Train pulled out, a gas well was spectacularly "blown off" beside the tracks.

West of the town, as they climbed the high rolling plains still green from the recent rain, a lone figure on a horse came into view, the rider sweeping off his wide-brimmed hat in a royal salute. It was the best sign yet that they had left the wheat lands behind and were heading into the farming and ranch lands of the Last Best West. The sky was the colour of corn-flowers, the sun brilliant, and the white schoolhouses that flashed by all had their Union Jacks flying. Alberta was another family reminder—named in 1905 for Her Royal Highness Louise Caroline Alberta, fourth daughter of Queen Victoria, wife of the Marquis of Lorne. But Carl Stone, a settler from Claresholm, was perhaps more representative of the area's down-to-earth outlook:

Our isolated settlement of 20 was wide open prairie for 55 miles to south, 25 miles to east, 25 miles north to the river and west 90 miles. Ride your horse all day and hardly see a fence. THAT WAS THE LIFE! . . . That morning of the Royal Tour I got up at 2 A.M. 4 was my usual time. Having arrived to see the King and Queen the train had pulled out and we didn't see them. To get up the hill out of the Hat took two engines and went slow. We rushed out there to the hill and there was a few others there. The Queen was the only one of the whole party came to the platform at the rear of the caboose and waved to us. I have loved her ever since!

King had been described as a 2x4 for a head, not at all like his brother who had a ranch in Alta and visited the odd time. He was a real good sport. He left word with his ranch boss to be sure and keep lots of good bulls and don't worry about them getting out. It was his way to improve the basic Alta cattle, the Texas Longhorn. He called it his "RONCH" he said the difference between a ronch and a ranch was the ranch was a money maker and the ronch wasn't.

Later in the morning, there was time for another walk along the railway ties, and for the Queen once more to lead the perspiring aides and equerries in a wind-sprint. Then on to Bassano, which guaranteed everyone a good view — 2,500 people fell into formation and marched past the observation platform while the King and Queen stood and waved. The King even got a chance to indulge his shaky mastery of the movie camera when seventy-five Blackfoot Indians showed up in feathers and warpaint.

Cowboys and Indians were waiting for them in large numbers in Calgary, "sunshine city of the foothills", although the royal party was keenly disappointed that there were no rodeo events. Never mind. Calgary had been chosen as one of only four stops (Port Arthur, Vancouver, and Brantford were the others) for the elaborate display of aboriginal costumes, dances, etc. The prospect excited the organizers, who felt local Indian bands could display costumes and other crafts unequalled anywhere in the world. The Alberta Director of Indian Agencies agreed. "I know the Indians will crowd in to see their King," he wrote his superiors in Ottawa, "the beloved Great White Mother's great grand-son":

> Old and young on the reserves are already mentioning and longing for the visit, and are anxious to see His Majesty, and his Royal Consort, the young Queen. This visit . . . makes the year 1939 a "high-light" in their lives; and with fine Spring weather in May, green grass growing, foliage coming out and all the excitement of the forthcoming visit of their Majesties, how can we possibly hold the Indians back from making the trip. . . .

Through the winter and early spring of 1939, Indian agents laboured to make arrangements. The chiefs, minor chiefs, head-men and their wives from the five Southern Alberta agencies were to be brought to Calgary as official guests — along with costumes, horses, travois, painted tepees, and lodge poles. Money was set aside for three days' supply of bread, meat, tea, and sugar for approximately 300, with a payment of 50 cents a day per person. Some vacant lots on 9th Avenue across from Mewata Stadium were to be used as the site for an "encampment" of thirty tepees; sanitary arrangements were made and a water-pipe was laid in for drinking and cooking. The aim was a sort of "historical enhancement". "I have insisted to the Agents that their horses be clean-limbed," wrote the Calgary Director, "no feather-legged Clydes or Shires — and that they have sleek hair, and are well-groomed." No democrats or wagons would be allowed on the main site to disturb the illusion. Two red-coated Mounties would be stationed like ceremonial guardians to watch over the proceedings. And there would be a main flagpole at the centre, in front of No. 15 tepee (belonging to Duck Chief of the Blackfoot), with a very large Union Jack (other chiefs would have smaller flags in front of their tepees). Finally, the grounds would be levelled, and sprinkled generously, to keep the dust down.

None of this sat well with one man, the principal of an Indian residential school, who thought the idea of Indians displayed in their "tribal finery" more appropriate to "the day of the buggy, band box wagon and saddle horse". But in 1939, when people travelled by "the latest model car and the de luxe Plane", a more modern portrayal of native people was needed as well. "For Their Majesties to receive homage from the Indian in full regalia is one thing," he argued, "but to portray before Them a living cavalcade in war-paint and feathers is another."

> By all means have the Indians (as Indians) to the forefront in all ceremonial ritual, devoid of nothing which might depict ancient pageantry in all its eloquent symbolism, in order that Their Majesties might review the aborigines of Western Canada, in all "Red Man significance". But there let it stop. That is the past. Then in due sequence, bring along the offspring of these mighty warriors, shorn of all "Indianism" but attired according to the groups they represent in our Schools today: Scouts — Girl Guides — Cadets — Band — Sports — Choir — Music and as such comprehensive pageantry, comprised from so many ranks of a modern Indian education. The results would, I think, show that the Review is composed of so many potential Canadians, being paraded before Their Majesties.

The Indian Department was not deaf to the argument (in fact it allowed Boy Scouts and Girl Guides to be present in modern dress), but remained distinctly hard of hearing when it came to tampering with what was clearly the centrepiece of the Calgary visit.

Expenses began to mount as the day of the visit neared. There were railway fares to be paid, as well as hay, oats, a flagpole, spruce trees for decorating, saddle-horses, etc. On May 20, nine dollars was paid to the Chief of the Sarcees as an advance "for tepee and travelling expenses". On May 26, five dollars each was paid to Duck Chief, One Gun, L. Many Bears, P. Backfat, T. Up Nose, T. Yellow Fly, P. Little Walker, J. Crowfoot, and Many Guns. May 26: horses rented for one dollar a head from Tom Two Horns, Black Rider, P. Good Eagle, D. White Elk, Max Three Suns, "a young man", Old Bull, S. Many Fires — 12 dollars in all. May 29: "Paid Peter Many Wounds for loan of two horses and 1 tepee . . . 4.50. Paid George Big Belly for loan of four horses . . . 4.00. Paid minor chief Man Who Smokes & wife . . . 2.50 (travel expenses from Peigan Reserve)." Many Guns paid five dollars "to help defray expenses". And so on.

Everything was in readiness when the Royal Train arrived at three in the afternoon of the 26th to be met by General George Pearkes, Mayor Andy ("the Singing Chief Magistrate") Davidson, and their wives. Claims were extravagant as always, but it was said that in a city with a normal population of 84,000 the royal procession had been greeted by as many as 200,000 Canadians, liberally sprinkled with Americans "up for a good time". The bleacher tycoons had been stung again as people chose cheaper and more comfortable views on the hillsides overlooking the eight-mile route. Cheers were flung down on the royal procession with the usual enthusiasm, some of them landing on the Prime Minister, who nevertheless discerned more "hard times . . . in the faces of the people than I had seen elsewhere", a consequence, he believed, of the radical Social Credit agenda of the Aberhart government.

"The day turned out bright," wrote Mackenzie King, "the cheering was good, and altogether, the impression toward the end was the best. The Indian Chiefs were, for the most part, fine looking men, and in their full costume, very colourful." White buckskin and headdresses of eagle feathers, faces painted in brilliant yellows and reds, costumes stitched with porcupine quills, elk-teeth, and bear claws. When they moved, they jingled with the dozens of bells that hung from their clothing on tassels. As the noise from the crowd began to run down the street, thirty-six of the Indians, sitting astride horses, were arranged in tableaux about the encampment — "which, I may say, took the eye of the press representatives," wrote the Indian Affairs Director in his report, "who took many pictures."

Two thousand Indians in all — Blackfoot, Blood, Sarcee, Peigan, and Stoney — stood on the fringes of the encampment to watch the royal limousine pull in. To the chanting and beating of drums, eight women in white buckskin ran forward and spread buffalo robes at the feet of the King and Queen. Duck Chief, Shot-on-Both-Sides, Yellow Horn, Moses Jimmy John, Jacob Two Young Men, and David Bearspaw stood by a giant portrait of Queen Victoria; behind them, sitting impassively on their ponies, were the minor chiefs, each with an elaborately beaded rifle case slung on the saddle in front of him. Some of the older men among them had taken part in the Blackfoot and Cree wars sixty years earlier, while many of the younger Indians wore Great War Service Medals. "I shook hands with your father," said Duck Chief to the King with simple dignity. "I shake hands with you, and for both times I am glad."

There was a magnificent headdress for the King, now Great Chief Albino, and a beaded tobacco belt — handed by mistake to the Queen by the two flustered grandchildren of Duck Chief. Dust rising from the nervous pacing of the horses peppered the King's pin-stripe suit (in spite of the water that had been sprinkled), but, to the disappointment of the royal party, neither the Indians nor the gaudily attired cowboys and cowgirls who bordered their encampment displayed anything more than Stetsons, feathers, buckskins, and jingle-bobs. Riding, roping, and bronco-busting would have to wait for another visit.

The only excitement around horses in fact came later, when some of the Strathconas' mounts shied dangerously at the station ("I had been prepared, once or twice, to rescue Her M. if need be," wrote Mackenzie King, "also Mrs. Davidson from one of the Mounted horses which behaved pretty badly"). Fortunately, the horses were brought under control, and the nation was spared the sight of its Prime Minister being trampled heroically underfoot; and the Royal Train left town, not to the sound of war whoops or thundering hooves, but to the lonely skirl of bagpipes.

"There were great crowds all along the railway for miles after leaving Calgary," wrote Mackenzie King. "One of the prettiest sights of all was to see numbers on the banks of the river, and some of them almost waiting in the water itself, with the sun setting in the distance behind. . . . like a scene from a Chapter in the Old Testament." Ten thousand people were waiting by the sanatorium outside town where the patients had been brought down to the tracks on stretchers. As the train slowed, a number of the men and women on the ground raised themselves up and waved their arms in greeting.

Through the late afternoon and early evening, the Royal Train climbed slowly above the foothills, following every bend and twist of the Bow River. The royal party arrived in Banff in time to see the sun setting behind the deep purple of the mountains — and to hear 1,500 schoolchildren warble "When It's Springtime in the Rockies". And, in spite of the hour, everyone on board the train *did* seem invigorated by the scenery.

Invigorated as well perhaps by the thought that for the next day and a half they would be safely tucked away in the luxurious Banff Springs Hotel behind a tight RCMP security cordon that had been thrown up around them.

Lord Eldon had scarcely dropped his bags he before disappeared over the hill to fish for trout; Mackenzie King mooned about the sulphur baths and the hatcheries with Arnold Heeney; and even the King and Queen — after a few moments together in their suite — came down for a stroll. The young constable who had set off in discreet pursuit was shooed away, and they were allowed to wander down by the Bow Falls alone before returning to the hotel for a buffalo-steak dinner. After ten days of continuous travel, they were going to have some time to themselves.

CHAPTER SEVEN

Washday in Savona

Saturday, May 27:

"THE EFFECT OF THE HILLS and the air and the quiet is marvellous," exulted Mackenzie King after sleeping the night with his window wide open to the cold mountain breeze. He spent a pleasant morning puttering about — reading, making a few phone calls — then settled back for a leisurely shave and haircut. Tassé the barber had just come from the King's suite, and was determined to shave him with the same razor ("I confess it cut as though he was running a bit of silk over my face"). Then, at Mackenzie King's suggestion, they phoned Tassé's wife long distance (the first time Tassé had ever done such a thing). One can imagine Madame Tassé's face when the Prime Minister suddenly burst onto the line to wish her a happy birthday. Nevertheless it gratified Tassé, who was already reeling from the experiences of the last ten days. "The poor fellow's eyes filled with tears," wrote Mackenzie King of his long-distance gesture, "and he was quite overcome." After persuading him to take five dollars for his time, the Prime Minister set off with his stenographer, Eddy Handy, for another turn by the fish hatchery ("got the history of development of the rainbow trout, etc.") before strolling back to the hotel for lunch.

This was to be a real day of rest. Protocol had more or less gone out the window, and people were expected to come and go as they pleased — King, Queen, Prime Minister, belted earls, and the 127 journalists, all of whom had the Banff Springs Hotel to themselves for the next day and a half. The corridors of the hotel (described in its own literature as having "a touch of Baronial, Jacobean, Gothic, and Georgian") stretched out endlessly, and led to unexpected meetings. One journalist chanced upon the King and Queen, who were lost and confused without an equerry or prime minister at hand, and steered them tactfully to the lobby. A woman newswriter was caught unawares by the Queen as she practised her curtsey before the mirror in one of the hotel's large public rooms; the Queen stayed long enough to show the red-faced young woman how it was done.

But, on a sun-filled day like this, with the air balmy, and with the Valley of the Bow stretched below them, and with Mount Rundle, Sulphur Mountain, and the Fairholmes ranged around on all sides, everyone wanted to be *outside*—glad to be free for a time from the cramped quarters of the Royal Train. Ernie Bushnell of the CBC took Pallie Pascoe golfing. "We got a thrill walking in between those huge giants," wrote Pallie in his memoir:

> And every once in a while a clap of thunder would roll out. We would look up and find the sky clear and bright. About the 14th hole the caddies who were enjoying our worrying . . . told us it was but the wind leaping from Mountain to Mountain playing hide and go seek.

For the King and Queen, with their almost religious belief in the healthful benefits of long walks, the day was to be spent in an energetic exploration of the area. Dressed in sports clothes, they went down to the front terrace of the hotel that morning where their guide, Jim Brewster, was waiting.

Brewster was a legend in the mountains. A genuine child of the frontier (his father had been a scout for General Middleton during the Riel Rebellion), he had lived in Banff since coming there in 1887 at the age of five. And while setting up his successful outfitting business, he had guided every visitor of note on treks through the wilderness for the past forty years—from the Queen of Siam to George V (when the then Duke of York and Cornwall came to Banff with his wife in 1901). Later, he had entertained the Duchess (later Queen Mary) while her husband took himself off to Manitoba to shoot ducks. The Prince of Wales and the Duke of Kent passed through, of course; and though the Duke of Gloucester, when he came, had not felt up to the challenge of a grizzly-bear hunt, Brewster had shown up at the lodge anyway, and whiled away the evening by telling the young prince every grizzly story he knew. Bertie had been "the last of the four boys to come to Banff", and Jim Brewster loyally rated him a fine chap.

That morning he set off with the King and Queen and a few others for a two-mile drive up Tunnel Mountain. From the top they had a splendid view of the region — east to the Three Sisters, northeast to Lake Minnewanka, north to the Cascade Mountains, northwest to Mount Brewster, west to the Borzeau Range, and south to Spray Valley and Mount Rundle. The mountain teemed with every kind of wildlife — moose, bear, mountain sheep, goats, deer, elk, and coyote. The King, behaving like any other tourist, ran off hundreds of feet of film on his movie camera. The Queen, not surprisingly (given her recent performance in foot-races), was rated by Brewster as being in better shape than anyone else in the party — even if he did have to pick up her purse each time she left it on the trail. There was no dawdling for Elizabeth; when she walked, she strode ahead with a purpose.

After leaving Tunnel Mountain, they motored across the valley to Mount Norquay and its famous ski jump, and the King took more pictures. Then, refreshed by the exercise and the mountain scenery, they returned to the hotel to dine on the fresh trout that Lord Eldon had caught the night before (more or less illegally, as the Queen pointed out). The Prime Minister had been invited to join their luncheon party but he could add little to the merriment. Even on a glorious day like this in the tranquillity of the mountains, he still found time to brood on the unjust treatment he had received at the hands of Hardinge and others on the Buckingham Palace staff during the planning of the royal tour. He spent much of the meal bending the Queen's ear on the matter — and it was to her great credit that no one ever saw her once roll her eyes. On the contrary, she listened carefully to the Prime Minister, reassuring him immensely by her sympathetic manner, without ever having said anything very much at all.

After lunch, a buggy ride had been arranged. But first, to the King's intense irritation, Tommy Lascelles had arranged a short session with the photographers, arguing that it was the only way to buy them off for the day. The King motioned the

Prime Minister into the pictures with them, and Mackenzie King happily obliged. The high wind scattered his wisps of hair, while his Scotch plaid suit ("which the Duke of Montrose gave me") made him look like a bookie on vacation.

The Queen had been much taken with the Canadian buggies she had seen in Quebec City, and Jim Brewster, notified of this in advance, had canvassed the whole countryside around Banff until he found an old democrat owned by his friend Joe Otter on the Sarcee Reserve. It was in rough shape, shaky in the joints, but he cleaned and oiled it as best he could, and covered the old spring seats with buffalo robes. After seeing that his two passengers were properly tucked up with scarlet rugs, he took them on a six-mile ride over the golf course (and later on, after returning the democrat, put five dollars in the mail for Joe Otter).

There was no question he had hit it off with the royals, for on Saturday evening he was back again — this time to take them up to Mount Norquay for the view and then along the Lake Louise Road to see the beaver lodges. Sighting a small black bear by the side of the highway, the King impulsively jumped out and gave chase with his camera, followed by his RCMP bodyguards. Then, for a time, they just walked along the road, the King in his brown slouch hat and tweeds, the Queen wearing a coat over a plain blue dress. Before returning to the hotel, however, they asked Brewster if he would take them to see his famous collection of mounted trophies. A short time later, Mrs. Brewster, at home, unprepared and probably in the middle of spring cleaning (there were no curtains up in the front room), watched the door open and the King and Queen walk in.

The Queen chatted pleasantly with Mrs. B. about this and that, until the poor woman had recovered sufficiently to keep up her end of the conversation (it was not uncommon for people to be reduced almost to gibberish in the royal presence; like the flustered wife of a mayor during one of the earlier tour stops who, on being asked by the Queen why her husband wasn't wearing his chain of office, replied that he wore it only "on special occasions"). Conversation with royalty was no problem for Jim Brewster. He told them stories about the early days in Banff when he would buy horses from the Indians and

drive them up to Edmonton (often multiplying his profit by
reselling the wild range ponies each time they escaped and
were caught). After viewing his collection of trophies, many of
which were world-record size, the King and Queen returned
to the hotel. There they made their final appearance of the day,
stepping into the banquet-room where Mackenzie King, on
behalf of the Dominion government, had been plying the press
with food and drink.

The fact that the reporters, photographers, radio men, and
camera crews from the pilot train had been accommodated
behind the security cordon in the same hotel as the royal party
only contributed to the feeling that the 1939 tour was a co-
operative effort between the two groups. Almost like a conspiracy, communicated in winks and nods, to make the whole
cross-continental affair a triumph. The King or Queen had
only to flash an occasional winning smile their way and many
of the journalists seemed ready to bury every trace of their
professional scepticism under a pile of effusive prose. To do
any less would seem somehow ungracious. Reuters reporter
Alaric Jacob, who had once accompanied the Prince of Wales
on one of his journeys, found that this attitude — of being a
part of the success or failure of the royal tour — had already
clouded the perceptions of his two travelling companions,
whom he called Wilkins and Garner. Both were affected, however, in different ways.

Wilkins was an Englishman, a wizened little man who had
also travelled with royal tours before, and who, as Jacob
pointed out, cherished "an exaggerated view of the importance
of royal patronage":

> "I wouldn't be surprised," he confided to me early on in
> the trip, "if certain people didn't Get Something out of this
> tour."
> "A pair of cuff-links?" I suggested.
> "I got those last time," said Wilkins, shooting his cuff to
> display some jewellery. . . .
> "I must say I'm surprised," he added in a tone of reproach,
> "that the Prince of Wales never gave you a pair of braces."
> "Are those what he usually gives?"
> "Oh, yes. Being a bachelor, you see. One couldn't expect

the same on this trip because the remembrance would in part
be on behalf of the Queen. And a pair of braces, well . . . I
mean to say . . . it wouldn't quite *do*, would it?"

"Indeed, no. So what do you anticipate?"

"I rather think," said Wilkins judicially, "that I might get
an M.V.O. Or there again, it might be no more than the
B.E.M."

Garner, on the other hand, was a sports reporter for a New
York tabloid, hauled off his usual beat with more-or-less-
explicit instructions to debunk the tour of the King and Queen,
"and expose their royal circus for the un-American, subversive
affair that it was." Unlike Wilkins, he was expecting nothing
more than "a loud horse laugh" from the trip. A man who
customarily wrote "at the top of his lungs" (he sounds a lot
like George Dixon), Garner had begun by slamming the ceremonies in Quebec City as snobbish and effete, and laying some
of the blame at the door of the Roman Catholic Church. This
had brought a quick cable from his editor: "Offlay Pope's nose.
Your canvas colorfuller cleaner without cardinals." Unde-
terred, Garner had continued his hard-boiled approach, until
Ottawa:

> He met the Queen at a tea-party and treated her to a long
> monologue, explaining why the Publicity Slant of the tour was
> all wrong; she contrived to give him the impression that he
> was the most amusing fellow in North America — a truly
> astonishing demonstration of queenly art — and he for his part
> returned quite satisfied that she was the Swellest Little Woman
> in the World. . . . Garner's Americanism had definitely been
> undermined. His editor did not like the fervid accounts of royal
> charm and sapience which he now began to send and retorted
> with some sharp cables. . . . [But] Garner escaped the worst
> consequences of his apostasy through his employer's natural
> assumption that he must have embarked upon a drinking bout.

Alcohol played a part in the proceedings that night in the
Banff Springs Hotel, very nearly destroying the fragile bond
between the press and the royal party — and almost leading to
an international incident. Following the press dinner, one of
the reporters, somewhat the worse for wear, had approached

the King and asked whether he thought this trip would produce American support for Britain in the event of war. Astoundingly, the King (relaxed somewhat by the occasion, perhaps) had replied in casual fashion, "It's in the bag." As Alaric Jacob reported:

> Soon afterwards the correspondent was found in a befuddled condition in a telephone booth trying to transmit this story to New York. The rest of us dragged him out of the booth by force and agreed among ourselves that on no account should the unfortunate aside be published anywhere, since to do so would not only constitute a breach of confidence but would also be dangerous politically.

A garbled version of the King's words eventually appeared in a New York weekly, but the damage was nothing to what it might have been. The swift action of the other reporters on the tour had undoubtedly prevented the American part of the tour from being torpedoed—and had preserved good relations with the royal party.

Mackenzie King did not stay up with the press that night. After seeing the King and Queen off to their rooms, he sank back into a pleasant, restful conversation with a Mrs. Lang, "who has charge of the flowers for the CPR from Vancouver to Winnipeg". They sat in front of one of the hotel's great fireplaces, and, when that became too hot, continued chatting in the conservatory. At 11:30 he turned in. It had been an idle, agreeable day.

A little before morning, while he still slept, he felt the presence of his mother come into the room, placing her cheek against his, on one side and then the other ("I held her in my arms. . . . It seemed to me that as I held her face close to mine, she was looking toward the Queen who was sitting nearby"). Even after waking, he remained convinced that the experience was genuine, still feeling her presence there with him in the room.

Sunday, May 28:

In the morning Jim Brewster drove the King and Queen to church. Then it was off with the whole royal party on a final motor excursion through the mountains to Field, where they would rendezvous with the Royal Train. At first, the weather was bright and warm, and they had a good view of the mountains and the wildlife — mountain goats looking back at them over the crest of a rock, some elk, a deer that ran across the road, and nests of ospreys. But at Lake Louise, the water was still lightly coated with ice and the famous view had been spoiled by the drizzle. By the time the group reached Kicking Horse Pass and the Great Divide ("where all the weather starts"), they had been forced to put up the car's top. In the increasing cold and wet, they took tea — and had a brief view of the Yoho Valley; then it was a last dash along the fine gravel roads and the hairpin turns, along the tumbling turbulence of the Kicking Horse River, and finally down to Field and the Royal Train.

"Like getting back home," according to Mackenzie King, who ate lunch with Ian Mackenzie, his Defence Minister, and then went back to the barbershop to hear firsthand the story of the Royal Train's only genuine accident so far. An upper berth, containing the considerable bulk of the barber, Roger Tassé, had collapsed one night onto the lower berth where the Queen's tiny hairdresser, Frank Powell, was sleeping. The Prime Minister got them each to tell his own version of the story ("I have never laughed harder in my life. . . . When I said I thought it would be nice if we let the photographer come in and go through it again, Powell asked me if I would take his part").

The press meanwhile had had little to laugh about. Thanks to a mix-up over scheduling, and to the dictates of protocol (which had regained its starch overnight), about fifty reporters had been stranded at the hotel that morning, unable to leave until Their Majesties did. Unshaven, bleary-eyed, many of them without their breakfasts (and apparently unrecovered from the night before), they stood fidgeting near three buses which had been piled high with their luggage. As the royal party said its last goodbyes and finally pulled away, the press broke for the buses, like drivers at a racing-car rally, and headed for the pilot train. What happened then, and over the next few hours, owed its inspiration chiefly to Mack Sennett.

Turning the final corner, they arrived at the station to find that the pilot train had gone, although those in the leading bus claimed afterwards to have gotten close enough to be racing even with the train's observation platform. But orders were orders: the schedule had stipulated a 10 a.m. departure and, given the higher mathematics of train-scheduling which affected the entire east-west transportation system, the dispatcher had sent the pilot train on its way. Cursing their luck and the CPR, the reporters piled back into the buses, and raced through the heavy rain in hopes of catching the train at Lake Louise. Again they were too late, but a Mountie ran over to them, shouting, "Drive like hell, you'll make her at Field!"

"Field or Heaven, Goal of Reporters in Banff" ran the headline the next day. No reporter was so terrified of this last race over the mountains that he couldn't see a story in it — even if it was to be his last. So while Their Majesties sipped tea at Lake Louise, and snapped pictures of the wildlife, the reporters hung on to the careening buses — and the words of a high-speed drama began forming in their minds, "sleet . . . dust billowing up from the vehicles ahead . . . a hairstanding slithering pace . . . beating hearts . . . driver stepping on the gas . . . the roadway curling under the radiator like some dirty grey ribbon . . . the race up the Kicking Horse Pass . . . waving pines . . . wheel-tossing road . . . greasy roads . . ."finally gazing at the half-mile drop into the Yoho Valley on the right ("the minute difference between one front-wheel skid and eternity") and the sight of their destination looming up a mile or so down in the river bottom, arriving hungry, filthy, and evil-tempered in Field, but managing a great cheer at the sight of the familiar pilot train standing at the station blowing big white puffs of smoke into the sky, and the immaculate Maxwell, porter of car 23, grinning at them from the car steps.

Both trains now proceeded west through the remaining mountains—the final hours of relaxation before the "full-dress dignity" of Vancouver and Victoria. Sixty-three miles west of Field at Beavermouth, the King and Queen, wearing their sports clothes again, climbed into the cab of the lead engine of their snorting "triple-header". It was a Selkirk-type oil-burning locomotive, one of the largest in Canada, and for the next thirteen miles it afforded the royal couple a spectacular view of some of the best mountain scenery in North America. They snaked through mountains and passes along 2.2 grades, climbing the spectacular Beaver River Canyon Gorge to Stoney Creek, looking down 275 feet at one point to the tumbling mountain stream below. Even with rain and low clouds, the beauties of the Selkirk Range, the mountain torrents, and the foaming cascades were apparent.

There were no ceremonies planned during the twenty-minute service stop at Revelstoke in the Central Interior. Nevertheless, a large crowd of 8,000 had come into town and now stood waiting in the heavy rain. The King put on his tan raincoat and slouch hat and the Queen held up her umbrella and together they splashed through the puddles as they walked along the ties. "We have come now to where the lakes are visible from the train," noted Mackenzie King, gazing out the window as they sped on. "The scenery is perfectly exquisite . . . green trees, luxurious shadows in water on the lakes. Crowds assembled as we passed."

They stopped at Craigellachie, where Donald Smith had driven in the last spike of the transcontinental railway; Salmon Arm, where children came up to the royal carriages with masses of wild flowers they had picked; and Monte Creek, where fifty people gathered around to sing "God Save the King" and where someone suggested they sing "O Canada". The King asked who would start and a small boy piped up:

"You lead it, mister."

"Sorry," said the King. "I can't."

Eddy, the son of the foreman of the sprawling Bostock ranch, handed the Queen a bouquet of wild flowers, and the train started to pull out.

"Don't wait so long next time before you visit us!" someone called out.

"I would like to get off right now," said the King.

At ten o'clock they were in Kamloops, where the Prime Minister hopped out to introduce the mayor and then walked about with the royal couple. Fifteen minutes stretched to half an hour for the veterans, the children waving Union Jacks, and the Rocky Mountain Rangers, who led the crowd in singing. Two Indian chiefs, Johnny Rapback of Lytton and Tommy Lick of Cooksferry, showed the King and Queen the blue flag

that had been given to their people by a representative of
Queen Victoria so many years ago. "A finer and even larger
crowd than Brandon," Mackenzie King noted in his diary. "A
great sight, deeply moving as the children had been massed in
that formation for hours" and clear proof that the King and
Queen were "winning everyone along the way."

It was a pleasant irony of the 1939 Royal Visit that while
many cities and towns across the country had been forced to
fight for every minute they had wrenched from the tour itinerary, it was the humbler settlements along the rail line that
often had the more memorable visits. At each service stop, the
King and Queen could hop out and chat for a few minutes
with the people — unencumbered by illuminated addresses,
honour guards, or formal presentations. As for the communities
themselves, the temporary stop of the Royal Train was an event
that quickly found its way into the local folklore — as it did for
one small settlement a few miles west of Kamloops.

Hours before the Royal Train arrived, the news that it would
stop to take on water in Savona had become an open secret in
the town. Word had spread to the farms and the ranches scattered up in the hills — and someone had even ridden over to
the baseball game to let everyone there know when the train
was expected. By eleven o'clock Sunday evening, about a
hundred people had gathered at the station — townspeople,
farm families, and Indians from the reserve at Deadman's
Creek, who sat impassively astride their ponies. Although it
was warm for that time of year, people could remember a
shimmering curtain of Northern Lights that danced overhead,
and there was moonlight shining on the still waters of Kamloops Lake. As they stood around chatting, someone noticed
Granny Villiers in the crowd. No dance or Christmas concert
between Ashcroft and Kamloops was complete without
Granny and her fiddle — and surely *this* was an occasion. So
one of the boys sped away on his bicycle, and returned a few
minutes later with the instrument, which Granny Villiers immediately tuned up.

It was just before midnight when the headlights of the train
finally flashed around a bend, and the illumination came running down the rails to Savona station. As the huge engine
rumbled slowly into the station, people swarmed over the fence

and ran along the railway track behind. Cries for the King and Queen had started almost immediately, and lights now flashed on above the observation platform on the rear coach. A moment later the door opened, and a woman in a white dress and a picture hat stepped out alone. Unable to see at first beyond the radius of the light, Elizabeth smiled and asked who was there. "Just everybody, Your Majesty!" came the reply. She waved, the cheers rained down, and then she stepped back inside — only to return a moment later with the King, dressed in a black suit. "What place is this?" he asked. The answer came back in a burst, "Savona!" and he went in for a minute and marked it on the large map on the carriage wall.

A number of the children had formed up by the water tank when the train first stopped; but then someone ("maybe a belted earl, maybe a barber, maybe the minister of defence") leaned out and made the familiar "Oi" gesture of "The Lambeth Walk", and the kids scurried back to the rear carriage, where the rest of the crowd was enjoying an impromptu chat with the royal couple. Then Granny Villiers stepped over the cross-ties to the end of the coach, tucked her violin under her chin, and played "God Save the King", "O Canada", and "The Maple Leaf Forever", and to each of these, Savona sang along:

> In days of yore
> From Britain's shore
> Wolfe the dauntless hero came
> And planted firm Britannia's flag
> On Canada's fair domain

With servicing complete, the train began to pull away, and Herbie Wilson, the boy who had fetched Granny's fiddle, shouted after them, "Good-bye, Your Majesties! Come again!"

"We will!" said the Queen, calling back to him before the train once more slipped into the darkness beyond the station lamps.

"Monday was not observed as washday in Savona!" declared G. H. T. Edwards in the next issue of the *Kamloops Sentinel*, referring to that night's events. "And did Savona enjoy it? Did Savona spend Monday talking it over to our hearts' content? Did we? We did!"

Monday, May 29:

By first light, the train was rolling down the Fraser River gorge, passing now and then through long tunnels under the mountains. "I thought of the significance of Faith in darkness, etc.," wrote Mackenzie King. By ten they had arrived at the CPR's western rail terminus in Vancouver.

Vancouver had stayed up all night to greet them. Bars and cabarets had opened one minute after midnight, theatres had continued running—and in Chinatown, where the Mayor had officially inaugurated festivities two nights before, jive-man Benny Yip and his orchestra were probably somewhere still "swinging out the hits".

In the pre-dawn darkness, people arrived to take up the best locations. They carried rugs, camp-stools, piano benches, apple boxes, lawn chairs—or just made do with the cold curbstone. They chatted, knitted, wrote letters, drank tea and coffee from their thermoses, and wandered up and down Granville Street to keep warm. Wrecking-cars patrolled the streets, ready to tow away any car found along the royal route. At 6:30, two little girls scrambled up a grassy bank on Cambie and settled down to wait. By 7, there were still some free seats on the curb near the brand-new Hotel Vancouver, directly in front of the grandstand ("See the King and Queen *three* times from here!"), where seating went for a stiff ten dollars apiece. Service stations and barbecue stands on Burrard at the south end of the bridge were doing a brisk trade, while elsewhere people peddled cold drinks, Union Jacks, and packaged lunches. On Burrard, a man had refused to sell his flags after discovering they had been made in Japan.

Not everyone was so scrupulous. Newspapers reported that 5-cent coffee had jumped to 10 cents, breakfast could cost as much as 50 cents, and the price of dinner had skyrocketed to 85 cents at some of the local fountains. An order of coffee and doughnuts would not be encouraged; customers who took up space at the counter were expected to buy full meals. And there was little time to ponder the menu when hundreds were waiting behind you in line ("neither will you be encouraged to sit over your coffee, dragging on a cigarette and discussing just how attractive the Queen really is"). The American papers played up these stories, reporting that because of the extortionary prices in Canada, box lunches were being sold on the Seattle wharf to people taking the ferry to Victoria.

Women in oriental dresses began to show up along the processional route, as well as men in morning coats and spats. Costumes seemed to be the order of the day. There were English Kindred Societies, loggers, Japanese fishermen, firemen, native Indians, and various national groups, all in their distinctive dress. Even Mayor Lyle Telford, who greeted the Royal Train at the station, had, for the first time, agreed to put on his purple robes, white jabot, and gold chain (until now, the symbols of his office had seemed too ostentatious for a city in hard times). "A pleasing feature was to see the Chinese in their costumes," wrote Mackenzie King; "we passed through a long street where all present were Scotch, many in kilts. . . . It was interesting to see many Japanese soldiers wearing war medals, also masses of little Chinese children. Some natives of India." At one point on the route, 25,000 Scots were massed on a hillside with 300 dancers and 200 pipers. The strong identification with things British was not so unusual in a city where gasoline was still advertised as "petrol" (and where cars until recently had been driven on the left-hand side of the road), broad Lancashire and Yorkshire accents were common, and the signs advertising a number of large British companies were prominently displayed. Less expected, and in many respects more moving, were the hundreds of Chinese children, none of them eligible for citizenship, who sang "God Save the King" as the procession passed.

In spite of the downpour that had soaked Vancouver the night before, the clouds had lifted from the mountains when the royal party arrived. This was typical of what was known as "King's Weather", a phenomenon which caused observers to swear that sunlight had inexplicably burst through heavy rainfall, lowering clouds had magically evaporated, or moisture had fallen in severely parched areas — and always at the precise moment when the monarch stepped into view. Certainly the day was bright, though as the King and Queen entered their car a blanket was placed across the royal knees to guard against a lingering chill in the air. For the first time on the tour the King wore his Royal Air Force uniform, while the Queen was again in blue, with a blue fox fur tossed over her shoulders.

"Everything is on a grand scale," wrote Mackenzie King of their forty-mile drive through the city that day. "Magnificent in fact. Enormous buildings, wide streets, great parks." Arbutus, dogwood, and the luxuriant hawthorn trees blossomed everywhere and provided a lushness that had been missing in other cities. At the foot of Burrard Street stood a massive arch, forty feet high and fifty feet across, made from thousands of cut flowers and potted plants donated by local florists. Flags and banners were everywhere, of course, and Vancouver's housewives had been asked *not* to do their Monday wash, for fear the fluttering clotheslines might detract from the pretty effect of the decorations.

There was a brief ceremony of welcome at the sparkling new City Hall, and then the royal couple met with a number of V.C. winners — the daily reminder that this tour was being conducted under the shadow of past and future wars. Doug Oliver, of *The Globe and Mail*, described the scene as the men stepped forward, "nearly all of them old men now, old sweats, old fragments stumbling in their walk, and slowed in the fistedness and cussedness that flattened all obstacles like butter some twenty years ago. . . . "

> There was MacGregor, who came down from the Peace River country, with the blessing of Toronto's Dinny Draper on everything he says and does; O'Rourke, the stretcher-bearer, who didn't know what death meant at Passchendaele; Hanna, of the 29th Battalion, whose grin at Hill 70 hid all the deadliness of his Lewis gun; Shankland, the Emma-Gee guy who carved his name indelibly on the now peaceful rise that is Bellevue Spur; Train, the two-striped London Scottisher, and Beet, who won his bronzed cross in the relief of Wagener, near the end of the Boer campaign. . . .

Afterwards, in the Mayor's office upstairs, the King had a cigarette while they took in the city's panorama of park, harbour, and mountains. Down in the plaza, a massed choir of 1,500 entertained the huge crowd with "Jerusalem" and "Land of Hope and Glory".

There were visits to Shaughnessy Military Hospital and the University of British Columbia, and then a luncheon at the ultra-modern new Hotel Vancouver, whose opening had been delayed some ten years by the Depression. Experienced staff from the Château Laurier, brought west for the occasion, served supreme of crab legs, consommé Madrilène, crown of spring lamb, and bombe aux fraises. In spite of the intensive drilling in protocol that guests underwent beforehand, there was no "swank" about the affair. The King chatted amiably while the Queen, her eyes twinkling, shared herself between the Mayor and the Defence Minister ("Mackenzie," noted the Prime Minister, "is almost intoxicated with delight of our Scottish Queen").

That afternoon, before leaving for Victoria, there was another drive through the City, over to the North Shore, where Marine Drive had been bordered by two hundred baskets of flowers, and back via the magnificent Lions Gate Bridge. Late in the day, the CPR's cruise ship *Princess Marguerite* carried them through the Narrows — accompanied by four destroyers, an RCAF escort, yachts, Japanese fishing boats, and twenty-four Indian war canoes, whose occupants paddled furiously through the waves to reach the *Marguerite*, and then gave great whoops as they skimmed along the water beside the ship. The scene brought out the best crowds of the day. People clustered along the shoreline and the docks, or stood on the tops of buildings to get a look. The bells of Holy Rosary Cathedral pealed out, trains and ships hooted and whistled, and cannons boomed out from Stanley Park, their white smoke blossoming against the green of the Brocton Point Cricket Ground. Traffic was reported to be "demoralized" for an hour (after which, according to less reliable reports, the streets were taken over by Scotsmen dancing Highland flings).

The *Princess Marguerite* steamed into the heart of the sunset and the westerly breeze. On deck, the royal party admired the lush green islands as they passed, while the press trained its glasses without success on a nudist colony. As darkness came down, the ghostly white of the Olympic range came into view, and from the headlands on Vancouver Island and on the American side, beacon fires were lit in welcome. Automobiles parked on the coast road near Victoria formed a long, glittering necklace of light. And in the city itself, thousands of electric light bulbs had been strung along the outlines of the Provincial

Legislature and the Empress Hotel, giving the otherwise invisible buildings a fairy-tale appearance. As the *Marguerite* entered Victoria harbour, it was greeted by whistles, horns, sirens, bagpipes, church bells, wild cheering — and rain.

Here, at the most westerly point of their tour, there was the sense of a long journey ended. When the royal party reached Carey Castle, the Lieutenant-Governor's residence, "the doors were thrown open and a great fire was blazing in the hall inside." According to Mackenzie King, "the most welcome of welcomes given T.M. on their entire tour. . . . like an Old Country residence." Immediately they sat down to a buffet supper. "One felt like having a good meal," said the Prime Minister, "and as I had skipped dinner, immensely enjoyed the tongue and trifle and a glass of Scotch."

While the King and Queen settled in at Government House, everyone else — including Pallie Pascoe — went off in search of their rooms at the Empress:

> The night in the hotel was used mostly to scrub two weeks dirt off. We lay in the tub for about an hour at a time. The hotel was a mystery, it had been all barricaded off to insure quietness for the Royal Party and we used every kind of door to get from room to room. Geo. Dixon asked me if I would like a drink, and I said "Sure". He said, "Here's my key, help yourself" and as I strode away he called — "If you find the —————— room, come back and get me and then we'll both have a snort."

Tuesday, May 30:

The day was brilliant and clear. Victoria, in Mackenzie King's mind, was "at its best, trees in full foliage. Flowers everywhere. Children wearing garlands in their hair. . . . " At the Legislature, Thomas Dufferin Pattullo, the former sourdough from the Trail of '98, extended the province's formal welcome to Their Majesties. There were other ceremonies, a welcome at City Hall, a visit to Oak Bay, and then luncheon at the Empress Hotel, where the King's new-found composure before the public received a stiff test.

He had been scheduled to make a speech, and his comments, as usual, were to be broadcast to the vast audience that had been following the daily events of the Royal Visit on radio. These were always moments of considerable tension, not only for the King but for everyone else in the royal entourage. There was the fear that he might suddenly be seized by nerves and begin stammering badly. And, in fact, there had been times in Quebec City when George VI had paused so long between words that Tommy Lascelles must have wondered if he were going to continue at all. Since then, of course, the King had gained immeasurably in confidence. But now, as he stepped to the microphone in the banquet-room of the Empress, a film crew suddenly materialized and, without warning, raked the head table with lights. Lascelles and the Prime Minister were furious, and both signalled frantically for the lights to be switched off. The King, however, carried on, refusing to be rattled either by the blinding glare or by the intense heat, which had caused him to perspire almost immediately. It was, in fact, one of his finest speeches of the entire tour:

> To travel through so grand a country is a privilege to any man; but to travel through it to the accompaniment of such an over-whelming testimony of good will, from young and old alike, is an experience that has, I believe, been granted to few people in this world. . . .
>
> In the course of this journey I have seen the old settled parts of the Dominion which have a long history behind them, and I have seen the newer parts, of which the first settlement is still within the memory of living men. When I remember that here I am as far from Ottawa, as Ottawa is from London, I realize something of the vastness of Canada. When I saw the broad plains, changed by pioneers to the uses of man, and the mighty mountain ranges through which they cut their roads, I began to understand the qualities of the Canadian people.

The success of the speech did little, however, to assuage the fury of the King's party. "Lascelles went for Pattullo pretty hard about the movietone having been permitted," wrote Mackenzie King afterwards, noting just how zealous the King's Acting Private Secretary had been in protecting his sovereign's dignity. "He said he was glad he had not a gun with him at the time, that it was an outrageous thing to turn the lights on the King in that fashion." An investigation was swiftly launched, the culprit responsible for the intrusion of the movie crew was fingered, and the Prime Minister could report that the press (in their new sense of themselves as proprietors of the royal image) were "treating the offender in a manner which would excommunicate him".

The King himself was so pleased with his performance that he seemed to take little notice of the fuss that had been raised afterwards. He had been hot under the lights, and had told the waiters not to remove the decorative ice sculpture (complete with two beavers rampant) from the table because of its cooling presence, but otherwise he was unaffected. He even turned to Mackenzie King when it was all over and, in a tone of almost childlike delight, pointed to a particular passage in the text, saying, "I worked that part in myself." But the success of the speech came not only from its eloquence (those parts of the text not claimed by the King had been drafted originally by Lord Tweedsmuir) but from the manner in which it had been spoken.

Overlooked in the continual anxiety over George VI's speech problems was the actual quality of his voice, which was rich and melodious — almost an actor's voice, though not so mannered. When he spoke well, as he did in Victoria, his slow, deliberate pace (which set up a slight suspense, even between words), his pleasing baritone voice, and the way he lisped slightly on his "r"s, all gave his performance a mildly hypnotic appeal — as when he said, for example: "the migh-ty moun-tain uh-ranges . . .". Of course, it helped the audience's receptiveness to know that it was the head of the British Empire talking.

But what the "movietone" incident at the Empress proved was that those who surrounded the Sovereign and made every attempt to "protect" him from uncomfortable moments occasionally underestimated the King's ability to cope on his own. The small boy who was forced to wear painful splints to correct his knock knees; the young Prince Bertie who struggled with severe gastric problems and a nervous stammer, who finished 68th out of 68 at the final examinations at the Royal Naval College at Osborne, and who showed during his service in the

Navy an alarming tendency to be seasick — this same young man had considerable reserves of character. He had acquitted himself honourably during one of the most famous naval engagements in history, the Battle of Jutland — where he helped man the big twelve-inch guns of "A" Turret and calmly made tea for his shipmates in the heat of the action — had learned to navigate the perilous flying machines of twenty years ago, and had been accomplished enough as a tennis player to compete at Wimbledon. The prince who had seemed to live perpetually in the shadow of his dazzling older brother David, and who broke down and wept when confronted with the prospect of becoming king in his place, had nevertheless shouldered the unwelcome burden of monarchy as best he could — *because it was his duty*. While the former Edward VIII would live out his years as the Duke of Windsor in increasing irrelevance, George VI would move modestly from strength to strength. And, eventually, as the North American tour would demonstrate, he would learn the art of reigning as a popular and well-loved sovereign.

And, like his tendency to seasickness, the King's love of the Navy would never completely desert him either. So it was that perhaps the one formal ceremony he welcomed on this Royal Visit was the presentation of colours to the Royal Canadian Navy Western Command. That afternoon, twenty thousand people had massed on the hillsides of Beacon Hill Park to watch the event. It was, as any reporter looking about him would realize, a perfect setting, with the golden broom, the oak trees, the blue of Juan de Fuca Strait, and, in the distance, the snow-capped Olympics. And, for the first time in this late-spring royal progress across the Dominion, it was warm enough for the Queen to break out her parasol.

The ceremony itself was brief, but impressive. The colours were brought in and laid on a drumhead, presented, and then blessed. The King, in his cocked hat and Admiral's frock coat, stood at the reviewing-stand for the march-past while the band played "Hearts of Oak". Then, as the Navy moved off with its new colours for the four-mile march back to Esquimalt, he wandered over to chat with the veterans. The simple event was, in Mackenzie King's mind, "a triumphal climax to this portion of the journey".

The only thing I could liken the whole tour to is a bit of grand opera like Parsifal or Tannhauser with the complete note of triumph at the end. I shall never forget the Royal Standard flying in the breeze — a wonderful scene.

Formal duties discharged, the King and Queen were whisked off in a closed car by the Lieutenant-Governor, Eric Hamber, and his wife to Hatley Park, on the grounds of the old Dunsmuir estate. There they sat down to a quiet picnic, with packages of sandwiches and hot thermoses of tea, before driving back through the countryside where the daisies and wild roses bloomed in profusion in the fields and along the hedgerows.

The picnic must have taken the edge off their appetites, for that night at Carey Castle, the Queen did little more than toy with her food, while the King contented himself for the most part with champagne and liqueurs. He was, however, by the end of the meal, in an excellent mood. When the ladies had withdrawn, he laughed and joked with the Lieutenant-Governor and Mackenzie King, both of whom told stories of rum-running days in Canada (one can only assume the tales were second-hand). But then, as it usually did, the talk came around to the situation in Europe:

> The King got on to the question of Munich. Told us how he and Chamberlain had talked the matter over at Balmoral. One can see he is really fearful about the situation still but is most concerned about who is to succeed Chamberlain in the event of anything happening to him. He said, quite frankly, "I hardly know what I shall do."

But the King had more immediate worries nagging at him. In spite of the sense of well-being everyone felt at reaching this symbolic half-way point in the tour, it was apparent that, for the King at least, the biggest challenge was still to come. The confidence he had gained travelling across the Dominion did little to reassure him that he and his wife would be equally well received by the people and politicians of Washington and New York. His concern showed itself in his edginess around American reporters. There had been the hushed-up incident at Banff with the drunken correspondent, and that night at Carey Castle the King told Mackenzie King about another awkward moment with the press:

> When he last saw the reporters, some fellow . . . from Boston,
> I think — had said something to him about his ancestors and
> the Boston tea party. He had turned him off by saying he was
> not thinking of the past, but of the future.

The encounter, however, had clearly rattled the King, although, as the Prime Minister pointed out, there had been only one or two of the reporters on the tour who had been "really embarrassing". But there had been inflammatory articles published recently in *Scribner's* and *Time* magazine ("he spoke about how completely they misrepresented and lied"), and it was only with difficulty that Hamber and Mackenzie King could persuade the King that in fact editorial opinion in the United States was overwhelmingly in favour of Their Majesties' visit.

Still, the King's preoccupation with press coverage could not help striking a responsive chord in the Prime Minister. Later that evening, as he sat in his suite at the Empress Hotel and noted the day's events in his diary, Mackenzie King reflected on "the curse" of the modern press. Certainly, while he had basked in the glow of the tour's triumphs to this point and shared in the crowd's warm applause, he had been aware of the inevitable slip-ups and misunderstandings. And these had been given a full airing in the newspapers. Editors, columnists, and newspaper readers had not waited until the Royal Visit was over before pointing fingers at those whom they thought responsible for what had already gone wrong. And they had *not*, contrary to what Lord Tweedsmuir had predicted, pinned the blame on the Interdepartmental Committee.

One reader had predicted a storm brewing at cyclone force for ninety per cent of the politicians and their families who had stepped forward to meet the King and Queen: "I have frequently heard the remark that people would like to have a picture of our King and Queen without our premier peeking over their shoulders. . . . A picture of Their Majesties without Premier King in it would be as valuable as one of the Canadian royalty postage stamps will be a thousand years hence."

Artists, businessmen, writers, and musicians had been

shoved aside in favour of "a lot of legislative members, their cousins and their aunts". And not only politicians but *Liberal* ones to boot: "Mr. Mackenzie King and his satellites monopolized the show" to the extent that it appeared Their Majesties had come "as guests of the National Liberal Federation". Another reader contrasted the way Mitch Hepburn had included his political opponent George Drew with the Prime Minister's shabby treatment of the Opposition Leader Robert Manion, CCF leader J. S. Woodsworth, and the former prime minister, Senator Arthur Meighen. There would have been time enough to recognize these distinguished gentlemen at the state lunch "by simply curtailing the speech of the Prime Minister, for it is noteworthy that he spoke longer than did His Majesty in both languages combined."

Predictably, *The Globe and Mail* led the attack. Judith Robinson pointed out that while Brockville and Cornwall had been dropped from the royal tour, Mackenzie King had gone ahead with his private luncheon at Laurier House, where the guests' only claim to distinction was that "they happened to be related to him." Even worse, when His Majesty had unveiled the memorial to the dead of 1914-1918, he had been attended by a prime minister who, in the words of one irate letter-writer, "was far from the theatre of war in those fitful days, serving, not the cause of Empire and democracy, but rather the interests of the Rockefellers." Another wrote of Mackenzie King's recent enthusiasm for royalty, wishing that during the Great War he "had displayed a little more of the fulsome devotion to the Throne and the Empire which he now parades."

Much of this was cruel and unfair (particularly the reference to the Prime Minister's private luncheon for the King and Queen, which displaced nothing on the itinerary). Much of it came from *The Globe and Mail* and other Tory newspapers. Still, the commentaries and letters showed something of Canada's current sentiments. Whatever disappointments people felt about the Royal Visit, they seemed utterly incapable of blaming the King and Queen. So they blamed Mackenzie King instead, a man whose political legerdemain and ability to keep the country together in difficult times was unequalled, but who could never be much loved by the electorate. More ominously, considering what was soon to sweep over the world, they demonstrated how much the Great War was seen as a litmus test of character, particularly in English Canada.

Wednesday, May 31:

That morning placid, stately Victoria gave the royal party an exuberant send-off reminiscent of the scene at the National War Memorial in Ottawa. Ten thousand people stood in the open area around the harbour, including three thousand returned soldiers who formed their own group across the driveway and sang to the crowd — "Tipperary", "Hail, Hail, The Gang's All Here", "Pack Up Your Troubles". The mood among the crowd was festive; everything that moved was cheered (including the cars carrying the royal baggage), and when the King and Queen drove along the waterfront, "they screamed —no decorous British hurrahs but a continuous mounting wild western yell," and the veterans began surging forward against the barriers and the police lines. And once again, to the dismay of the officials, the King and Queen abandoned formality for five minutes and walked over to the men in medals and berets. Again they were instantly swallowed up. The King recognized one man he had served with in the war, and chatted for a time with another — a one-hundred-and-one-year-old veteran, wounded in the Fenian Raids. Leaning over him as they were about to leave, the King said gently, "It's about time that you were thinking of marrying again."

Moments after the royal couple finally retreated to the dock, the veterans broke through the barriers and led the crowd to the foot of the gangplank. As the last ropes holding the SS *Prince Robert* to shore dropped away, the Queen appeared again at the rail and waved to the veterans. Then the King stepped up beside her in his Admiral's uniform and saluted; the crowd sang "Auld Lang Syne"; the guns boomed; sirens and whistles sounded; and five thousand children on the pier at Ogden Head sang "Will Ye No' Come Back Again" as the ship moved slowly out. The Queen waved and waved again until she and the King dwindled into tiny light and dark figures barely discernible against the blue summer horizon.

The day was bright and clear, the eighty-two-mile voyage through the island-dotted Strait of Georgia accomplished in a record three hours and ten minutes. The royal couple dined on

B.C. halibut and lamb and kept their movie camera clicking at the scenery. In the afternoon, as the *Prince Robert* and its destroyer escort entered the Narrows and moved under the arching span of the Lions Gate Bridge, a squadron of Blackburn Shark seaplanes from Jericho Beach zoomed low in salute, and the inner harbour set up the now-familiar cacophony of greeting. From the Vancouver wharf, the royal party drove through the east-end business section and Burnaby directly to the port of New Westminster on the north bank of the Fraser River.

This visit, like so many, was more symbolic than real. The royal procession simply motored through the business section of town (past the spot where the first legislature for the mainland colony was established eighty years ago) to where the Royal Train waited, a scheduled visit of just twelve minutes. But New Westminster had squeezed as much into these minutes as possible. Flags flew everywhere, royal arches had been erected along the streets (which, it was claimed, held twice the Royal City's normal population of twenty thousand), and the route was lined by a diverse mix of uniforms. Seaforth Highlanders, B.C. Hussars, the New Westminster Regiment, American Legionnaires, Old Contemptibles, Army and Navy Veterans, Imperial Comrades, South African Campaigners, Japanese war veterans, and the Salvation Army were all lined up. And assembled among the logs and debris of the Fraser south of the railway tracks, and decorated stem to stern with flags and pennants, were dozens of boats owned by "Scandinavian, Canadian, Japanese, and Indian" fishermen.

Leaving New Westminster on the CNR track, the Royal Train began its eastern run, steaming through the patchwork farms of the Fraser Valley and reaching Chilliwack in the late afternoon. There, at the final official stop in the province, ten thousand people waited behind the barrier ropes, "an enormous crowd, including as everywhere else many war veterans; an old man brought out on a stretcher; an old lady of ninety-eight talking with the King and Queen". Now they began the long overnight climb to Jasper — through the Fraser Canyon, into the Rockies again. Except for brief stops for coal and water, there were no scheduled stops until they reached Mount Robson, near the Alberta border.

Pulled now by a giant CNR engine, they steamed through

Hell's Gate Canyon, Boston Bar (named for the men who swarmed here during the gold rush), Red Pass Junction, Yellowhead Pass, and across the Great Divide. Largely unseen by the passengers were the dramatic features of the rugged B.C. interior—boiling rapids, ice-cold tunnels, dizzyingly high bridges, and the higher mountain peaks — and the watchers who stood with lanterns every four hundred yards to warn against boulders on the track. At one of the servicing-stops, a small, quiet crowd came down from their log cabin homes on the mountain to stand by the observation car. When the King and Queen came out on the platform, they cheered a little, waved handkerchiefs and flags, and shook hands awkwardly. There seemed nothing more to say, until the moon drifted out from behind a mountain peak and an inspired voice in the crowd began to sing, "When the Moon Comes Over the Mountain". And everyone, the King and Queen included, joined in. Then the Royal Train moved on, leaving the small group in the mountains, in the moonlight, standing by the railway tracks.

Thursday, June 1:

The royal couple were up early to see Mount Robson, ice-capped, surrounded by cumulus clouds at 12,972 feet. At Jasper, they were led to a small, luxuriously furnished log house, Outlook Cabin, with its pine floors, bearskin rugs, stone fireplace, and splendid views of Lake Beaver, Mount Edith Cavell, and Mount Pyramid from its windows. Flowers of every kind bloomed around the royal lodge, the work of old Bill Glass, who had barely slept for the past four nights, worried that his winter's work would be nipped by frost.

"In Banff you are surrounded by mountains," wrote Pallie Pascoe, "and I can understand why a prairie man would like Jasper a little better. The mountains seem to have been pushed back a little further and you can take a deep breath without swallowing a mountain or two."

> The King and Queen had a wonderful rest. It was arranged that they would pose for the camera men at a certain hour, and then for the rest of the day they would be free to come and go without finding some photographer snapping them

when they were not looking. Later in the day word got out that some of the fellows had not played fair and had taken a lot of pictures. The Police got busy and they grabbed all the cameras that had been used by those rascals and I'm darned if some smart guy did not get a picture of all the cameras piled on a table. You can't beat those birds when they think there is a story in the air.

I had really never seen the Royal Couple at close range up to this point and it was becoming quite a joke. I was out playing Golf at Jasper with Geo. Dixon and another chap and at one place we had to cross a road. I saw a car coming and as I walked across the road the car gave a toot and without looking I waved my hand kind of, "don't be in a hurry like", and passed over. After I caught up to my partners they said, "They looked kind of cold." I said, "Who looked cold?" The boys said, "That was the King and Queen." I was so excited I missed a six inch putt on the next green.

While the rest of the party from the two trains occupied themselves with fishing or swimming or golf (reporting an encounter with a bear and a brief chase from a moose), or just sitting about, the King and Queen set out on a tour of the area. They walked through Maligne Canyon, climbed from the floor of the Athabaska Valley to the foot of Mount Edith Cavell, and were caught in a brief snowstorm on the Angel Glacier. Safe for the moment from the photographers, the King wandered about in a battered old hat and tweeds, and the Queen in a blue tweed coat and dark glasses. He ran off hundreds more feet of film on his movie camera; she picked flowers and collected coloured rocks for her daughters.

There were limits, of course, to how much royalty could be expected to rough it in the mountains. Back at Outlook Cabin (special family rate, $125 a day), besides the roses from Bill Glass's greenhouse, meals arrived from the lodge kitchen in heated pushcarts to be placed in electrically heated cabinets and later served on gold service from the Château Laurier by the two personal servants who were staying in the cabin with Their Majesties. The King and Queen made use of the red-and-gold phone to call the two princesses at Buckingham Palace (they had *their* adventures to tell as well: visiting the London

Zoo, riding the Tube for the first time, swimming at the Royal Lodge, Windsor).

The King spent the evening with the head bellman at Jasper Park Lodge happily splicing his film together and running it through a projector. Outside, the work of cleaning the cars of the Royal Train was completed, the sixteen members of the RCMP (who had come up from Banff on their motorcycles over gravel roads) stood guard, and Mackenzie King and Eddy Handy walked the two or three miles around Lake Beauvert in the bright moonlight.

Meanwhile, far away, aboard the liner *St. Louis* in Havana harbour, the 907 German Jews pondered their next move, having had their entrance visas cancelled unexpectedly by the Cuban government. The Havana officials had been unmoved even by threats of mass suicide, and frantic appeals to Argentina, Uruguay, Paraguay, and Panama had been turned down. Tomorrow they would be forced out of harbour, and they must pin their last hopes on some action from the Canadian or American governments.

CHAPTER EIGHT

"Lost Children, Fainting Women, Bewildered Visitors . . ."

Friday, June 2:

"ONE OF THE GREAT SURPRISES OF THE TRIP," wrote Mackenzie King after their reception in Edmonton. He meant the immense crowds that seemed to have doubled the city's population of 90,000 overnight, but he might just as well have been talking about the political scrapping that went on all day not very far from the King's elbow. Relations between John Campbell Bowen, the stiffly proper Lieutenant-Governor of Alberta, and William Aberhart's radical-talking Social Credit administration had been going steadily and swiftly downhill since 1937 when the Premier had turned Bowen out of Government House as a cost-cutting move. The enmity between the two men, coupled with the political strains the province was undergoing because of hard times, threatened to sour the atmosphere of the visit.

Aberhart had stepped on the Lieutenant-Governor's toes when he took it upon himself to organize and host the evening's banquet for Their Majesties at the Macdonald Hotel — rightfully Bowen's prerogative, since officially the King and Queen were *his* guests. The Lieutenant-Governor had then taken steps of his own to get even with the Premier, who meantime had been bruised by the loud outcry over the choosing of his granddaughter — from *Vancouver!* — to present the bouquet to the Queen on behalf of the province. And, if this state of affairs wasn't disruptive enough, there was also apparent confusion over many of the arrangements for the King and Queen. Eventually, in some exasperation, like a stage director confronted with two leading actors engaged in a bitter spat, Mackenzie King would be forced to step in and clear up the chaos.

Meanwhile, unknowing and likely uncaring about this behind-the-scenes feuding, half the population of the province was emptying itself into Edmonton for the Great Day: 300 schoolchildren from the Peace River, 900 people from Grande Prairie, 2,500 from Red Deer. People arrived by special trains, on buses, in cars, or by any other conveyance available. The Premier had even winked at his own law against children riding in the back of trucks. Everyone had a story to tell of the day's events; and sometimes of the adversity they had overcome to get to the city. The *Edmonton Journal* reported the misadventures of one teacher with two small children who drove to Monitor, missed the train by minutes, raced on to Consort — and again arrived too late. According to the *Journal*, the obliging CPR agent then piled them into his own, faster, car and they set off again, chasing the train down the tracks for twenty miles. The agent had just caught up to the speeding locomotive when one of his tires blew out. By then, however, they had been spotted and the train was halted in time for the teacher and her children to climb aboard.

A young woman from Lacombe, Lillian Sharpe, got up early that morning to get a ride into Edmonton with her neighbours, and later wrote down her impressions of the Royal Visit. The group began "the Great Trek" by turning onto the Edmonton Highway at McKibbon's Corner to join "modern Cars & Buggies (mostly Engine) — Truck-Loads of Children — & Persons walking to nearby R.R. Sidings". Moving past Wetaskiwin, "we were in a fairly close Procession allowing no speeding — nearing Edmonton, some Democrats & 'Bennett Buggies' joined us — & Indians in Farm-Wagons." The small group from Lacombe arrived at 9:20 that morning, wandered around the business section looking at the decorations, then drove to the bleachers on Portage Avenue, where a Mountie showed them where to find the picnic grounds. After "Eats" they strolled over to the airport to watch the planes:

> Then it was time to be seated, to listen to the Broadcast Auto informing us of the near approach of the Royal Train, preceded by the Pilot-Train bearing the News-Reporters. We stood up & cheered the Train — visible from the back of the Stands. Then warned by the Radio Loud-Speaker, we prepared

for "Their Majesties". We stood up and sat down at least 3 times as the Radio broadcasted the Cheers & Singing of "God Save the King" by the Crowd Down-Town.

The Royal Train arrived in the city at three o'clock in the afternoon. The first sign of Aberhart's partisan touch was at the station, where the 49th Highlanders stood glumly by while the white-coated Social Credit band boomed out "The Side-walks of New York" for the crowd. After being greeted by both Lieutenant-Governor Bowen and the Premier, and pass-ing down the rows of the Edmonton Fusiliers, the King and Queen got into their limousine for the drive to the Legislature.

Turning onto Portage Avenue with their escort of Dragoons, they came upon what Mackenzie King called "the finest sight in the whole trip thus far", rows of grandstand seats, erected for a distance of two miles down both sides of the street and filled with 70,000 people from every corner of the province — Hardisty, Red Deer, Lougheed, and Lacombe. Laid out for a housing boom that died with the Depression, twice used by Wiley Post as a runway to begin his round-the-world flights, Portage Avenue was renamed the Kingsway that day in honour of the King's visit. Lillian Sharpe remembered the scene:

> Then the Drive up *two-mile* Portage Ave — with a double line of Well-Filled Stands — waving flags of People backed by a Marvellous Line of larger Flag-Backed Bleachers — as far as the eye could see. A gracious wave from our King & Queen en route, for one side of this People-Made Valley — then a few minutes later as the Return Loop was made a Gracious Wave, for the other side — Our Side. We stood upright & waved anything handy. I had given my Flag to a crying youngster, which stopped the tears. So had to wave my white gloves. By the way I represented "The Red White and Blue" in my own costume — Red Fuschia Hat — White-Silk pleated Dress, with short-jacket of Pale-Blue Silk trimmed in dark-Blue Silk — Blue-Grey Hose & White-Kid Shoes. Anyway the gayest attire for "Dress-Up" I ever wore. . . .

At 101st Street, the royal procession stopped at a large Indian demonstration. The men, women, and children had turned up with their chief, Joe Samson — in spite of the Indian

Department's refusal to invite them officially to Edmonton, as the southern Alberta tribes had been invited to Calgary ("they are liable to say that we asked them up & we have got to feed them as they have no money or grub. Otherwise they are very liable to start begging around the city . . . "). Samson and his group had a few moments with the royal couple, presented them with a gun case, tobacco pouch, and belt (all buckskin and beaded), and rounded off the short visit with a rendition of "God Save the King" in Cree.

It was during this impromptu halt that the royal party got its first taste of the volatility of the crowds in Edmonton. People came plunging down from the bleachers and surrounded the royal auto, although maintaining a discreet distance — either from a belated feeling of awe, or because of the increasingly nervous behaviour of the Dragoons' horses. Police, fearing that children might be trampled and crushed, sent in "shock" reinforcements who joined hands with the beleaguered Boy Scouts to push the crowds back. With the way finally cleared, the royal party continued on to the far end of the Kingsway. Here they paused at the display of aircraft (which reflected Edmonton's importance in the world of aviation) and talked to a number of bush pilots, including the legendary Wop May.

The Premier meanwhile was having his own problems. Hurrying ahead of the King and Queen, he had arrived at the Alberta Legislature (where he was soundly booed by the waiting throngs) only to discover that all the doors had been locked by zealous security forces. Only the main entrance remained open. So he had been forced to scurry around the building to the front steps, where the royal procession had already halted, uncertain what to do next. Puffing and perspiring slightly (and perhaps slightly mortified), the Premier read the proclamation of welcome to Their Majesties. Next, a bouquet of roses was presented to the Queen by a little girl from the Kiwanis Home (chosen at the last moment to replace Aberhart's granddaughter). Rigged out in a blue silk dress for the occasion and rehearsed overnight, she performed her task "very beautifully", according to Mackenzie King (always sentimental where children were concerned), "curtseying twice in a lovely way in the open before the large crowds. . . . "

Following a short reception in the Legislature, Their Majesties adjourned to the Lieutenant-Governor's suite for tea. This at last was Bowen's chance to exact some small revenge on his meddlesome premier. As the official party moved into the suite, William Aberhart and his wife were left standing at the door in some embarrassment. The Premier of Alberta had not been invited in, because, as Bowen blandly explained to Mackenzie King, "they had to limit the numbers." This was too much for the Prime Minister, who, with the grace he could summon up at times like this, simply took the Aberharts by the arm and sashayed in. He made his feelings even plainer by chatting conspicuously with them over the tea-cups, and even made arrangements to have the two Aberhart daughters presented. When the King, who had been observing a great deal out of the corner of his eye, asked the Prime Minister (with perhaps a ghost of a smile) if he was trying to get him to take sides, Mackenzie King answered truthfully that he was simply anxious to prevent the situation becoming "too much of a broncho".

There was a clear affection and respect between the Prime Minister and the maverick premier in spite of their political differences. And it helped that both held a dim view generally of lieutenant-governors who conducted themselves as local grandees. Bowen had in fact been troublesome for some time about the arrangements; "I suppose his amour-propre has been offended," said Mackenzie King, who could see that there could be no truce such as had existed between himself and Hepburn in Toronto. What was needed most, however, was not just an end to the petty sniping, but an end as well to the air of disorganization that clung to each succeeding event.

Aberhart did not even seem have a clear idea of the seating-plan for that evening's provincial banquet. And control of the enthusiastic crowds continued to be a problem. At the veterans' hospital that afternoon, people pressed in so closely that the Queen for the first time showed alarm, which caused the security people to cut the visit short. Later that afternoon, as the official party made their way back to the railway station through the crush of onlookers, it was discovered that the Premier and his wife had been left without a car. Arnold Heeney went off to look after that problem. "Meanwhile," Mackenzie King recorded, "movies were taken of Aberhart and myself, [and] when they told us to get a little closer together, I said if we get any closer, we will be forming a Union Government."

Lascelles and the King's party were in no mood for making jokes, however, being in a fury about "the terrible lack of organization" (although Mackenzie King tended to blame Aberhart and not the welcoming committee). What was needed, the Prime Minister realized, was someone to step in, "someone who understands ceremonial, to take matters of this kind in hand." He would remain alert to see that everything else was carried on more smoothly from this point on.

The dinner itself went off well enough, and the King and Queen, conscious of the need to soothe feelings, paid special attention to the Premier and his wife. Afterwards, as the Aberharts were presented with the customary autographed photographs of the royal couple, the King turned to the Prime Minister and said, "Bowen is lost to sight again." Mackenzie King plunged through the milling guests and located the Lieutenant-Governor with his overcoat, hat, and scarf already on, and on the point of leaving. After a few moments, he coaxed him to return for some final words with the King and Queen. Then it was discovered that the Lieutenant-Governor and his wife had no transport, and the Prime Minister once again took the initiative, packing everyone into his own limousine for the trip to the station. They were forced to make their way through the curious mobs who had packed the small enclosed area around the Macdonald Hotel throughout the evening. The entire area had become so congested with people that, for a time, the royal procession could not move off, and the Army had to be called in to help with what was very close to becoming a dangerous situation. It was left to the ever-reliable Heeney to look after the Premier and his wife in the confusion; "Arnold had literally to throw Aberhart into a car to get him away from the Hotel."

Meanwhile, Lillian Sharpe and her friends from Lacombe had spent an enjoyable afternoon, listening to a band concert and then eating their picnic supper at the Exhibition Grounds.

After they had "strolled around the Property" for a time, they attended the basketball game between the famous Edmonton Grads and a visiting women's team from Chicago (who beat Edmonton by a basket, 35 to 33). Making their way out of the city, the Lacombe group had been stopped by the huge crowds blocking the royal route, and so had one last glimpse of royalty making its way to the Royal Train ("The Queen had her Ermine Capelet on Her shoulders and a Diamond Tiara or Coronet glittering on Her dark hair. What a Cheer, we gave (!!!)").

> We had a good trip home — passing Trucks of sleepy, quiet youngsters who had literally yelled themselves to sleep — quite happily. I was left at our Home about 12.30 a.m. The first train back arrived at 11.30 p.m. The next train was delayed at Ponoka, owing to a faulty wheel — no harm done — but some Red Deer Citizens did not arrive home until 5.30 a.m. next morning.

"Rest!?" the Queen had said with some emphasis when the Prime Minister had asked her earlier about their stay in Jasper, much of it spent walking and climbing. The King, it was true, looked much fresher and more rested than he had at the beginning of their visit (Jasper would remain perhaps his favourite memory of the Royal Visit), but the Queen, while she seemed effervescent as always, had, to Mackenzie King's eyes, "lost a little of the constant smile which she wore at the beginning." And whatever benefits the royal couple derived from their short relaxation in the mountains, these seemed to vanish almost immediately in the hurly-burly of their first day back on the tour. There were the usual goodbyes to the dignitaries at the station that night, and the last sight of the King and Queen waving from the observation platform as the Royal Train headed out into the darkness east of Edmonton. And then the entire royal party must have trooped wearily to their beds.

Only the Prime Minister seemed to be gaining in strength and confidence as the tour wore on. The task of managing events — as he had done that day — likely invigorated him. And, in spite of the unpleasantness between Bowen and Aberhart, the city's reception for the royal couple had been truly spectacular. "Altogether," he wrote in his diary that night,

"Edmonton has left a wonderful picture in the minds of all." His final tasks completed, Mackenzie King drifted off to sleep, to dream of Neville Chamberlain and celery soup.

Saturday, June 3:

That morning, the King and Queen were up early to stretch their legs during a servicing stop at Taho. It was a gorgeous day and there was the temptation to linger in the warm sunshine and cool Western air. At Artland, they were still mingling with the crowd on the railway platform when the Royal Train began to move away. In Wainwright, the royal couple took time to walk the whole length of the station yard to see the mountain buffalo and to greet the greatest crowd that town had ever known, on the "greatest day in Wainwright's history". At Unity, "literally a couple of miles of people, mostly children," from all parts of northern Saskatchewan had gathered at the station — "one of the greatest sights of the whole tour," according to Mackenzie King:

> They were a lovely sight, standing along the side of the track. Great open sky and bright sunshine overhead. I got great cheers from many of them as I looked out of my own car. The train stopped for a couple of minutes, then went slowly past rows and rows of children. There were also large numbers of Indians and settlers. . . . There is something particularly appealing about these people of the plains, who have come great distances just to catch a glimpse of the King and Queen.

Outside Unity, the entire royal party (even Mackenzie King, who had risen somewhat later than his sovereign) emerged from their carriages once more to walk along the rail line and to breathe the refreshing prairie air. A family with a dog came up and chatted shyly with the King and Queen, but otherwise they were alone in the immense Saskatchewan landscape. At Biggar, which they reached about 12:30, the Prime Minister's popular Minister of Agriculture, Jimmy Gardiner, climbed aboard. Here there was another huge turnout — one of the largest so far from the small towns — and the King and Queen again walked happily along the platform to greet those who cheered and waved.

In Saskatoon, the royal party was greeted at the station by a choir of seven hundred high school girls who had formed an enormous "singing flag" in red, white, and blue middies and berets. An ear-splitting scream greeted the King and Queen as they appeared, then the girls launched into a spirited rendering of "God Save the King", and rounded this off with a seven-hundred-voice pep-rally cheer that must have been heard on the other side of the city. "KING GEORGE — HOORAY!!! QUEEN ELIZABETH — HOORAY!!!" It was a charming and unforgettable scene. As the noise died away, the music teacher's piano sounded the first chords of "Land of Hope and Glory", the singing flag took up the words, and the ceremony, slightly jolted out of its stiff predictability, went on again.

"Curtseying isn't a very common practice in Saskatoon," said the CBC announcer, "or I guess in most cities in Canada:

> We're having a lot of fun here watching the curtseys to the Queen. Everyone was down here practising yesterday. Not quite sure whether to put the left foot back or the right foot back. So we're watching with a great deal of interest today — to see what happens. . . .

Archie McNab had shown up with Senator Horner and other worthies — "if anything, more demonstrative en route than while in Regina," according to Mackenzie King. "Once he stood up in his car and waved his silk hat, keeping on his grey gloves all the time." Again the crowds were enormous, having come from as far as three or four hundred miles away by box and baggage cars, special coaches, buses, trucks, and private autos. One couple was said to have ridden three hundred miles on bicycles to be there.

Saskatoon had provided more than crowds along the processional route. Trucks were parked in strategic locations to afford the King and Queen a momentary glimpse of the area's prize cattle, sheep, horses, and poultry. There were also threshers and combines in operation and golden wheat, the symbol of the good years in the West, piled on the side of the streets. The official party paid a flying visit to the University of Saskatchewan and the Sanitarium, watched another Indian demonstration, and endured the inevitable ceremony of welcome at City Hall. Signing the visitors' book, the King paused for a moment at the date and Mackenzie King, always at his elbow, reminded him it was June 3—the birth date of his late father, George V. The King paused for another moment and uttered a cryptic, "Yes." The Prime Minister, for whom dates (like everything else) were fraught with significance, was stricken to learn later that this was also the second anniversary of the Duke of Windsor's marriage to Wallis Simpson. Had he put a foot wrong? he wondered.

After the obligatory procession of dignitaries (in royal dreams, the faces of nervous, smiling aldermen stretched in an unbroken line right back to Quebec City), it must have been a relief to shake the hand of the short, lean, white-bearded man who had come from his settler's shack outside the city for the day. This was Thomas Swain, son of an English father and a Cree mother, who had fought in the Riel Rebellion. He claimed to be all of one hundred and four years old, which meant he had been born when George VI's great-great-grandfather, William IV, was still on the throne.

Back at the station, the crowd, which had been pressing in, suddenly broke through the barriers and surged around the royal party. "It was almost a miracle that there was not a crush," wrote the Prime Minister, who could not make his way back to the other coaches, and who was instead beckoned aboard the royal car by the Queen. The King, while giving a cold stare to the inebriated veterans who had crowded right up to the observation platform, nevertheless seemed to take a perverse enjoyment in the excitement. As he later told Mackenzie King, "he saw the ranks breaking and was interested in watching them come forward."

Early in the evening they reached Watrous, with its population lining the bank opposite the train. Two little girls presented bouquets, one of lilacs and the other of lady's slippers, and were lifted onto the platform. "After they came down," Mackenzie King wrote, "I told them they were the only two young people who had been up on the platform of the King's and Queen's car, and that they had done exceedingly well. One said to me without any further words: 'Are you the Prime Minister of Canada?' I said I was. She said: 'I am very pleased indeed to meet you.' It was quite a surprise."

The King was in fine humour that evening, demonstrating

over dinner the best method of shaking hands — which was to catch just the ends of the fingers, and thus avoid possible injury. This of course was a subject of consuming interest to royals and to professional politicians alike. The Prime Minister, who was a guest in the Married Quarters that night, showed the King the way his brother, the Prince of Wales, had accomplished the same gesture while touring Canada, and how the ordeal of having his hand wrung too vigorously had caused it eventually to be put into a sling. "Oh, I remember," said the King, "he had to shake hands with hundreds and thousands." Still, in spite of the risk of injury, the King enjoyed the immediate contact with people that handshaking brought him. There had been entirely too much formality for his taste (and not enough entertainment either, as he told his own people), and he continued to shock local officials by the manner in which he virtually brushed aside welcoming ceremonies in order to plunge into the masses of ordinary people. He was like a politician or a public entertainer discovering for the first time the power his presence had on a crowd.

The King's mood was so buoyant that evening that Mackenzie King did not have the heart to show him that day's dispatches from the Foreign Office: more warlike noises from Mussolini; the Polish situation beginning to shape up like Czechoslovakia; the British making conciliatory statements; the Russians showing ambivalence. Europe was about to stumble into another war scare.

At ten o'clock they stopped at Melville and got a reception that managed to outdo every other community in the country in heartfelt enthusiasm. "Over the entire town hung a huge cloud of dust raised by automobiles, horses, and people," reported Pallie Pascoe; "the people had gathered in so close that even a pick-pocket had no option but to keep his hands in the air." The King and Queen, "almost taken off their feet by surprise", mounted the dais to the cheers of ten thousand or more people, many of whom had originally come from central and eastern Europe. Said Mackenzie King, "I never saw a more radiant look on the face of the Queen. . . . she and the King threw up their hands in acknowledgement of the cheers . . ."

Pallie, who had narrowly avoided being carted off by the

local police after his pal George Dixon had identified him as an unauthorized person, found himself a good vantage point to watch Melville's welcome:

> The King and Queen just stood waving and smiling with this huge spotlight playing on Them. The Queen shaded her eyes and looked over at a group of kiddies and quick as a wink, the spotlight focussed on the spot where she was looking. Then the King looked over the other way and the light moved there. Well it seemed like the King and Queen decided to have fun because every time the light showed in one place, They would look somewhere else and that spot light starting flashing thither and yon with the King and Queen laughing and really enjoying themselves.

Then, as they had so many times, the royal couple stepped down into the mob—again agitating the RCMP officers and the men from Scotland Yard, Cameron, Canning, and Giles. Once again there was tongue-tied respect mixed with the occasional over-enthusiastic response of loyal subjects who embraced the Queen, or thumped the King on the back. So unlike the Court of St. James. What could they be thinking as they pressed deeper into the crowd? "One old soldier who had served in the Black Watch in Scotland ... called out, 'How are you Lady Bethy?' Quick as a flash the Queen ... pushed through the crowd and chatted away to the Old Sweat. ... "

After ten minutes they were back safely on the platform. The vets had sung "Soldiers of the Queen", there had been fireworks, the massed band of seventy played "Will Ye No' Come Back Again"—and still the people refused to go home. "Until you've seen 40,000 farm folk gathered at one spot on the bald prairies singing 'Britannia Rules the Waves',"" wrote a reporter, marvelling at the enthusiastic reception, "you cannot know the triumph of this Royal tour through Canada." The Royal Train was to have stayed the night in the railway yards, but because of the crowds, the decision was made to pull out of Melville—a signal for people to break through the police lines and follow the waving King and Queen until they were out of sight. Only in the early morning hours could the train be shunted back into town for servicing.

Finally, when the excitement had died down, people who had come to Melville for the day to see the King and Queen wearily started for home. For many of them the hour was now so late that they parked on the side of the highway and went to sleep in their cars; others simply lay down and slept on the open prairie under the same bright moon that shone on the Royal Train.

Sunday, June 4:

This was a travelling day. In Portage la Prairie, a ten-minute stop stretched to an hour as the King and Queen attended Divine Service at the United Church. Thousands lined the street to see them come and go — the Queen in a grey crêpe ensemble, the King wearing a grey double-breasted lounge suit.

No ceremonies had been planned for Winnipeg on the return journey east, but, thanks to the efforts of the Manitoba premier, John Bracken, one brief event had been squeezed into the royal itinerary. A little over one hundred Great War veterans from Deer Lodge Hospital, who had been overlooked on the previous visit, were brought down to the CNR station on Main Street, where the train had halted for servicing. Those who were not on stretchers raised themselves up as best they could when Their Majesties entered the main foyer. "Please ask the men to sit down," said the King gently, "they must be tired." Then, following slightly behind the Queen, he circled the echoing rotunda to chat with them. A short time later, as the Royal Train left Winnipeg, it moved through the large crowds that had gathered along the railway line in the warm sunshine. Thousands more people had clustered at the back of the grandstand at Whittier Park to get a view of the train as it passed by.

At Redditt, there were more crowds, including thousands who had driven in from Kenora and Keewatin. Alexander Murray, who was conducting the Legion band as the Royal Train pulled in, was invited aboard for a short chat with the King and Queen ("Then they allighted, Dad first, who instinctively took his white handkerchief from its pocket and wiped the railing of the coach and then held his hand for the Queen.

He later said to Mother 'Never wash that handkerchief because I doubt I will ever wash my hand again.'").

Amost the entire population of Sioux Lookout was at the station when the Royal Train pulled in that evening, including seven-year-old Daphne Redding, who showed up on six-foot-high stilts so she could get a better view. Also among the crowd were seventy-two youngsters from the mining towns of Red Lake and McKenzie Island who had travelled for thirty-six hours to be there (and whose adventures included a wild trip by scow over rough and wind-blown Lac Seul). Two nuggets of Northern Ontario gold were presented to Their Majesties as gifts for the two princesses, before the royal couple once again slipped into the crowd to chat. The King was tired and anxious to get back to his dinner, but the Queen persuaded him to talk with the veterans ("including an old man of 98 who had been in the Zulu war and who had come 200 miles to see them"). Afterwards, the men grouped around the train's observation platform and sang a farewell song from the Great War:

Don't cry-ee, don't sigh-ee,
There's a silver lining in the sky-ee,
Bonsoir, old thing, cheer-i-o, chin, chin,
Nap-poo, toodle-oo, Goodbye-ee.

"There seems to be a lump in the throat of Sioux Lookout tonight," said the CBC commentator as the Royal Train pulled slowly out of the station, "and it's a last farewell, I suppose, for most of them. But the flags and the bunting still wave brightly":

The silver and blue of the Royal Train fade into the night. The dark sky blue, but not lowering. One might even call it a happy evening sky. And we hope what holds for Their Majesties is indeed for us an imperishable portrait of this lovely northern spot. . . . And so the band plays as the crowd slowly wends its way home again after the greatest day in Sioux Lookout's history. And as the cheering dies, the picture is but a memory. The Royal Train has faded from our view. . . . God speed Your Majesties!

A few miles down the track, where the train had moved into a secluded siding for the night, Mackenzie King looked up from his dinner to see "two mothers, each with their baby wrapped in a shawl, running over the rocks and sand to get near the end of the train. . . . it made one think of the story of 'Lorna Doone'. . . . "

Monday, June 5:

The day was spent speeding through the cavernous rock cuts and bush of Northern Ontario, stopping only at sparsely populated settlements for servicing. The turnout at Fire River established an attendance record that could not be surpassed anywhere — the entire population of twelve made it down to the tracks. Gogama pushed *two* girls forward to present bouquets, one each for the public and separate schools. At Capreol, fifty-three veterans showed up during the thirty-minute stop and got a chance to chat with the royal party. The King and Queen lingered here and there so that by early evening when the Royal Train reached Garson Junction (five miles from Sudbury, but in sight of the towering plumes of the city's smokestacks) everything was running hours behind schedule.

Among the huge crowd in the stands at Athletic Park was Alderman Isaac Bradley's daughter, Lorraine, dressed in her Girl Guides uniform and bitterly disappointed that the mayor's little girl had been chosen instead of her to present the bouquet to the Queen. Her parents were to be presented, however, and her mother — five months pregnant — had been practising her curtsey for weeks ("After the ceremony was all over, both my parents talked for months — or maybe years — about how impressed they had been, but most of all, it was the blue of the Queen's blue eyes that they marvelled at"). The Queen, wearing a light dress that matched her incomparable eyes, employed the familiar motion of the hand to wave to the crowd, while the King, in pin-stripes and bowler hat, waved and then batted futilely at the mosquitoes around him.

After the bands and welcomes and presentations at Athletic Park, the royal party was whisked away for a short "unscheduled" visit to the Frood mine north of town (like other apparently spontaneous moments during the Royal Visit, it had in fact been meticulously planned ahead of time). The men put on overalls and helmets, the women donned stylish silk waterproofs, and together they entered the small miners' cage for the drop to the 2,800-foot level. INCO had prudently arranged for the company's chief surgeon to meet them when they emerged below, having dropped more than half a mile in about two minutes. The party was then taken by a small train through scrupulously cleaned and whitewashed tunnels to watch a demonstration of miners drilling at the main ore face. After watching the ore being dumped into the crusher, they returned to the surface, faces smiling and streaked with dust.

Driving back to their train at Garson Junction, the King and Queen passed members of the Sault Ste. Marie and Sudbury Regiment posted along the gravel road who had been stationed there since eight in the morning. "We stood there all day long," recalled Roy Leonard, a fifteen-year-old recruit at the time, "sweating and covered with mosquitoes. Too afraid of the RSM to relax or talk to the fellow beside us. . . . We had World War I uniforms, with the collars done right up, and Ross rifles. . . . When the King and Queen did go by it was just a blur, since we weren't allowed even to turn our heads, and it was dark. By that time, nobody cared where the hell they went. We were just glad to get back to the Armouries and sleep."

Tuesday, June 6:

That morning the royal party braced itself for the two most densely packed days of the tour. The Interdepartmental Committee's notion of the King and Queen "being seen" by their people was about to be realized as never before. More than two million men, women, and children would watch, if only for a moment or two, as the Royal Train made a sweep through Ontario's industrial and agricultural heartland. They would see the King and Queen return from the West with a new confidence that made their appearances in the early days of the Royal Visit look stiff and wooden by comparison. And the crowds themselves seemed to have changed. They were less awestruck than before, more friendly and outgoing in the American manner—a fact noted by *The Globe and Mail*'s Ralph Allen:

An anonymous keynoter at Washago, early morning watering place for the big blue engine, hit the note of informality on which this easy jog through territory skirted once before was conducted.

"Hi'ya, King?" he enquired from the packed station with a deplorable lack of feeling for the conventions but an obvious depth of good-will.

Before the sparsely distributed representatives of dignity and order had recovered from the first horrified recoil, His Majesty was grinning back:

"I am fine, thank you. How are you?"

Happy spectators had gathered through the night and early morning along the CNR line to Toronto, often scampering down the track until the train was out of sight. At Beaverton, a crowd of twenty thousand, including the Prime Minister's sister ("Jennie waving for all she was worth, and calling 'Willie, Willie'"), cheered the two figures on the observation platform. As the train was moving out, the Queen caught a bouquet tossed to her by ten-year-old Lillian Danes. Her twin sister Betty ran down the tracks and tossed the second, which the King clutched at and missed. "Playing out the string, Betty scooped up the bouquet on first bounce, took half a dozen more steps to make up lost ground, and fired again. This time His Majesty used two hands and the side was retired." Six young women summering at Jackson's Point screeched up in a roadster at Zephyr, tumbled out with cameras only to find that the train had just gone by, and then tumbled back into the car to race to the next stop. Near Vandorf, Lady Eaton came cantering across the fields with the Toronto and North York Hunt as the train steamed by. Then Mount Albert and Richmond Hill — William Lyon Mackenzie's old riding. At Todmorden, the crowd cheered a newspaper photographer who had fallen into the Don River, but who kept his camera dry and managed to snap the picture.

In Toronto, where an unofficial stop had been scheduled, several thousand people climbed down the embankment from Fleet Street and lined the eastern entrance to Union Station. As the train pulled in, the mob swarmed over the tracks—only to be met by Chief Constable D. C. Draper, attired in a glossy silk hat and morning coat, who swung his cane like a sword as he led his men in a futile battle to restore order. The stampede was slowed temporarily when someone began singing "God Save the King", and everyone stood to attention while the men took off their hats. But almost immediately the mob pressed forward again. While the King and Queen kept waving from the observation platform, police on horses attempted to hold the perimeter, people perched on boxcars gawked, children put pennies on the tracks, and the Chief Constable continued to wave his cane, and ask *please*, would everyone move back. As the Royal Train finally left, a woman began to sing "Will Ye No' Come Back Again", and once again the milling, noisy crowd fell silent, listened until she finished, then cheered louder than before.

From here, the tour meandered through the densely populated areas of south-western Ontario — past well-cultivated fields of sugar beets and tomatoes, painted barns, lush pastures, small woodlots and orchards, towns and villages with humming factories, and relatively prosperous inhabitants who had none of the pinched and strained look of people from the Depression-scarred prairies. For much of the 250-mile journey that day, the King in a plaid pattern suit, the Queen in pastel pink, stood at the back of the train to wave to what Mackenzie King described as "a continuous stream of people from Toronto to Windsor". The stops included Guelph ("enormous crowd. . . . I was sorry that the King seemed a little hurried"), Kitchener ("enormous crowds, but everything was so congested that the place was anything but a pleasant [experience]"), Stratford ("an enormous crowd. . . . The King was a little anxious to get on further. . . . the multitudes have surpassed all expectations"), Chatham ("great crowds") and, finally, Windsor ("enormous crowds").

The day was very hot, the air heavy and sticky. And behind the heartfelt cheering, there were the usual resentments ("and why civic employees, who have always been well paid for their services to the community, should be presented ahead of the wearers of the Silver Cross and others . . ."). "Is it the intention of the city council," inquired DISAPPOINTED in withering tones, "to hold a private party on the occasion of the visit . . . of Their Majesties?" Letters flowed in to rural newspaper edi-

Canadian Pacific

Star Weekly

The Royal Train steams through the Rockies west of Field.

May 27. The royal couple give in to the demands of the press and pose for photographs with Mackenzie King on the wind-swept terrace of the Banff Springs Hotel.

May 29. A veteran of the Seaforth Highlanders holds up a Japanese Canadian girl during the royal visit to Vancouver.

Star Weekly

May 30. In a ceremony conducted at Beacon Park in Victoria, George VI presents new colours to the Pacific Command of the Royal Canadian Navy.

NFB/National Archives of Canada/PA-148552

*June 1. The King and Queen, about to step down from the observation platform
of the Royal Train, near Mount Robson, Alberta, early in the morning.*

*Aboard the Royal Train, a steward fills a decanter of wine in the luxurious
"married quarters" occupied by the King and Queen.*

June 3. The "singing flag" of Saskatchewan schoolgirls who welcomed Their Majesties to Saskatoon.

Lakewood Studio

June 4. The King and Queen stroll down the tracks to meet the people of Reddit in northern Ontario.

National Archives of Canada/C85097

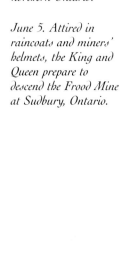

June 5. Attired in raincoats and miners' helmets, the King and Queen prepare to descend the Frood Mine at Sudbury, Ontario.

June 8. In the sweltering heat of a Washington summer, American President Franklin Roosevelt greets Queen Elizabeth. Beside him, in her heavy woollen dress, is Eleanor Roosevelt.

Associated Press

June 13. Marjory Davidson presents the Queen with a bouquet of flowers on the welcoming platform at Newcastle, New Brunswick.

June 14. The King and Queen chat with veterans of the Great War in Charlottetown, Prince Edward Island.

June 15. On their last day in Canada, the King and Queen stand with their RCMP escort in front of Government House in Halifax.

One of the many welcoming arches built along the royal route to welcome the King and Queen to Newfoundland.

June 17. The King lays a wreath at the War Memorial in St. John's, Newfoundland.

Schoolchildren waiting along the royal route for the arrival of the King and Queen.

tors from BRITISH FAIR PLAY, stickler for FAIR PLAY, JUST JAMES, A GOOD CITIZEN, and DEMOCRATIC ("The place where the platform is now being erected is used to load and unload coal, scrap iron, etc. The surroundings are disgraceful with the smelly old subway just below the platform, and dirt and dust and germs flying about. . . . What's the idea? Who is behind this ignorant mix-up? Where are the ex-mayors, war heroes, old citizens?"). The welcoming committees were under siege.

In Guelph, the decorations so lovingly mounted along Wyndham Street had blown down two days before, then hurriedly been slapped up again; Ann Jamison, "celebrated star of Hollywood and New York", was prevented by the musicians' union from singing for her old home town because she intended to do it for free; and Mackenzie King pulled George Drew out of the crowd to meet Their Majesties. At Guelph Junction, where bridges crossed the Speed River, a policeman lifted up child after child in the blazing heat to see the royal couple. In Kitchener, one hundred thousand people jammed around the station and gave a special cheer for their native son who had gone on to become the prime minister — and Indians who showed up wearing fierce warpaint later admitted that it was in fact their wives' lipstick. In Stratford, the Royal Train was an hour late and came into the station at about fifteen to twenty mph, and consequently children from Goderich, Southampton, Walkerton, and New Hamburg, who had waited three and a half hours with their flags just outside the town, never saw anything but a flashing blue and silver train, and went home weeping.

"Windsor Excited" ran the newspaper headline, "Detroit . . . Near Frenzy". Canadian newspapers seemed happiest when suggesting that American reaction to the Royal Visit next door was, well, slightly hysterical compared to that of Canadians. Whose King was it, anyway? All day long, a big signboard across from Windsor had been flashing "Detroit Welcomes Their Majesties", while a huge flotilla of boats from the Detroit Yacht Club made last-minute preparations to sail down the river as the Royal Train arrived. Wildest predictions stated that a million Americans would come flowing north by auto, ferry, and excursion steamer, or on foot, over the bridge or through the tunnel under the Detroit River — and *they* were flying more Union Jacks than the Canadians were. The advance estimates were later toned down a little — by three-quarters of a million; nevertheless, immigration officers had been hastily summoned from Fort Erie, Sarnia, Niagara Falls, and other nearby posts to handle the monarchical enthusiasm of those south of the border. Unlike those in the prairie cities, where onlookers had room to spread out, Windsor's royal route was less than five miles long. After a few hours, people who had been jammed into sweaty proximity with one another under a hot sun began fainting in large numbers.

Still, as the Royal Train came trundling in, the city presented "easily the finest display of the whole tour," according to Mackenzie King (who, admittedly, had said this before), "with the river on one side and people between the train and the river . . . skyline of Detroit visible on one side; on the other, people and children massed on banks for a couple of miles before we reached *Windsor* itself." Twenty-five military bands were on hand at the station, and the King and Queen were greeted by David Croll, who had shined shoes when he first came to Canada as an immigrant and who had since gone on to become the city's mayor and a provincial Cabinet minister. The King brushed off moths and mosquitoes in the gathering night to sign the guest book. "Again the King insisted on going down the steps and talking to some of the veterans," wrote the Prime Minister afterwards. "This was positively dangerous as the crowds were enormous. . . . I was afraid once or twice we were going to get into a jam that was almost impassable." The King was looking out across the river to Detroit when a voice called out, "Them's your allies over there, George," and he smiled in response. Eventually, the RCMP moved in and got the royal couple back to the platform. "At the end of the afternoon," wrote Windsor MP Paul Martin, "just as they were about to leave, a tardy Mayor Richard Reading of Detroit rushed into the railway station for an unscheduled presentation."

> Word was passed, and the king and queen held up their departure to meet him. Strutting onto the platform and backed up by his own musical ensemble, Reading was formally presented to their majesties . . . and curtseyed! After he had taken his

leave and a rather weary king was boarding the train, the Detroit band again blared forth the royal anthem. Standing close by, I heard King George mutter to his queen, "There's that song again!"

Grilled immediately afterwards by Gordon Sinclair of the *Toronto Daily Star*, Mayor Reading seemed as puzzled as anyone else by his manoeuvre—the envy of any debutante ("Curtsey? Who, me? Well I guess I did, but by gosh I didn't know what I was doing. . . . just out of surprise or instinct or something"). That wasn't the only mystery. Reading, who was to be jailed for racketeering a few years later, had also introduced to Their Majesties a woman he called his wife, although the Detroit reporters on the scene didn't recognize her.

Meanwhile, outside Windsor, up to thirty thousand children had been assembled in the extreme heat that afternoon to wait for the Royal Train to slow, and perhaps even stop, as it made its way north again to London. By now, however, everything was running very late, and tour officials had become alarmed that the children — hot, tired, and over-excited — might be stampeded in the darkness when the train arrived, and trample through the snow fences—and possibly even crawl under the cars. Fearing the consequences of even slowing down, they commanded the big blue and silver train to steam by quickly — a painful, but probably wiser decision which led to more bitterness and tears than any other action on the tour.

Wednesday, June 7:

In the morning, the Royal Train shunted a few hundred yards west from the London freight yards, where the royal party had spent the night, and glided into the city's railway station. This was to be an even more strenuous day than the previous one, with scheduled stops in Ingersoll ("another huge crowd"), Woodstock ("tremendous crowd"), Brantford ("still larger crowds"), Hamilton ("great crowds through city"), St. Catharines, and Niagara Falls. The weather was near-tropical — and, if possible, even hotter and muggier than the day before. In London, the Royal Canadian Regiment, wearing red coats and white helmets, formed the honour guard, and, this being Loyalist country, there was a large contingent of veterans from the Fenian Raids, the North-West Rebellion, and the South African war waiting to greet the King and Queen. Among them was ninety-five-year-old Dr. Solon Woolverton, who could remember the visit of the Prince of Wales (later Edward VII) in 1860, when his mother had taken the carpet off her parlour floor and laid it on the Grimsby station platform.

At Ingersoll, twenty miles along the Thames Valley, the Tillsonburg Citizens' Band played the royal salute when the Royal Train arrived. While Their Majesties chatted with the town's notables, dairy farmers carried two twelve-pound rounds of cheese to the dining-car. The temperature meanwhile was hovering at 85 and the humidity was suffocating.

The heat was taking its toll in Brantford too, where many people in the crowd had already fainted. Ken Lefebvre, a fourteen-year-old Boy Scout assigned to provide first aid, gave the heat victims water until his canteen ran out. Then, with Boy Scout ingenuity, he began selling Cokes from a nearby store for ten cents, netting himself a tidy five-cent profit on each bottle. The young Lefebvre was so busy in his new enterprise, in fact, that he failed to notice that the Royal Train had arrived.

> I slipped behind the "Advance Guard" to refurbish my supply of Coca-Cola and to my utter surprise found myself five feet from my reigning Monarch, King George VI and his lovely consort Queen Elizabeth standing on the rear platform of the Royal Train. The King was dressed in a magnificent uniform with many, many medals and the Queen was far better looking than her pictures showed. I had no idea of what my role was so I snapped to attention and saluted. The King and Queen paid no attention to me and when the civic officials arrived to escort them to the reception platform I sidled over and took up my position as the first member of the Honour Guard.

The Honour Guard consisted of veterans of the First World War, wearing their medals and berets, and they stood at ramrod attention throughout the short stop. The Mayor's daughter, not quite three, presented the bouquet, bowed to the crowd instead of Their Majesties, and got a kiss from the Queen. The

Mayor, against all instructions, then presented the King with a solid silver telephone. The highlight of the Brantford stop was the signing of the historic Queen Anne's Bible, which had been given to Her Majesty's Chapel of the Mohawks in 1712, in recognition of the loyalty of the Six Nations to the Crown.

Ken Lefebvre recalled the only jarring incident:

> As the Royal Train was departing, one of the Veterans standing near me suddenly broke from attention, pulled the medal cap badge from his beret and flung it onto the rear platform, simultaneously calling out "Here King". King George bent his right knee slightly in attempting to scoop up the medal and received a nudge from the Queen and he immediately returned to an erect posture standstill at attention. The Veterans were furious. . . .

Some time later, before the local Legion branch could get around to drumming out the offending vet (who may have been emotionally disturbed, but was not expressing disloyal sentiments), a letter arrived that smoothed over matters brilliantly. It was from one of the royal equerries, thanking the man on behalf of the King, who was known, of course, as a keen collector of military memorabilia.

Brantford was distinguished by more than one military demonstration that day. The Dunnville Company of the 37th Haldimand Rifles, most of whom were members of the Six Nations Reserve, had been drawn up in a hollow square around the welcoming platform to witness the signing of the Queen Anne's Bible by the King and Queen. At that moment, a battery of First World War howitzers had begun firing a royal salute, but unfortunately "some of the guns were too old and did not fire at all," according to Bill Macartney, who was with the Haldimands that day. "As a result the twenty-one-gun salute continued all the time the King and Queen were present and was still going on when they were leaving."

> Meanwhile the officers of the 37th were not visible to their troops. The Brantford school children could not see the King and Queen so we let them inside our hollow square. The troops put small children on their shoulders so they also could see.
> One of the sergeants — I think Charley Pitts, ex-U.S.A.

Marine — gave the order for the regiment to fire a feu de joie. We all started firing with the right hand, holding our rifle up in the air and a small child held on our left shoulder. The school children were around us, in front of us, back of us and in between us — all screaming with excitement, cheering the King and Queen. The Royal Couple, as well as [Six Nations Reserve representative] Walter Liquors and his mother, kept their composure in a very admirable manner.

When the royal train was leaving, the children were cheering and waving flags, the Brantford Battery was still trying to finish the twenty-one gun salute, the 37th were still firing any blank cartridge in their possession — I am sure the King and Queen never forgot the "wild Canadians" of Brantford, Ontario!

There was an altogether more sedate reception down the track at Paris Junction, where they had a ten-minute operating stop and where the road foreman served ice chips to the wilting crowd. Then, to the cheers of the hundreds who had gathered there, the Royal Train once more moved out, and "the bright silver and blue coaches, drawn by the massive 6400, wound down the Copetown grade, past the beautiful Dundas Valley to Hamilton, where a visit of an hour and a half was made."

In Hamilton, there were thousands of Scottish flags fluttering, the band played "Coming Through the Rye", and the crowd, as if disdaining the sweltering heat, sang "In the Good Old Summertime". Their Majesties visited the UEL Monument, and met Hugh Keenleyside's twelve-year-old daughter Mary, who had been unable to see them earlier in Ottawa because she had measles.

Twenty-five thousand schoolchildren were at Scott's Park to watch the King and Queen as they watched the rhythmic drill demonstration by high school students. After which, the King stepped up to the microphone and, exercising one of the most popular of his remaining royal prerogatives, gave them all the next day off school. While the Hamilton teenagers were still going through their strenuous drills, Mackenzie King turned to the King and said he thought there had not been enough in the way of entertainment. "The King laughed and said, '*We* have been the whole show,' but then remarked that 'the Regina Musical Ride and cowboy exhibition at Calgary would have added to the entertainment. . . . '"

The heat and the ceremony had taken its toll on the royal couple as much as it had on the spectators, and by the time the Royal Train arrived in St. Catharines, the King had shed his suffocating military uniform for a suit, and the Queen's grey ensemble had been replaced by an Alice-blue dress. Concerning the Garden City's preparations, the *Buffalo Times* wrote:

> Rome with a first night show at the Coliseum, was a sleepy dull town compared to St. Catharines, completely agog as Royalty momentarily moved nearer. Sidewalks were a medley of bright colours, facades of downtown buildings had been completely hidden from view by Union Jacks and Scottish emblems; everywhere flags were flying. Many men wore cutaways, striped ties and trousers, hours in advance of the ceremony; not a single top hat was to be begged, bought, borrowed or stolen in all St. Catharines today.

One hundred thousand people watched as the royal party left their train and rode in limousines through the twisting streets of St. Catharines, which had been lined for the occasion with returned soldiers, uniformed postmen, firemen, militiamen, and "pert cadets from Ridley College". People perched on rooftops, viaducts, fences, cenotaphs, and curbstones. A Ukrainian girls' choir sang "God Save the King". At the edge of the city, the royal car broke an electric beam that officially opened the Queen Elizabeth Way, Canada's first super-highway. Then there was a leisurely paced drive through the orchards, vineyards, and fields of the great Niagara fruit belt. The royal procession slowed at Port Weller and the Welland Canal, jogged through Niagara-on-the-Lake, slipped past squat Fort George, scaled Queenston Heights, and, joined by an escort of Dragoons, arrived finally at Table Rock, below Niagara Falls.

There, above the great whirlpool, oblivious to the Americans shouting to them from across the river, the King and Queen stood for a few minutes with all the absorbed wonder of any tourists. Then, turning their backs on the Falls, they drove on to the General Brock Hotel, once again tripping electric eyes that unveiled a memorial, opened some formal gardens, and set in motion the machinery that laid the foundation stone for the city's new "Honeymoon Bridge".

Among those "street lining" that day in Niagara Falls was T. R. Yaeger, who had enlisted in the RCAF in April, had been posted to the base at Trenton, and had been preparing for the Royal Visit ever since. "We stripped our rifles, had the metal parts re-blued and endlessly French-polished the wooden pieces . . . and practised endlessly on the parade square." On the big day, they were up at five to board a special train, arrived at the Falls, were given lunch, took up their positions on the Niagara Parkway — and waited.

> It was a beautiful sunny warm day which made us feel our heavy blue serge uniforms but we had become conditioned to this. The large crowd many of whom were Americans was friendly and in a festive mood. During the wait when we were allowed to relax slightly they talked to us and offered soft drinks. But being young and considering this an important duty I refused the offers.
>
> Then the crowd tensed and a ripple of "Here they come" moved toward us. Our orders came in succession; "ATTEN-TION," "SLOPE-ARMS," and then "PRESENT-ARMS." As I stood rigidly at the PRESENT the car with the King and Queen slowly passed. Did they smile? Did they wave? I don't remember. It was enough that I was there!!
>
> Later events are vague but I do remember the peaceful feeling in the early evening as we marched along the river bank to the train in our squadrons with the band playing and the falls on the right illuminated in soft pastel coloured light.

Preparations had also been under way for some time at the General Brock, which had spared no expense in providing every convenience for Their Majesties during the few hours they would spend in the hotel. An interior decorator had been imported from New York City, and had taken one look at the royal suites and decreed bone-white walls, deep-green carpets, lemon-coloured drapes, and a *habitant* weave on the bedspreads. The Rainbow Room on the tenth floor, where the royal visitors would eat, had been draped with gold and blue satin with gold braid. A specially designed silver service in the Coronation pattern had been purchased, along with gold-inlaid china and glassware. The Brock's head chef had been labouring all day long with his assistants to prepare a meal of artichoke hearts stuffed with beluga caviar, roast beef, Lake Superior whitefish, baby guinea hen, and asparagus tips, followed by vanilla mousse royale, ice cream, and Grand Marnier. Luigi Romanelli and his Orchestra had been engaged to provide music for the occasion.

Unfortunately, the King was tired. He had already cancelled the scheduled walk under the Falls, pleading exhaustion, and at the moment he just wanted a haircut. What he emphatically did not want was an elaborate formal dinner with toasts and speeches and so on. And so, while a weeping maître d' stood by, carpenters sawed up the horseshoe configuration of the tables and rearranged them in a more conventional manner while hotel staff carted off bushels of rare blossoms. Dinner was to be an altogether more intimate affair, pleasant enough with the view of the coloured lights playing on the Falls, and with the orchestra's presence "softened" at the King's request. Among the guests were Lady Lindsay, wife of the British Ambassador to Washington, and Daniel Roper, the United States' new Ambassador to Ottawa who came over the border with a screaming motorcycle escort of New York State police and, after the meal, asked the Queen to autograph his menu. On two occasions, the King and Queen left their company to appear before the crowds and acknowledge the ovations. In one case, it was a special gesture for a trainload of schoolchildren from Welland who had arrived too late to see them earlier. Mackenzie King was, as usual, storing up the occasion for his diary that night:

> I said to the King [that] these little "chippers" outside shouting for the King made the greatest noise. H.M. said: the other night when I was taking my bath, I could hear them in my ears "We want the King", and said out loud: You have him, what more do you want. He mentioned the noise of the streets keeps dinning in his ears for some time after.

With dinner completed, the royal party entered their cars and drove the short distance to where the Royal Train was waiting for them on the Canadian side of the Suspension Bridge. The carriages had been meticulously inspected by U.S. railroad inspectors before being hitched up to the American locomotive that would haul them across the border. Before climbing aboard, the King inspected a Guard of Honour from the RCAF and the Lincoln and Welland Regiment. In the distance, a twenty-one-gun salute reverberated down the Gorge as the royal coaches gave a sudden lurch and began to move forward.

"Halfway across the plain iron bridge," said the announcer on the American side, "two flags draped and touching . . . the Stars and Stripes and the Union Jack. . . . And now we can see the headlight of the Royal Train coming . . . and crossing the halfway mark of the bridge."

Five minutes after their journey had begun, the royal couple stepped out of their carriage onto a red carpet on the platform of a dingy railroad station. There to welcome them in a courtly Tennessee drawl was the tall, white-haired Secretary of State, Cordell Hull. Everyone shook hands, the Queen looking, in the words of the *New York Times*, "fresh as a debutante before her first big party . . . her costume as crisp and her manner as gracious as if she were beginning—instead of entering the final phase of her tour." Along the roadway, Americans cheered and sang "God Save the King" as best they could. Inside the Royal Train, the corridors were suddenly filled with cigar smoke and bulky, serious-looking men.

The King had arrived in America.

CHAPTER NINE

"That Honeychile Missus Queen"

DURING THE NIGHT OF JUNE 7, the Royal Train moved steadily south and west through New York State, Pennsylvania, and Maryland on its way to Washington. At Buffalo, Tommy Lascelles knelt before the King, was tapped lightly on each shoulder, and rose again — Sir Alan Lascelles. It seemed an odd bit of timing, the Acting Private Secretary being rewarded apparently for a so-far-successful visit to the Dominion, when a far more daunting task lay ahead of the royal party in the American capital. British statesmen and British newspapers had been awakened suddenly from the torpor induced by the endless applause that had echoed successively along the entire Canadian route, and they now tensed in anticipation, too. "Canada, the Empire — that is all in a day's work," as the Earl of Crawford had so bluntly put it to Lord Tweedsmuir, "but a visit to Washington sounds imposing."

Certainly the visit had started well. In the dwindling summer light, a million curious Americans had massed on the Niagara frontier, forking out as much as five dollars apiece for choice seats on lawns, porches, and rooftops overlooking the route of the Royal Train. The crowds seemed just as friendly and almost as large as they had for the previous five hundred miles through southern Ontario, the only discernible difference being the absence of flags and bunting at the railroad stations — and the extraordinary measures the Americans were taking to protect Their Britannic Majesties. Twenty miles of undefended border had been temporarily placed under arms, and more than 1,600 National Guardsmen and state and county police officers were stationed every hundred yards along the route, each man armed and his bayonet fixed. Railway crossings were under double guard, and portions of the highway running along the track had been closed to traffic.

The American press had also stepped up its efforts. Two Pullman cars full of reporters had been hitched on to the pilot train shortly after it crossed the border. And there were other, less welcome, changes to the old cosiness. The twenty red-coated RCMP officers on the pilot train were gone now, replaced by humourless Secret Service men and New York State troopers who swaggered about with loaded revolvers. "I never saw so many big men carrying so many guns in my life," wrote Pallie Pascoe. "I'm sure we took less with us when we went over the top in France." He had been replaced as well when the Americans took over the mail car and now, after a bath, was sitting in the smoker enjoying "a real quiet cigarette". But the guns made everyone a bit nervous, and one of the porters was only half joking when he told Pallie that each time he went to make up a berth he found another loaded revolver. The Special Branch men, Canning, Giles, and Cameron, had always been coy about whether they carried firearms, and the RCMP predictably tightlipped, but Pallie was adamant that he had not seen so much as a hand-gun up to that point.

Their Majesties had given up their own special RCMP constables (the four men who had travelled with them since Quebec City), but not without a fight — "a very friendly quarrel", as the Queen put it. She had become "suddenly more vivacious and assertive than I have seen her at any time," according to Mackenzie King, who witnessed the contest of wills that had taken place the day before as the train rocked along between Toronto and Kitchener:

> In the loveliest way, she said that . . . we must not on any account leave them behind. Began to speak of how much they added to the security and pleasure of trip. . . . The King then joined in, saying: "We must have them. We cannot think of going to the States without them." I could see that both the King and Queen felt they were absolutely necessary for their baggage; knew where everything was, etc.

On this point, the Canadian and British tour officials (as they had already done a number of times during the tour) ranged themselves against their royal and political masters.

Keenleyside, Commissioner Wood, and Lascelles were in complete agreement, Wood arguing that "it would lead to real jealousies and difficulties . . . the Americans were determined to handle all the police end of things." Still, the King, using what passed for forceful language among royals, asserted that he was "really most anxious about having them come on." Mackenzie King was inclined to agree, believing the Americans would not mind a few strapping, red-coated Mounties in the entourage. But then — "another shock" — the Americans had taken over all the available accommodation on board (even here, Mackenzie King might have felt his power starting to slip away — a little hint of what was to come in Washington). Lascelles set about calming the King's famous temper, and then played his ace by reminding His Majesty of what the "sensationalist press" might make of the fact that he apparently did not trust the Americans to protect him. At this, the King, disappointed and doubtless grumbling at once more being thwarted by his own people, gave in. "Officials," muttered Mackenzie King in some sympathy, "always narrow and troublesome."

Lascelles, however, knew what he was doing. Along with other British officials, he was haunted by the thought that any perceived slight to their American hosts, any minor indiscretion, might turn this vital part of the tour into a diplomatic and political shambles. Whatever concerns the British may have had in 1939 about wooing Canada back into the imperial fold, they were as nothing compared to the importance placed on re-establishing strong links with the Americans. The Roosevelts understood this. "My husband invited them to Washington," wrote Eleanor Roosevelt afterwards, "largely because, believing that we all might soon be engaged in a life and death struggle, in which Great Britain would be our first line of defence, he hoped that the visit would create a bond of friendship between the people of the two countries." By now, war was a certainty as far as FDR and Cordell Hull were concerned. This belief, however, was not shared by the majority of Congress, or by millions of Americans who remained deeply suspicious of British motives. As the *New York Times* put it, "the British are never polite to us except when they want something. . . ."

Believing themselves to be safe behind the walls of their

oceans, Americans wanted no more of costly foreign entanglements. They still harboured bitter memories of the Great War,
an essentially European quarrel as far as they were concerned,
and the isolationist Senator William Borah had gone so far as
to suggest the President find a suitable moment during the royal
visit to draw the King aside and ask him about the 21 billion
dollars borrowed by the British from 1914 to 1918. Even more
significant was the resolution introduced in Congress just eighteen months before, which stated that the United States should
not declare war until a majority of Americans had voted on
the matter in a nationwide referendum. The motion was
obviously unrealistic and unworkable, yet it struck a responsive chord across the United States. A national poll claimed
that an astounding seventy-three per cent of the population
supported the idea. And beyond the sturdy isolationism of
America preached by the likes of Charles Lindbergh and the
America Firsters, there was the pro-Nazi sentiments of more
sinister organizations such as Father Coughlin's "Crusaders",
the Citizen's Protective League, the Christian Front, American
Patriots, Inc., and the German-American *Bund*.

Then there was the matter of how Americans viewed the
British themselves. People remained keenly aware that the
United States of America had its beginnings in the "military
resistance to a British king" (*New York Times* again). And in
1939 there was between the United States and Great Britain
the mixed admiration and resentment of competitors jostling
for world influence. The brashness and confidence that America could exude as a growing power was still coloured at times
by an unwilling deference to things British. The United States
had not yet learned to stride the global stage with complete
self-assurance, and Americans were liable to rage at anything
that smacked of interference by their former colonial master.
So, it was hardly surprising then that the rabidly anti-British
Chicago *Tribune* spoke of the King as "the image of a feudal
mediaevalism":

Nor can a larger acquaintance with the institutions preserved
by the British caste system for its own protection be very stim-
ulating to the American belief that a man's worth is wholly in
his own qualities.

And it was hardly unexpected that New York Congressman Hamilton Fish would predict that with this visit America was on the road to becoming once again a British colony; or that Congressman George Holden Tinkham of Boston would mutter darkly that "a sinister secret diplomacy is now directing American foreign policy." At the same time, despite their own isolationist sympathies, Americans were intensely critical of how Neville Chamberlain had sacrificed Czechoslovakia at Munich in order to appease Hitler. Last but not least, there were Americans still offended by the British treatment of Wallis Simpson during the Abdication Crisis.

Fortunately for the royal party, Americans seemed able to separate their view of British foreign policy from their opinion of George VI and his consort, Queen Elizabeth (more so, in fact, than the British themselves). Reaction to the news of the visit had been surprisingly positive (although the *New York Times* was left to wonder "whether the King and Queen shall take with them their English mediaeval suites of ladies of the bedchamber, groom of chambers, master of horse and so forth"). Columnist Walter Lippmann was a notable exception to the warm sentiments expressed in most newspapers, writing that a royal tour, however brief, would "revive suspicion of foreign interference and would disunite and distract American public opinion. . . . It would mislead the innocent without impressing the mighty."

The view of the average American was the key. As Lord Tweedsmuir had already pointed out, "American public opinion is a very delicate plant, and may suddenly develop curious growths." The British would have to be careful not to overplay their hand — or tip it — in such a way as to squander American goodwill. "[Public opinion in the U.S.] has a virginal fear of being coerced," Tweedsmuir had informed the Palace before the tour; "it can suddenly and violently alter its direction if there is any suspicion that it is being guided from the outside." So there must be no evidence of strong-arm tactics. The Foreign Secretary had already been dropped from the royal party, and now the Mounties were sacrificed for the sake of appearances.

Franklin Roosevelt also had to be careful not to overplay his hand during the visit of the King and Queen. To some extent, his problems mirrored those of Mackenzie King; he was a politically vulnerable leader searching for a way to lead his country unified into the war that he now believed was unavoidable — and that would inevitably involve the United States. Like the Canadian prime minister, he had to be devious — to toe the neutralist and isolationist line while gradually bringing American public opinion around to accepting the idea of war against Hitler. And part of the strategy obviously involved a successful royal visit which he hoped would strengthen American sympathy for the British position. So, for him, as for the British, it still came down to how the average American reacted to the King and Queen.

In this regard, a remarkable article had appeared in the February 7 issue of *Scribner's Magazine* called "Selling George VI to the U.S.". The author, Joseph Israels II, did not mince his words. "A large part of this country," he wrote, "still believes that Edward, Duke of Windsor, is the rightful owner of the British throne, and that King George VI is a colorless, weak personality largely on probation in the public mind of Great Britain, as well as of the United States." Israels also stated what no one in Washington or London dared to say out loud:

> Even though the American part of the trip is supposed to be a side excursion from the royal visit to Canada, it does not detract from the fact that in the eyes of the world, and of America in particular, the few days the King and Queen will spend on American soil and in contact with Americans will be the most potentially important part of the entire trip. . . .
>
> The slightest slip-up can easily be magnified by an uncontrolled and often irreverent press into a major diplomatic catastrophe. . . . in future years the American people shall think of the British Empire in terms of the personalities of George and Elizabeth and shall feel at times when danger might threaten the British Empire that George and Elizabeth are nice friendly people, are like Americans and worthy of our sympathy, our financial support and, if necessary, our arms.

Often facetious in tone and dressed up with gag headlines, the article nevertheless mapped out a shrewd strategy for "selling" the Sovereign to the American public. One can imagine the blood rushing to the faces of the mandarins at the Foreign

Office, their eyes bulging in apoplexy as they dissected "Selling George VI" word by word. In fact, Israels's observations might have been called eerily prophetic, if it were not obvious that the British, ignoring his jibes, had gone ahead and used the article as a virtual blueprint in the planning of the North American tour.

What Israels proposed was a broad strategy that would "strike an accurate and careful balance between dignified regal reserve on the one hand and democratic friendliness on the other." There was, he wrote, much damage to be undone: the image of "perfidious Albion" after the "Chamberlain sellout at Munich", and, of course, the matter of Edward and Mrs. Simpson:

> You must remember that the United States was much disturbed by the abdication of Edward VIII and the circumstances which surrounded that event. Edward was much liked in this country and his marriage to an American woman, as well as the generally romantic aura which enveloped his abdication, added greatly to his popularity.

On the other hand:

> Edward as Prince of Wales sold nothing to the United States on his 1924 visit except the personality of Edward. He was young, handsome, irresponsible, and romantically appealing. He spent most of his time in night clubs and in what we now call "café society".

In order to sell the royal couple, Israels argued, greater attention must be paid to managing and cultivating the American press, including daily press briefings and mimeographed information sheets, close personal contact with the royals, and photographic sessions — otherwise "the easy human character which will make the average American feel that George and Elizabeth are flesh and blood will never appear." In this regard, he believed the Queen was as much a problem as the King. In contrast to the "chic and charmingly American" Mrs. Simpson, Elizabeth seemed too plump and dowdy — at least by Park Avenue standards. She must be smartened up.

Much of this was conventional wisdom, at least on the American side of the ocean, and, whether inspired by Israels or not, had already been applied during the Canadian tour. It was in the American "side-trip" that the *Scribner's* article made some telling points, serious and otherwise:

> It must be borne in mind that many ignorant Americans, particularly among those of Irish extraction, still believe the English people, and British royalty especially, to be evil-intentioned. . . . Thus a graceful method should be found of remembering that the British burned the White House during the War of 1812. The King and Queen might bring some house gift. . . .

Because there would be wide publicity given to the White House menus, Israels suggested that the King find some way to convey "his pleasure at being introduced to such American foods as baked beans, scrapple, or scrambled eggs and bacon." This could of course be taken too far; the King on no account must be photographed eating a hot dog at the World's Fair ("largely classified in the New York mind as a show for hicks"). A nice democratic gesture would be to hold a large garden party, to ease the pressure of the thousands who would be clamouring to meet the King and Queen.

> At some point during the visit, it should be reported that the King and President Roosevelt have had an entirely private conversation in which international matters of the greatest importance may be supposed to have been discussed. There need never be any actual report of what happened at this conversation, but it makes a good focal point for future memories of the visit.

Of course, Israels was not the only one presuming to advise on the American visit. William Bullitt, head of the U.S. Mission in France, dispatched a secret memorandum to the Roosevelts, based on what he had been able to find out about the visit of the King and Queen to Paris the year before. If George was furious at what the *Scribner's* article had to say, he would undoubtedly have been reduced to an incoherent rage by Bullitt's blunt assessment:

> The little Queen is now on her way to you together with the little King. She is a nice girl . . . and you will like her, in spite

of the fact that her sister-in-law, the Princess Royal, goes around England talking about "her cheap public smile". She resembles so much the female caddies who used to carry my clubs at Pitlochry in Scotland many years ago that I find her pleasant. . . . The little King is beginning to feel his oats, but still remains a rather frightened boy. Best not to mention the Windsors since about a month ago the Duke of Windsor wrote to Queen Mary that Bertie had behaved toward him in such an ungentlemanly way because of "the influence of that common little woman" the Queen, that he could have no further relations with Bertie. Brotherly love, therefore, not at fever heat.

Still, Bullitt took the whole matter so seriously it's hard not to imagine the French laughing up their sleeves at the detailed instructions he passed on to the White House. "Among other things," according to Eleanor Roosevelt, "he listed the furniture which should be in rooms used by the king and queen, told me what I should have in the bathrooms and even the way the comfortables on the beds should be folded!"

But while the Roosevelts were chuckling over the Ambassador's advice, Eleanor went to work ("Lord, what details!"), dutifully hunting up suitable eiderdowns, and advising the White House servants on royal tastes (no ice in their water, and tea with bread and butter to be served before breakfast). "[Bullitt] admonished me to have a hot-water bottle in every bed, which I did, though the heat of Washington must have made them unbearable. One thing that was listed and that I was never able to find was a linen blanket for the queen's couch. Nobody I asked on this side of the ocean knew what it might be." The White House went so far as to have London tap water analysed for its exact chemical content in hopes of providing the King and Queen with an ideal cup of tea. But after a number of bottles were made up, they were examined by medical authorities, "and I think it was finally decided that even if the tea did not taste so good to them it was safer for their majesties to use Potomac River water."

There was in fact no end to the advice flowing into the White House, much of it concerned with etiquette. "There'll be no curtseys or low bows and so on," the President had insisted

("Franklin always behaved as though we were simply going to have two very nice young people to stay with us"), but many Americans were clearly worried that they might appear provincial when judged by more exacting British standards—and inevitably the President had some difficult moments with the State Department protocol people. Slowly, however, things pulled themselves into shape. Even the poker-playing, bourbon-loving Vice President, "Cactus Jack" Garner, noted for his dislike of "the fuss and feathers of society", had agreed to struggle into a stiff shirt for the occasion.

The biggest controversy surrounding the royal visit to the United States came with the announcement that Their Majesties would be served that quintessential American dish, the "red hot", when they visited the Roosevelt estate at Hyde Park. People were scandalized—no one more so than the President's formidable mother, for whom propriety was life itself, and who worried FDR so constantly on matters concerning the visit that he had eventually taken to his bed with a sinus attack. Eleanor published a sly rebuttal to the anti-hot-dog lobby in her newspaper column, which here and there showed the steel she was capable of employing in dealing with the elder Mrs. Roosevelt:

> Oh dear, oh dear, so many people are worried that "the dignity of our country will be imperilled" by inviting Royalty to a picnic, particularly a hot dog picnic! My mother-in-law has sent me a letter which begs that she control me in some way and in order to spare my feelings, she has written on the back a little message: "Only one of many such". But she did not know, poor darling, that I have "many such" right here in Washington. Let me assure you, dear readers, that if it is hot there will be no hot dogs, and even if it is cool there will be plenty of other food, and the elder members of the family and the more important guests will be served with due formality.

To this she added (though it was not published):

> I should not be at all surprised if some of the things which the King and Queen will remember and laugh over, when they return to their fireside, are the differences between the English way of doing certain things and the way they are done here.

Nevertheless, Eleanor Roosevelt was concerned enough about the differences that, one day before the King and Queen were due to arrive in Washington, she had tea with the British Ambassador's American-born wife, Lady Lindsay, and asked her for any last-minute tips on protocol. "Yes," replied Lady L., "Sir Alan Lascelles has been to stay with us and he has told us that the King must be served at meals thirty seconds ahead of the Queen. He added that the King does not like capers or suet pudding. I told him we did not often have suet pudding in the United States and that I really had not expected the King to like capers."

After their tête-à-tête, Eleanor hurried to consult the President about what Lady Lindsay had said:

> I told Franklin that British protocol required that the head butler, Fields, stand with a stop watch in his hand and, thirty seconds after he and the king had been served, dispatch a butler to serve the queen and myself, and I inquired what was to happen about the White House rule that the president was always served first. He looked at me with firmness: "We will not require Fields to have a stop watch. The king and I will be served simultaneously and you and the queen will be served next."

The President had more important things to think about than when the soup was to be served. Sitting at that moment in a detention cell in Detroit was an Irishman named Sean Russell whom the FBI and Scotland Yard suspected of being involved in a plot to blow up the Royal Train. Russell, who was Chief of Staff of the Irish Republican Army, had been in the United States since April, drumming up money and support for the IRA's campaign to drive the British out of the six counties of Northern Ireland. At public meetings, which he attended with an IRA sympathizer named Joseph McGarrity, he had boasted that he was the man behind the more than one hundred bombs set off in England that year, many of which had killed or maimed a number of innocent people. The Foreign Office and Scotland Yard's Special Branch, already nervous at the possibility of "Irish outrages" during the royal visit, had asked the FBI in May to keep an eye on Russell. American agents complied with the British request and their surveillance soon turned up a number of disturbing details—all pointing to a conspiracy to assassinate George VI. But if the talk they heard was true, and not just revolutionary bluster, then Russell and his companions were being incredibly indiscreet.

In Los Angeles, a hotel worker at the Hayward Hotel had overheard Russell's friends "boasting about the reception the British monarch will receive from the 'Irishers' under the command of RUSSELL and McGARRITY." In addition, Russell's close links with the Nazi Party had led to a not-very-secret meeting with the head of the German-American *Bund* in California and with the German consul general in San Francisco. Agents eavesdropping on the conversation reported that plans had been made to sabotage British shipping on the west coast and to "waylay the Royal couple". Russell had been kept under an often haphazard surveillance as he made his way up the Pacific coast, travelling through Seattle, Pendleton, Walla Walla, and Anaconda. The RCMP, having been alerted by the FBI, watched for him at the Canadian border in British Columbia. Instead, the stocky, genial Irishman chose to go east, to Butte, Montana, where he registered at the Finlen Hotel. Then, on May 30, he was observed boarding the Northern Pacific train to Chicago.

American authorities had been content up to this point simply to keep track of Russell's movements. With no solid evidence linking him to any plot, the State Department in particular was anxious that the IRA chief not become a *cause célèbre* for Irish-American groups. Now, however, they decided to act. The New York City Police Alien Squad had received information that the IRA had a cache of explosives hidden in a house on 607 Orange Street in Newark, New Jersey, which were to be used for blowing up the Royal Train. Russell meanwhile was headed for Detroit, where it would be a fairly simple matter to cross into Canada undetected among the hundreds of thousands of Americans who were planning to visit Windsor to see the King and Queen. On the morning of June 5, the day before the Royal Train was due to arrive in the Canadian city, federal Immigration officers swooped down on the Michigan Central Railway Station and arrested the IRA leader and another man as they were about to climb into a taxi. Russell was charged with having made "certain false statements" when he had entered the country in April, and with overstaying his thirty-day visitor's permit. The same day, police raided the home on Orange Street, although U.S. government records no longer reveal what, if anything, was found.

On June 6, while guns across the river could be heard booming out their salutes to George VI, Russell polished brass at Immigration Headquarters and chatted with reporters. His presence in Detroit was a coincidence, he told them. He was not aware the royal couple were even in the vicinity, and he had never had any intention of going to Windsor: "the King and Queen after all did not invite us." News of his arrest had raised a predictable storm of anger among Irish-American patriotic organizations throughout the United States. Clan-na-Gael was outraged that a law-abiding visitor to the country should be jailed and held incommunicado. There was some inflamed rhetoric in Congress, and three Congressmen, led by James P. McGranery, went straight to the President to protest the "inexcusable" situation. Then McGranery informed the press that because of the grave injustice being done to an innocent man, seventy-six members of Congress who were of Irish descent might refuse to meet the King unless Sean Russell were released. Roosevelt, realizing that the Russell incident now threatened the success of the royal visit, quickly gave in to the pressure. Sean Russell was granted bail on funds raised by Clan-na-Gael — and promptly disappeared (he later surfaced in Berlin, and died in 1940 aboard a German submarine carrying him to Ireland).

A diplomatic incident had been averted, and Washington was at last ready to greet Their Majesties. People had been pouring into the capital for days, and hotel rooms along the parade route were now going for twenty and thirty dollars each. The day before the King and Queen were due to arrive, the President got his morning suit back from the cleaners and Eleanor Roosevelt, after supervising last-minute preparations, retired late in the evening with her copy of John Steinbeck's *The Grapes of Wrath* ("a wonderful piece of work but I can hardly bear to read it. I dread to start each new chapter").

Aboard the Royal Train, now speeding towards Washington, all was in readiness as well — thanks to the efforts of the conscientious Lascelles and others. There was one small concern, which threatened only faintly to intrude on the smooth running of the next day's itinerary. Both President Roosevelt and Mackenzie King had been approached about the predicament of the passengers aboard the *St. Louis*, which was now steaming north towards the eastern seaboard of the United States. That very night, a letter signed by some of Canada's most prominent citizens had been delivered to the Prime Minister on the Royal Train. The contents were published by Judith Robinson in *The Globe and Mail*:

> As a mark of gratitude to God for the happiness which has been vouchsafed the Canadian people in the visit of their King and Queen, and as evidence of the Christian charity of the people of this most fortunate country, we, the undersigned Christian citizens of Canada respectfully suggest that, under the power vested in you as Prime Minister of our country, you forthwith offer to the 907 homeless exiles on board the Hamburg-American ship *St. Louis* sanctuary in Canada.

Among the signatures were those of historian George M. Wrong, Sir Robert Falconer, Bishop R. J. Renison, *Saturday Night* editor B. K. Sandwell, Canon Plumptre, and Andrew Brewin. Robinson concluded her summary of the letter's contents by writing, "There might be added Jesus of Nazareth, still considered as carrying some weight in the counsels of this country's First Ministers."

The only entry Mackenzie King made in his diary was: "Received, this morning, a message about immigrants."

Thursday, June 8:

"Well, at last I greet you," said the President, smiling as he took the King's hand in his own. They stood, the Roosevelts and the King and Queen, in the President's blue and gold reception room in Union Station, where the royal couple had been led by Cordell Hull and the British Ambassador from their train on Track No. 20. Washington was hot and steamy that morning and the air about them was like warm broth. The President's Cabinet were all present, and wilting visibly in their cutaway coats (many of them rented for the occasion). Roosevelt (in spite of the infantile paralysis which had crippled him) stood upright with the discreet support of the brigadier general at his shoulder. It was a huge moment in his life, "a radiantly magnificent interlude". He towered over his royal visitors as he chatted with them, flashing his broad, familiar smile and gesturing like a show-business impresario about to give them his personal tour of America.

Thirty thousand people had managed to jam into the plaza outside, and they erupted in a great roar when the two heads of state finally appeared on the front steps of the station. The official cars swung onto Delaware Avenue, and were joined there by thirty rumbling army tanks and a cavalry escort. Ten Flying Fortresses and forty-two fighters from Langley Field, Virginia, swooped overhead. Six thousand soldiers, sailors, and marines lined the streets, facing the crowd with fixed bayonets. As the mile-long procession journeyed up Pennsylvania Avenue, a phalanx of grim-faced Secret Service agents ran alongside or stood poised on the running-boards of the two lead cars. America was taking no chances with its royal visitors. High up on the rooftops crouched a swarm of sharpshooters, men who would accompany them for the whole visit and who the Queen, quickly picking up the lingo, would call "swell" fellows.

And beyond the grinding roar and stifling fumes of the baby tanks, the low whine of the aircraft, the clop of the cavalry, the hot-footing, florid-faced "G-men", and the heat waves lifting from the asphalt was the crowd. Eight hundred thousand people, clinging to the pavement "like wet paper", fainting in large numbers, but cheering themselves hoarse in the 97-degree heat. "I have seen many important events in Washington," wrote Eleanor Roosevelt that night, "but never have I seen a crowd such as lined the whole route between the Union Station and the White House. . . . "

Farther back in the procession was Mackenzie King, dressed in the warm wool and gold braid of his Windsor uniform. In spite of the sun which sizzled down on him and made the open car in which he was riding feel "almost like the top of a stove", he could size up this reception with a practised eye: "beautiful bright day; magnificent buildings; people clustered about the buildings, around monuments, on balconies, etc." Any concern in the royal party about America's reception for British royalty evaporated during that hot half-hour drive.

Just as important, the King and the President seemed to have struck up an immediate friendship. By the time the motorcade (another American expression) had swung past the steps of the Capitol Building, the two men were conversing like old chums, turning aside every few moments to wave to the shouting crowd and, in Roosevelt's case, to tip his topper. The President, perhaps recalling his mother's rigid social ideas drummed into him since childhood, continued to address the man beside him in the car as "Your Majesty" until eventually the King said it was too hot for this sort of thing and asked to be called "George". And so he was, for the rest of the American tour. Said one veteran Washington reporter watching Roosevelt chat with the King that day, "I never saw the old boy look happier."

Eventually the motorcade arrived at the White House, named of course for the 1814 repainting done to the blackened walls of Virginia freestone after British troops burned it to a mere shell of its former self — and where, today, the magnolia tree planted by Andrew Jackson was in full bloom. After another brief reception of welcome, the King and Queen had a short time to themselves before once again meeting the Roosevelts for a "family luncheon" — American-style — which included Mackenzie King as well as the extensive Roosevelt clan. It was a relaxed, pleasant meal, and the President seemed charmed by the royal couple and their evident poise, gained no doubt from the experience of the Canadian tour. Somehow, in the light and cheerful conversation that floated about the table, the matter of the *St. Louis* and its unfortunate passengers was broached. The President explained the American position to the King (gunboats had been sent out in case the liner tried to approach American waters), and added for Mackenzie King's benefit that Canada too was restricted by its immigration laws. The Prime Minister kept quiet during the discussion ("I said nothing about the wire which I had received or about the situation itself. It is much less our problem than that of the U.S. and Cuba").

After lunch, there was a White House tour conducted by Mrs. Roosevelt, and then, the sun having come blazing out after a short, heavy rain, it was time for some sightseeing in Washington. First, they visited the Lincoln Memorial on the banks of the Potomac, where five thousand had gathered to cheer them, then drove past the reflecting pool to Rock Creek Park and Pierce Mill on Beach Drive, and then to the National Cathedral of Saints Peter and Paul (where twenty thousand people had assembled). Back at the White House, there was time for a short rest from the heat before the King and Queen set out for the British Embassy, where they were to be the centre of the most eagerly anticipated social event of the year.

The Garden Party to be held on the spacious grounds of the British Embassy was (as the *Scribner's* article had foreseen) an occasion to satisfy the urgent desire of some of the country's most influential and powerful citizens to meet, or mingle with — or at least catch sight of — the King and Queen on their brief visit. For weeks the press had been gleefully chronicling the sometimes undignified scramble by members of the Social Register to be among the fortunate "1300" with the coveted invitations ("Washington Agog As Royal Garden Party Approaches"). The small gilt-edged card with the crown had divided plutocratic America into the "haves" and "have-nots". The Vanderbilts, the Morgans, and the Rockefellers would be there of course but other names in the Blue Book were not so lucky. Sir Ronald Lindsay took it upon himself to explain the situation to reporters. "It's like heaven," he announced airily. "Some get in, some don't."

The fascination of seeing the rich and powerful jostling for favour made the British Embassy Garden Party a singular occasion on the royal tour. Yet in Canadian communities where the King and Queen received any sort of formal welcome, from the largest cities to the smallest villages, the struggle had been no less intense, nor the humiliation any less real for those who were not invited onto the station platform to make a brief bow or curtsey. If anything, given the importance of status in small communities, it may even have been worse ("Everyone presentable was presented," as James Reaney wrote, "And those who weren't have resented it, and will to their dying day"). Of course, in Washington as everywhere else, some took rejection harder than others. Gossip writer Count Igor Cassini was tarred and feathered on a remote country road in Virginia — allegedly because in his column "Petit Point" he had mentioned that a certain leading figure in that state had *not* been invited to the do at the British Embassy.

"A garden party that might pay off Canada's National Debt

and not feel it" was how one journalist summed up the occasion on the green, rolling lawn of the Embassy grounds. And while the party was handled with enough pomp to suit a coronation (servants circulated in red breeches, blue coats, and white stockings under the steely glare of Lady Lindsay — the type of woman "even butlers fear"), the British Ambassador's wife had nevertheless made one concession to the stifling Washington heat. Gentlemen were permitted to wear white Palm Beach suits instead of formal morning suits and pin-striped trousers. Some even came with straw boaters and defied all notions of civilized behaviour by wearing belts instead of braces. A senator from South Dakota, who arrived sporting a ten-gallon hat, was quickly overshadowed by the Congressman wearing a grey sombrero and flowing necktie and smoking a long black cigar. Among the ladies, crinolines were often favoured, underscoring the fact that this was, in 1939, still a southern city where people sat on verandahs in the evenings and sipped mint juleps. They strolled about in the 89-degree heat among the roses of Sharon and mock orange, looking like extras from the movie *Gone With The Wind* (which was due to open in a few months), while the FBI, in plain business suits, hid in the shrubbery or stood vigilantly at every entrance to the Embassy grounds.

At five o'clock, while the heat was still strong enough to make people giddy, the royal couple arrived at the imposing doors of the red-brick mansion on Massachusetts Avenue to be met by Sir Ronald and Lady Lindsay, and escorted through the drawing-room with its portrait of George III and onto the portico. As they stepped into view, the band struck up "God Save the King", and the guests, with as much dignity as they could muster, rushed forward for a look. Dixon of the *Daily News* was not impressed by the behaviour of his fellow Americans:

> The biggest and snootiest our land has to offer react the same fundamentally as the poor farmers out in Saskatchewan. . . . when the King and Queen arrived [everyone] broke off as if a fire alarm had sounded and joined the crush to get a gander at Britannia's rulers. The King and Queen, meeting our chosen people, got a look at more teeth than a professor at a dental college.

The Queen, also in a white crinoline dress, and, to the intense interest of fashion mavens, twirling a dainty ruffled parasol, was led among the guests by Lady Lindsay, while a short distance away, the towering, moustachioed figure of Sir Ronald could be seen doing the same for the King (who, oblivious to the heat, had worn a grey morning coat and a grey topper). When introduced, the English either bowed or curtseyed; the Americans for the most part firmly shook hands.

John Wheeler-Bennett, the future official biographer of George VI, had been dragooned into acting as a temporary equerry, and was following in the Queen's party that afternoon. Elizabeth was radiating her famous charm as she strolled about, "and the guests succumbed to it in swathes. . . . " Everything was going extremely well, in fact, until the group arrived at the marquee where refreshments had been laid out — under strict orders not to be touched until Their Majesties had completed their rounds and returned to the terrace:

> We had just reached the entrance when an unfortunate man came out carrying two glasses of iced tea. Before him he beheld the Queen of England and, like a peccant schoolboy caught at the jam-jar, his nerve forsook him. "My God, the Queen," he ejaculated, and dropped both glasses! The Queen laughed delightedly and passed on her triumphant way.

Their promenade concluded, the royal couple sat on the pillared portico of the Embassy, where the Queen had an orange punch and the King sipped iced tea. Thirty selected guests — a favoured few of "the 1300" — were then invited up to be presented. Among these were the Cordell Hulls, J. P. Morgan, assorted state governors, and the widow of Woodrow Wilson. The Queen chatted with the polar explorer Admiral Byrd, and of course Cactus Jack Garner got the King laughing at one of his tall stories and then followed up by slapping the startled Englishman on the back. Mrs. Cornelius Vanderbilt, waving a gold fan, held the King's attention for five minutes. Mackenzie King, up among the favoured, enjoyed a reunion with his old employer, John Rockefeller, and introduced him to the King. Those below the portico discreetly craned their necks for a view, while spooning the fresh Virginia strawberries and cream (25,000 strawberries shipped in for the occasion).

Concealed among the forsythia and other flowering shrubs, the orchestra played on.

The intense heat that had blanketed the capital was broken in the evening by a torrential storm of wind and rain. While lightning streaked over the city and struck the lofty Washington Monument, and thunder crashed outside the White House, the King and Queen dined as guests of the President. The royal party (which included Mackenzie King and Arnold Heeney) had been spared the oppressive weight of court uniforms and gratefully bent over their clam cocktail and boned capon in the relative informality of evening dress.

Among those dining that night off the White House's gold plate and Irish linen was Cabinet member Harold Ickes. A veteran New Dealer, Ickes looked on the royal visit with his usual sour disposition (which had earned him the title "the old curmudgeon" — although Roosevelt referred to him as "Donald Duck" behind his back). He had passed up the formal doings at the British Embassy ("a lot of uninteresting, climbing, and supercilious people") to attend a shirt-sleeves cocktail party at Lyndon Johnson's. Ickes and his wife had gone willingly, however, to the White House dinner, though he found his evening spoiled by, among other things, the behaviour of Cactus Jack Garner:

> He is the type of democrat who thinks that a showing of familiarity and bad breeding is necessary to impress others with his democracy. He sat on the Queen's right at the dinner and he was as full of life as a kitten. He has no breeding or natural dignity and I doubt if he exercised any more self-restraint than he would have shown at a church supper in Uvalde, Texas.

After the last course had been cleared away ("Mrs. Nesbitt's kitchen lived down to its reputation," as the Roosevelts' son Elliott drily observed), it was time for the toasts. The President had in his pocket a few scribbled notes to use as an outline: "Life of nation. . . . Give thanks — bonds of friendship. Greatest contrib. civiliz. neither aggress. no race episodes. . . . May understanding grow closer — friendship closer — Drink to health." Instead, FDR struggled to his feet with the help of an aide, discarded his notes, and spoke simply and eloquently to

the assembled guests about the relations between the two countries. Then it was the King's turn. Standing behind his chair to
speak, George managed, with a few hesitations, to get through
the carefully drafted sentiments which, like the President's,
touched on the idea of eternal friendship and understanding
among English-speaking nations.

Formalities over, the ladies moved to the Green Room, where
the Queen sat on a couch and chatted (mainly about the
weather) with guests who took turns sitting with her. In the
dining-room, FDR, the King, and the rest of the male contingent
talked man-to-man over liqueurs and coffee. With growing
distaste, Ickes watched the Vice President "paw at the long-
suffering royal guest, grab the King by the forearm and on
another occasion reach his arm behind his back as if in a
semiembrace":

> Garner monopolized the King until we went in to join the
> ladies. The only one who was able to break in was the
> Speaker, who thrust his face over Garner's shoulder almost
> into the face of the King the while he talked and laughed in
> loud tones. I suppose that to Speaker Bankhead and to Garner
> the King was simply a visiting Elk.

Then it was to the steaming East Room to join three hundred
additional guests for a musicale organized by Eleanor Roosevelt. The concert was to be a kind of sampling of New Deal
America, although Mackenzie King referred to it simply as
"folk songs, et cetera". A nervous Alan Lomax sang "Git Along
Little Dogie", still shaken by the experience of being frisked
by Secret Service men whose suspicions had been aroused as
much by his long hair and absence of socks as by his political
beliefs. The "Washington singer of swing", Kate Smith, sang,
at the royals' request, "When the Moon Comes Over the
Mountain" ("a type one would expect to hear in a cheap music
hall," sniffed Ickes). But the hit of the evening was the contralto
Marian Anderson, who only weeks earlier had been prevented
from performing in the Daughters of the American Revolution
Auditorium because of her race. She sang "Ave Maria" and
"Trampin'". "As beautiful a voice as I have ever heard," wrote
Mackenzie King, who thought she sang like a medium inter-
preting "voices from another world"; even Harold Ickes was

moved, saying Anderson "can thrill me more than any other singer that I have ever listened to." The concert lasted till after midnight, when both national anthems were played, and the evening broke up.

Eleanor Roosevelt, tired and drained by the oppressive heat, could congratulate herself that the first day was "over & fairly well over". The King and FDR were getting along famously — in fact had disappeared into the President's study after the musicale to talk about the European situation until the early hours of the morning. The First Lady's own opinions of the royal couple were less straightforward than her husband's. "The Queen reminds me of Queen Victoria!" she wrote, commenting on Elizabeth's "self-consciously regal" manner. "He is very nice & doesn't stutter *badly* when speaking aloud & not at all in quiet conversation."

If, beneath her breezy good humour, Eleanor Roosevelt seemed mildly irritated by the Queen's manner, the reasons were not hard to understand. The two women could not have been less alike. Eleanor, fifty-four years old, extremely tall, intellectually engaged, and undeniably homely; Elizabeth, still, at thirty-eight, with the bloom of youth about her, engaging and flirtatious, brilliant at small talk, dainty and pretty (and nearly a foot shorter than Eleanor) in her dressy hats, jewels, matching accessories, and very high heels. Their differences had been underlined that morning at Union Station. Eleanor, in the interest of good will among English-speaking nations, had gamely agreed to show up at the station in a woollen dress contributed from sheep in Canada, New Zealand, Australia, and England. Elizabeth, too, had a dress made from the same material expressly for the occasion but, pragmatically, had chosen something lighter. All the way to the White House then, while the President's wife sweltered for international understanding, the Queen coolly twirled her parasol and smiled seductively at the crowds.

The American press had no such doubts or equivocations about the royal couple. "THE BRITISH RE-TAKE WASHINGTON" was how the New York *World-Telegram* summed it up next morning, referring to the tumultuous welcome the King and Queen had received from crowds in the capital. Americans had been reassured by the royal couple's absence of "shirt-front stuff", their simple and unaffected ways, and their well-groomed good looks. Jack Garner pronounced them the "salt of the earth", and someone else had come away dazzled that they weren't "high-hat" at all. The King, "young, strong and earnest", impressed people with his lack of swank, his firm handshake, and the sincere interest he took in doing his "King-job" well. As for Elizabeth (or "that honeychile Missus Queen", as a servant at the White House had described her), she was "winning everyone's heart with her gracious bonnie ways"; indeed, she was "the perfect Queen: eyes a snapping blue, chin tilted confidently . . . fingers raised in a greeting as girlish as it was regal. Her long-handled parasol seemed out of a story book." It was a far cry from Elizabeth's previously frumpy image.

American reporters, who had made fun of the Canadian newspapers for overdoing their coverage of the royal tour in Canada, now vied with each other to ferret out each and every detail of the visit. Nothing was too insignificant to pass on to their readers (102 men and 18 trucks had been employed to pick up the debris from the triumphant motorcade to the White House, and one of the street cleaners or "white wings" declared "it was the biggest mess since President Roosevelt's first Inauguration"). The fiercely isolationist *Washington Post* had to admit that the effusive welcome was "not the result of calculated government dragooning to create the effect of popular enthusiasm but wholly voluntary and sincere." Even the Hearst newspapers had been charmed into submission. According to the *Daily Mirror*, "George VI . . . has already won a warm welcome here that makes us forget there ever was a King named George III."

But then, worried about what readers would make of the fashion news, etiquette tips, and general welling up of pro-monarchical sentiment on their front pages, the press took pains once again to distinguish between British royalty and British foreign policy. The august *New York Times* stressed that the King represented all "the people of England — not merely Mr. Chamberlain or Parliament, but also the men and women in shops, stores, factories and mines, on farms, in millions of homes set in the ancient sea, from which so many of our traditions have come."

Friday, June 9:

The second day in Washington was one of the hardest of the entire tour — ten engagements in just eleven hours, and all of it kept on schedule by the $1.25 watch of the White House Secret Service chief. It began with a visit with the "newsgals" at Mrs. Roosevelt's regular press conference — really just a stroll through a double line of reporters with the royal couple offering up an occasional "Good morning", but it was enough to make the British Embassy furious. Then a quick step into the furnace of the Washington summer, and a drive to the Embassy to meet the local British community. As always, given the American penchant for high drama in security arrangements, they were accompanied by a screaming motorcycle escort and a carload of jittery Secret Service men.

Then it was on to the Capitol Building, where virtually all the 330 Senators and members of the House of Representatives waited to greet them. Arriving at the entrance to the east portico, the royal party threaded its way through the "angry wives" (as Sir Ronald Lindsay called them), who, having been excluded from the ceremony, had to content themselves with sitting on camp chairs outside. At the top of the steps of the Capitol Building they were greeted by the Vice President ("Here come the British," cackled Cactus Jack) and the Speaker of the House, who ushered them into the delightful cool of the Rotunda. The Queen smiled around her, and looked up to the painted dome above her head and at the huge paintings depicting scenes from early American history. As befitting politicians, there had been a compromise between correct formal wear and the more practical linen suits, although, surprisingly, Senator Borah from Idaho, normally inclined to see kings and queens as slightly sinister figures, had reclaimed his morning coat after thirty-five years in mothballs to wear for the occasion.

Representative Nat Patton greeted the King with a hearty Texas handshake and said, "How do you do, Cousin George?", then took in the Queen in her white silk frock, double strand of pearls, and wide picture hat and told her she was a thousand times more beautiful than her pictures "and nearly as beautiful as the Blue Bonnet girls of Texas". Another Senator grabbed the King's hand and confided, "My, you're a great Queen-picker." Knowing what was at stake and understanding the influence over foreign policy wielded by these men (and one woman, Mrs. Hattie Carraway from Arkansas), the King and Queen carried it off with surprising grace, shaking everyone's hand as they stood in front of a mural of Pocahontas, and winning points for their friendliness and "democratic" manners. For their part, the Senators and Congressmen mostly confined themselves to a handshake and a greeting. Even the ancient Senator Borah swallowed his isolationist sentiments for the moment, although many, like Congressman Schwartz of Wyoming, were quick to assure the folks back home that "we still have our feet on the ground, and are not of a mind to pull anybody's chestnuts, if you know what I mean. . . . " New York Congressman Barry on the other hand simply stayed away, saying the royal couple seemed nice enough but "their visit at this time is obviously a part of the British propaganda to entangle us with them to preserve the British Empire in the event of war."

Through all this, Canada's Mackenzie King, as Minister in Attendance, stood behind Their Majesties and, partly shielded by a bank of ferns, urgently attempted to fix one of his braces which had come undone. The predicament seemed appropriate to his situation somehow, and to everything that had happened to him since they had arrived in Washington. Just that morning, he had been forced to attach himself rather clumsily to the royal entourage on its way to the Capitol Building, after being advised that he would "not be expected" during the presentations of members of the British Colony. He had been relegated to the sidelines during the great doings of the day, always present but somehow obscured by the shrubbery. Control of the tour had been snatched out of his hands, and things were being shuffled about behind the scenes by the Americans and the British, who, regardless of what had been agreed to by Buckingham Palace and the Foreign Office, obviously saw the visit as *their* show. Unknown officials in anonymous offices were making decisions and they had the Prime Minister at

their mercy. "I continuously find that someone has told someone else that I am not wishing to go here and there with the
result that I feel great embarrassment. . . . "

As to who was responsible for this miserable state of affairs,
Mackenzie King needed to look no farther than the tall and
imperious Lindsays. While "punctilious" about granting the
Prime Minister his proper precedence at unimportant
moments, one or other of the Lindsays always managed to
manoeuvre him into a less prominent place during public
events. He couldn't help comparing their actions with the con-
duct of the Americans, particularly the Howes and the Roosevelts, who had been conspicuously well-mannered towards
him. However, he noticed that even the Americans had seated
him some distance away from the royals' table during luncheon
that afternoon on the President's yacht ("I am not quite sure
of these arrangements") as they sailed down the beautiful Potomac River to Mount Vernon.

They were on their way to the riverside mansion that had
once been the home of George Washington, and where the
United States' first president was buried in a red-brick tomb
surrounded by cedars and pine. This was a national shrine for
Americans; in 1860, Prince Albert had planted a chestnut tree
here to symbolize the rapprochement between the two English-
speaking countries. That relationship was reinforced by
George VI, who laid a wreath of lilies and irises tied with the
colours of the Brigade of Guards on Washington's grave. After
that, the official party strolled up the terraced lawns to the
Georgian-style mansion with its green shutters and eight-
column porch. Complementing the King's position as a direct
descendant of George III was the Queen's convenient connection with George Washington, authenticated by the College of
Arms in London. She could claim with him a common ancestor,
Colonel Augustus Warner of Virginia, which made her a second cousin, six times removed, of the American President (and
a distant relation as well of the Confederate general Robert E.
Lee). While the group inspected Martha Washington's sitting-
room, and visited the slave quarters, the Prime Minister made
his own claim to history while chatting with one of Washington's descendants. Mackenzie King's grandfather had been for
a time "President of a provisional government of the Republic

of Canada", and he noted the irony of having "this particular conversation in this particular place in the presence of the King and Queen."

After the presentation of bouquets of heliotrope and pinks to the Queen and Mrs. Roosevelt by the gardener (a veteran of the Fourth Canadian Mounted Rifles in the Great War), members of the official party got into their limousines for the trip back to the White House. There was a brief stop at Fort Hunt to tour a Civilian Conservation Corps camp where boys from the slums were apprenticed to work on conservation projects. It was a showcase of the President's New Deal, and one that particularly interested the King, who had worked in similar programs in England (one boy, showing old-fashioned enterprise, shook hands with the King, then "sold" his handshake to those around him for cigarettes, pop, and a shoeshine). There was also a short memorial service at the National Cemetery at Arlington, where thirty thousand of the nation's war dead lay buried and where the King laid wreaths on the Tomb of the Unknown Soldier and at the Canadian Cross.

Later in the afternoon there was tea on the White House lawn with three hundred Girl Scouts and five hundred Boy Scouts. Also there, at Eleanor Roosevelt's invitation, were several leaders of the New Deal. Their presence did not escape the notice of the German News Bureau, which professed shock that "the Left Radical members of the Federal Government" should have had conversations with the royal couple. It was typical of the attitude struck by Nazi newspapers, anxious to discredit every aspect of the royal visit to the United States. The *New York Times* published a brief survey of the German coverage:

According to the press headlines . . . "the unroyal reception in Washington" was free of courtly manners and was accompanied by "the painful music" of "compliments, nigger songs and swing," to which "a Jewish-led strike in the news reel industry and the Irish counter demonstration" added further disharmony.

Popolo di Roma took a more genteel approach, noting that "Mrs. Roosevelt did not kneel when introduced to Queen Elizabeth," and concluding gravely, "this is the greatest scandal of the present era."

Large-boned, ungainly Eleanor, unconcerned about scandal, wondered instead how the Queen "never had a crease in her dress nor a hair out of place," able to remain "so perfectly in character all the time," but in fact the royal couple was under terrific strain. The crowds, the unaccustomed heat and overwhelming humidity, the exhaustion after weeks of touring, were now beginning to tell on them. It was the Queen, unexpectedly, who was showing signs of playing out, leaving a reception line at one point, slipping away from another event to rest, her face scarlet from the heat. The King mopped his brow and carried on. But they had begun dividing up the duties between them, talking with alternate persons in an inspection line, and pacing themselves through each event.

The last official Washington engagement was dinner at the British Embassy, where the President and Mrs. Roosevelt were entertained by the King and Queen. Refreshed by a short rest, Elizabeth was once again a proper-looking Queen, prepared to make one final conquest. The eight-year-old daughter of Secretary of Commerce Harry Hopkins had watched as the royal couple arrived at the White House the day before, and had been disappointed by their somewhat ordinary appearance. Learning of this, Eleanor Roosevelt made sure the little girl was in the hallway that evening when the King and Queen prepared to leave for the Embassy. What Diana Hopkins saw was the Queen dressed in a Victorian gown of white tulle, wearing a diamond tiara and a necklace and earrings made of diamonds and pigeon-blood rubies. As Eleanor Roosevelt noted, "the illusion was so perfect that she curtseyed to the Queen and ignored the King." The royal couple spoke with her for a few moments, and when they left, Diana turned to her father and said, "Oh, Daddy, Daddy! I have seen the Fairy Queen."

Just thirty-six guests gathered around the huge walnut table in the Embassy dining-room which had been decorated with mounds of "Better Time" roses and old silver dating back to George IV. Once again there were toasts to better understanding among all peoples, but, on this evening (undoubtedly to the King's relief), no orchestra and no musicale. And with the dinner concluded at 11:30, the royal party left directly for Union Station to board the Royal Train for the overnight journey to New York.

Poor Mackenzie King—he had had another frustrating evening. The original plan to have him accompany Their Majesties from the White House that evening had been scrapped. Instead, he arrived alone and was shunted into an anteroom to cool his heels with members of the American Cabinet and miscellaneous British Embassy staff, while everyone waited for the main party to arrive. Like a bachelor uncle, he had been paired with the wife of a Kentucky Senator for dinner — far from the chatter of the royals and the Roosevelts. More humiliations lay ahead. After the banquet, the King and Queen disappeared behind the firmly closed doors of the library. Lascelles made some excuses, but it was clear to Mackenzie King that the British wanted some private conversations without the King's Minister. It was even suggested that he go on ahead to the station without waiting.

He stood alone by the Embassy entrance for a while, a somewhat pathetic figure, ignored and unregarded by those who remained, left to talk with "chauffeurs and others". Eventually the Lindsays came out and gave him a lift to the station, where he said goodbye to the Hulls, who, as always, were extremely kind and attentive to him. He climbed aboard, "glad to be back on the Royal Train again", with familiar and even respectful faces around him. Most of the reporters and officials had long since returned, driven from their hotel rooms and residences by the extreme Washington heat to the comfort of the air-conditioned carriages.

Pallie Pascoe and other members of the Royal Visit crew were already aboard the two trains by the time Mackenzie King arrived. Like everyone else with time to kill, he had taken in the sights of the American capital, including the White House, though the strict security in force had blocked off so many streets that it sometimes made moving around the city difficult. But the Americans had been friendly, and the affection they had shown for the King and Queen was nothing short of astonishing. Sitting in a Washington movie-house with a friend, Pallie had watched newsreels of the royal couple in Banff, "and do you know that we two Canadians were the only ones sitting down. Yes Sir, about two thousand people were standing applauding for all they were worth. I was so thrilled, I broke out in goose pimples."

After appropriate goodbyes to the American Cabinet and to the Roosevelts, who were going on to Hyde Park, the Royal Train slowly pulled out of the station to the cheers of thousands. Eleanor Roosevelt was as tired as anyone in the royal party by the event-filled day and the suffocating heat, but as she confided to her diary, "This day is also over & has gone well. . . . "

> Even FDR is content and I am glad for him. The young royalties are most intelligent. At the tea they asked everyone questions and left them with a feeling that their subject was of interest and well understood. At dinner the King told me he felt that he had learned a great deal. She seems equally interested. I begin to think there is something in training.

CHAPTER TEN

"New York Goes King Crazy"

Saturday, June 10:

IN THE MORNING, the Royal Train rested on a siding at Red Bank, New Jersey, surrounded by armed guards while workers swarmed over the carriages, cleaning every surface and bringing up blocks of ice for the air-conditioning. When the Queen looked out a window, a brass band hovering near by broke into "Let Me Call You Sweetheart". At nine o'clock, the King and Queen emerged from the royal carriage for a brief reception with the governors of New York and New Jersey. The royal party then drove by automobile the fourteen miles south to Sandy Hook, where they boarded the U.S. destroyer *Warrington* for the short sea journey to New York City. The U.S. Navy still being "dry", the King was served a strange, reddish-brown beverage. Hugh Keenleyside happened to be close by when His Majesty "turned to an aide and asked quietly if not surreptitiously what was in his glass. 'That, Sir, is known as Coca-Cola; it is the folk-drink of the lower orders in America.'"

Entering New York harbour, the King and Queen could see the Statue of Liberty looming up on the port side and in front of them the famous skyscrapers of New York, their towers lost in the haze. A twenty-one-gun salute boomed out from Governors Island; ten bombers rumbled overhead in formation; speedboats raced around the *Warrington*; ships in the harbour set off a terrific noise; day rockets trailed across the sky; and three silver blimps let loose thousands of small balloons on the city. Persistent reports that the harbour had been swept for mines and that anti-aircraft guns had been wheeled into position had been firmly denied by the authorities, but there was no doubt that security remained an important concern.

Every foot of the official route had been plotted and photographed under the supervision of Scotland Yard. All roofs had been inspected, and only known persons were allowed into buildings along the route. The largest detail of policemen in the city's history, 13,482, had been assigned for the five-hour visit, and the majority of these, who were on street duty, had been ordered to stand with their backs to the motorcade to watch the crowds for dangerous elements. "White wings" had worked far into the night to scrub every foot of pavement on the fifty-one-mile official route, and the estimated three million onlookers (the Police Commissioner's estimate) lined the streets everywhere. One million schoolchildren waited in Central Park alone, and 60,000 tickets had been distributed for choice viewing spots along the West Side Express Highway. Among the crowds was the world's greatest tap-dancer, Bill "Bojangles" Robinson, who a week earlier had danced down Broadway with Cab Calloway to celebrate his sixty-first birthday and to publicize his show, *The Hot Mikado*. To a reporter he explained that his famous "stairs dance" had originated in a dream he had one night after performing before the Prince of Wales at London's Coliseum. He had dreamt of being knighted, "and I danced up the stairs to the throne to get my badge and danced right down again."

As the King and Queen stepped ashore at the Battery about 11:30 that morning, New Yorkers "forgot to be blasé." Foghorns, factory whistles, and wild cheering greeted them as they strode up the three-hundred-foot carpet, a stone's throw from where American Revolutionary soldiers had once pulled down an equestrian statue of George III (and been upbraided for the deed by George Washington). New York's legendary mayor, Fiorello LaGuardia was on hand to greet them and show them to their limousines. For reasons of safety and speed, the royal party had been denied a good view of the Empire State Building and a ticker-tape parade up Broadway ("They used to throw down ticker-tape," Roosevelt had told the British Ambassador, "but now they drop telephone directories"). Even so, everyone said it was the best reception since Lindbergh's. New Yorkers, "sophisticated, hard-boiled but sentimental", hung over the roofs, and dangled dangerously from windows and fire-escapes for a good view of the motorcade, and threw down ticker-tape and torn paper in defiance of the police. British journalists seemed particularly impressed, settling on the word "crazy" to describe what was going on ("New York Goes Crazy Over King and Queen", "King Gets Craziest Welcome Ever", "New York Goes King Crazy"). New York journalists, on the other hand, kept their admiring prose hard-boiled ("They Wowed The Big Burg — Their Majesties Did", "Ain't She Gorgeous — Huh?").

Only Jack Lait of the *Mirror* bucked the generally gushing tone, writing ungallantly of the Queen that she was a "cute, cuddly, homey-looking girl, in an ice-blue ensemble that looked neat and becoming, but wouldn't have rated a second glance in a Broadway lobby."

Even racing up the West Side Highway at 30 mph, which reduced their view of the city to a blur, the party was still more than a half-hour behind schedule by the time they reached the World's Fair site at Flushing Meadow. Admiring the 200-foot Perisphere and the 700-foot three-sided Trylon, the King and Queen stepped from their bullet-proof limousine and into the heat and crush and noise of the exposition. Rockets roared, bands played, red Indians whooped, and to the Queen's surprise the crowd sang "Rule Britannia" and "Land of Hope and Glory". The Italian Commissioner General gave them the Fascist salute; they posed for photographers before a giant illuminated map of Canada; an RCMP band played "Rose Marie, I Love You"; and Australians gave "typical Australian yells". An over-long reception line composed in large part of the friends and flunkeys of their guide Grover Whalen ("Avoid letting such entrepreneurs as Grover Whalen . . . intrude into the picture," the *Scribner's* article had warned) embarrassed American officials, incensed British ones, and forced the King and Queen to improvise by just strolling along and shaking a few hands. Travelling on a trackless train, they admired the forty-five-foot-tall statue of George Washington (the 150th anniversary of his death had provided the excuse for the exposition), and visited the exhibition of the Irish Free State, where the Queen asked — perhaps a little too ingenuously — about the granite monument to Padraic Pearse and the men executed in the 1916 Easter Rebellion.

At the British exhibition there were replicas of the crown

jewels, and an original copy of Magna Carta (one of only four in existence), with a chart that explained its importance as the source of American Freedom and Liberty. Opposite this (another cunning move by the British to establish solidarity), there were two charts: one showing how George Washington was descended from one British king and nine princes, and the other demonstrating the connection between the Royal Coat of Arms and the design of the Stars and Stripes.

Escaping the mobs and heat of Flushing Meadow, the royal party sped in a long, screaming motorcade to Columbia University (originally King's College), where there was another short ceremony of welcome. Mackenzie King, who liked to think of himself as fading graciously into the background on these occasions, felt differently when it came to being nudged backwards by the perfidious British, and seeing his place on the platform being taken by Lord Eldon:

> I hesitate to push myself forward in these matters and felt embarrassed in the presence of Sir Ronald and Lady Lindsay along the way, though Sir Ronald had kept pushing me ahead. I noticed his wife Lady Lindsay had always preceded me. In this way the precedence of the Embassy has, I suppose, been preserved in their minds.

The Prime Minister's disappointment was soon forgotten, however, as the procession made its way out of New York City for the seclusion of the Roosevelt estate some sixty miles away. Even travelling at high speed, and hemmed in by motorcycles and Secret Service agents, the royal couple got a chance to see a little of suburban and rural America. Church bells rang, and people clapped, cheered, waved, and tooted their car horns all along the route. On one brief stretch near Hawthorne, someone had trailed daisies over the road, while near Poughkeepsie the motorcade passed over a carpet of roses. The King and Queen caught a glimpse of America relaxing on a summer weekend: girls in beach pyjamas, families camping, fishing, playing baseball, or just sitting on their verandahs sipping lemonade. Everyone — diners, cooks, and waiters — deserted the Oaks Roadhouse as they passed, while the customers at Willie's leaned out of the windows and waved.

Over the Henry Hudson Parkway, the Saw Mill River Park-

way, the Bronx River Parkway; from Cortland by the Crom-
pound Road to Peekskill; past Fishkill where the branches of
overhanging trees were formed in a heart; then up the Albany
Post Road to Dutchess County; till finally, at six o'clock, as
the church bells of Hyde Park rang, the sixteen automobiles
swept into the Roosevelt estate, where Franklin, Eleanor, and
the President's eighty-five-year-old mother, Sara, stood on the
porch of the Big House to greet them, and to offer a little refuge
from the public world for the next twenty-four hours.

"They are coming away for a quiet weekend with me," the
President had said with characteristic charm. "I'll put the King
into an old pair of flannels and just drive him about in my old
Ford." His mother, whose entire life had been shaped and
anchored by the rules of proper social behaviour (the older the
rules, the better), had other ideas. Here, finally, Sara Delano
Roosevelt might exert her formidable influence, and rescue
some dignity for the American tour — beginning with a real
English tea when the royal party arrived, even though it was
now eight o'clock, and her son the President was ordering
cocktails.

"My mother thinks that you should have a cup of tea," said
FDR as the weary King walked into the room. "She doesn't
approve of cocktails."

"Neither does my mother," said George, gratefully taking
the glass. He didn't bother to mention that it was not the alcohol
itself that his mother objected to, but the cocktail as an example
of creeping Americanism.

There had been problems with the help. Sara Roosevelt's
English butler had gone off on a holiday at the prospect of
seeing the President's "coloured" staff serving his Sovereign.
Dinner, which they sat down to at 9:30 that evening, was a
series of catastrophes. Behind the serving-screen, a side table
collapsed, reducing the Limoges china service to bits of expensive trash. After dinner, the waiter carrying drinks into the
drawing-room slipped, and arrived before the King and the
President on his backside, accompanied by a slithering tray,
various bottles, decanters, glasses, ice, and rivers of alcohol.
Sara kept a stony composure throughout the evening, but to
the end of her life looked back on the whole affair with undis-
guised regret.

Once again, Roosevelt and the King sat down for a long talk, tactfully including Mackenzie King in their conversation. They concerned themselves almost exclusively with the international situation and the war, which both the King and the President now frankly talked of as inevitable. Gone was the cagey manner of a politician at fundamental odds with his country's mood in foreign matters. Roosevelt allowed himself to be blunt, sounding almost Churchillian in his sweeping statements, belligerent attitudes (which at times approached bloody-mindedness), and fascination with military (and especially naval) tactics. The King, meticulous in these matters, wrote it all down for the Foreign Office to examine and ponder:

> He was definitely anti-Russian. I told him so were we but if we could not have an understanding with her, Germany would probably make one. ... He showed me his naval patrols in greater detail about which he is terribly keen. If he saw a U-boat he would sink her at once & wait for the consequences. ... If London was bombed USA would come in. Offensive air warfare was better than defensive & he hoped we should do the same on Berlin.

FDR's great charm and easy manner had broken down the King's natural reserve ("Why don't my Ministers talk to me as the President did tonight?" the King later asked Mackenzie King). The two men spoke as equals, not so much because FDR was President of the United States, but because he was a member of America's ruling class, one of the "unsnubbable" Roosevelts (with the brimming confidence of someone who had once arrived at boarding-school in his own private railroad car). The talk went on for hours, ranging over the ways the British and Americans could stand together and pool their military resources. Some have even claimed these discussions were the first steps towards the Lend-Lease arrangements that enabled the United States to help prop up Britain's early defence against Hitler. But whether or not they achieved anything so significant, there was no doubt that Anglo-American relations were improved by the genuine feelings of friendship between the two men.

Sitting back, saying little, Mackenzie King drank in the flow of conversation as it ran here and there over the events and

personalities of the day — and of course, he later put down all
the private and unguarded comments in his diary:

> The King spoke very frankly about how the Germans for
> many years past had been spying on England. Gave his own
> experience and said his own family relations in Germany had
> been used to try and spy to get particulars from other members
> of the family. . . . Said his father never shook hands with the
> German Ambassador . . . after the way he had been betrayed
> by him. . . . There was a family feeling as well as a national
> feeling.
>
> He spoke very intimately about some of the things that hap-
> pened during the war. Of how Winston Churchill had dis-
> missed Prince Louis of Battenberg [father of Louis Mount-
> batten] from the command of the navy on the score he was a
> German but had later admitted he had done it in order to have
> the control of the whole situation himself. . . . He told how
> prior to the Dardanelles attack, Churchill had been told over
> and over again not to make the attack too soon, to wait some
> time, but was determined to go at it. At the time he had made
> up his mind, he had still to study the maps. The King indicated
> he would never wish to appoint Churchill to any office unless
> it was absolutely necessary in time of war. I confess I was glad
> to hear him say that because I think Churchill is one of the
> most dangerous men I have ever known.

And once again Roosevelt came to the aid and support of
his Canadian friend, Mackenzie, aware of the rough ride the
Prime Minister had had from the etiquette- and status-
conscious officials who perpetually surrounded and exasper-
ated all three men. One can imagine the scene, the three of
them sitting over drinks in the drawing-room, their large, comfortable chairs pushed together. The President talking, the King
nodding, Mackenzie King almost purring aloud with what he
was hearing:

> He told the King repeatedly that he and I understood each
> other perfectly and worked together on all matters of mutual
> relationship . . . and was very strong about not paying too
> much attention to the diplomatic services. Said they were
> always saying things were impossible and making it difficult.

... The President spoke of me as Minister in Attendance. ... "Mackenzie and I know each other so well that I was most anxious he should come." ... I naturally said nothing, and some remark was made to the effect that all had worked out quite obviously for the best.

The talk went until 1:30 in the morning, when the President finally laid a hand on the King's knee and said, "Young man, it's time for you to go to bed!"

The three men made their way to bed, although it is reasonable to suppose the Prime Minister did not actually climb the stairs, but instead floated along a few feet off the ground, having heard the President of the United States tell the King of England at some length what a grand fellow he was. Before retiring, however, George wanted to talk a little more, and so Mackenzie King, drifting over the threshold, followed the Sovereign into his bedroom:

> There was a door between us, and the door was not locked. So I went into the bedroom with him, and he opened the door into my bedroom, and came through and talked with me there a few minutes, and then walked back to his room. Shook hands and said: good-night there. On the other side of the King's room was an open door opening into the Queen's room. As we said good-night, I said to the King that doing so much in so short a time might be very trying on the Queen and himself, but that I hoped he would realize that while it might be necessarily trying, it was helping to save the world.
>
> The King said to me: this means very much for us. I interpreted this as meaning much for the British Empire, but he followed it up by saying it means very much for the Queen and myself. I could see that he was tremendously pleased that they had been personally able to play a very real part, and standing on their own feet, and getting recognition on account of themselves in a foreign country. ...

While the King and his prime minister turned gratefully to their beds, to sleep in the cool, serene air of the Hudson River Valley, far away in New York City some of the less elevated companions on the Royal Train were still casting about for ways to amuse themselves. Since early that morning, Pallie

Pascoe, Lou Gignac, Bill Ross, and a few others had been in the Big City to see the sights and do some shopping. Two of the men took off to see Sally Rand's Bubble Show, but the rest chose to take in a ball game—and whatever else came up later. As usual, Pallie got the whole adventure down on paper, and a few insights on the great American metropolis as well:

> I don't wonder there are pick-pockets in New York, because in a jam it's a darn sight easier to get your hands in someone else's pocket than it is to get into your own. . . . What a reception those New Yorkers gave to our King and Queen. . . . I never heard one single smart crack all morning. The King and Queen were introduced to 400 or 500 people and boy was it hot, but at the end the Queen was still smiling and knocking the people dead.

After some lunch, the men hired a cab, with the idea of taking the scenic route to Yankee Stadium:

> Told [the cabbie] we were three hayseeds from Canada and to give us the works. What a ride! He drove through traffic and between police and around people, past buses and trams and actually there was not enough room to push a baby carriage. The driver said, "you hold on and let me do the driving." He took us through Harlem, showed us the different places where, if you cared to, you could go at night. They ranged from opera down to as far as you wanted to go. The ball game was fair, but nothing spectacular. After the game we went into one of those places on Broadway where you can drink tea or anything. We stuck to John Collins. Later we got a bus and went for a ride. If you're ever in New York and want to see the town, get on a bus and make friends with the conductor. We had a bunch of fun and I'm darned if after hours of travel, we did not land back at the Fair. The conductor, when he found we had been there, put us on another bus and told the conductor to look after us and he sure did just that. We were riding along singing some old war songs when a man moved back to us and told us that if we really wanted to enjoy a sing-song to go to a night club called some Radio Club, I forget the name and never did know the address, but anyway we went and what a time was had.

Having heard all about the charges in such places, I took the head waiter aside and asked him for the low down on charges. He said it will cost you $2.50 for your dinner, no matter what you eat and 75¢ for each drink, from water to champagne, then he said, "when you get your bill add 10% for the waiter, they don't expect any more, but, incidentally, they don't expect any less." So we said "Let's go." The entertainment was good and the two boys who said they owned the joint were fine fellows. About half way through the evening, I think it was 1.30, I dropped my cigarette and the waiter incidentally gave me another, and one of the boys with the party said "That's right, you better look after him, he's the King's Postmaster." Well, Sir, did that rip it wide open! They found out we were all on the Royal Train and nothing was too good for us. We inspected the kitchen, condemned the food, led the Orchestra, bossed the singing and finally, at about 3.30, we headed homeward, really happy and swearing allegiance to everybody and everything.

Sunday, June 11:

In the morning, the royal party attended the old ivy-covered church at St. James, Hyde Park, where the vicar, faced with an unprecedented call to faith by thousands anxious to reserve one of the 200 seats, had had his phone disconnected the week before. FDR drove the King to church in his specially built Ford with the hand brakes, insisting that Mackenzie King hop in the back, and saying to George, "We have a new designation for Mackenzie. He is the official interpreter between the President and the King in relation to the affairs of the United States and Great Britain."

Five thousand people had clustered around the old church; which dated back to 1812; many had slept that night on the clipped and tidy lawns of the churchyard. An attempt to sing the unfamiliar "God Save the King" as the royal couple arrived died, although the Canadians present helped it along. The Episcopal service was, to the Queen's considerable surprise, strongly reminiscent of divine service back home, and included for this occasion prayers for the King and the royal family. The opening hymn was "Come, thou Almighty King"; the lesson was read by the Rev. Raymond Smith, rector of the Roosevelts' church on Campobello Island in New Brunswick; and the service concluded with Kipling's "Recessional" ("The captains and the kings depart . . . "). During the collection, the King and Queen dropped crisp new American banknotes into the plate.

Coming back from church, this time with the Queen beside him and the King and Sara Roosevelt in the back, the exuberant President drove so fast that George was forced to hold on to his hat. An American-style picnic had been arranged at Dutchess Hill — the very one Sara and so many others in the country had feared would compromise the dignity of the visit. There were the famous hot dogs (which the White House had assured the reporters were union-made), as well as smoked turkey, baked beans, pork, ham, lettuce-and-tomato salad, strawberry shortcake, green- and-orange-coloured soft drinks, iced coffee, iced tea, and cold beer. The royals sat on the stone porch and ate from paper plates, while Eleanor could be seen "dashing about in a little brown gingham dress, seeing that lunch was properly served and that everybody was comfortable, just as though it were only a family party." The guest list included Astors, Morgenthaus, ambassadors, bishops, a governor, some of the Roosevelt family servants, and neighbours, some of whom showed up in open-necked shirts and even galluses. People sat on the porch or at tables on the lawn, and a few took pictures surreptitiously with their cameras while pretending to eat.

The sensation over "America's favourite snack food" continued to fascinate the country — and remained the single biggest story of the entire visit to the United States. That afternoon, the press besieged the royal staff with questions as to whether either the King or the Queen had actually bitten into one. Lascelles' staff reacted as if they were dealing with a potential scandal, and it was not until evening that it was confirmed that both Their Majesties had in fact tried them. "Red Hots Relished by Royalty" trumpeted *The Globe and Mail*, while vendors at Coney Island immediately put up signs reading "By Appointment to His Majesty the King".

When the picnic meal was over, there was another one of Eleanor's concerts, with an Indian princess, Te Ata, and a young refugee singer, Charlotte Kraus; while this was going on, the King persisted in taking more home movies with his camera. Then the royal couple climbed once again into the back of FDR's little car (according to James Roosevelt, looking "little bigger than midgets next to the lofty Roosevelts"), and off they went to Val-Kill Cottage, like old family friends, for tea. Mackenzie King, who had followed along with a few others, was dismayed when the President suddenly called out to him to put on a bathing-suit and come swimming. Feeling tired, and imagining how good a nap would be back at the Big House, he made his excuses. "I was much disappointed later on to find out that the invitation had been really to join the President and the King in swimming without any others being present. Had I known this I would have certainly stayed." FDR and the King frolicked in the Roosevelts' spring-fed swimming-pool, then went on a tour of the estate, looked at the presidential timber, and generally talked like the simple countrymen they pretended to be. To Mackenzie King's further chagrin, he missed not only the swim and the drive but an hour in the President's library before dinner when Roosevelt and the King again spoke frankly with each other about their mutual problems.

By any standard of expectation, the four days in the United States had been a resounding success for all concerned. Even Walter Winchell had been impressed, saying, "Well, Great Britain picked the right pair at that." And the radio evangelist Father Coughlin was forced to admit the royals were "lovely personalities" while reiterating that they were there of course to help "nullify our basic foreign policy of no entanglements." As Eleanor wrote to a friend:

> FDR was satisfied and all went well. I like them both but what a life! They are happy together and that must make a difference even in the life they have to lead. Mackenzie King is jubilant over the whole trip. I should think it might give Hitler and Mussolini food for thought.

Certainly there was reaction from the German and Italian press. *Muenchener Neueste Nachrichten* suggested the tour had been conceived by Roosevelt, "democratic world reformer no. 1" as a way of luring America into a world war, and thereby winning for himself a third term. Another familiar German theme was how the Americans were playing into wily British hands. "Even in the days of the pharaohs," reported *Bremer Neueste Nachrichten*, "no court was so diligently fawned upon as the White House during the Royal Tour." Another tack was to suggest that the King and Queen had been subjected to a near-barbaric reception by the Americans. "All that was lacking in the reception given the British Sovereigns in the United States," reported the newspaper *Rheinfort*, "was an honour escort of gangsters."

> We turn pale with jealousy, we poor slaves of Fascist dictatorship. We console ourselves, however, by thinking that we shall never go so far, for we are without a wild west tradition. As an example of the highest American civilization, during the banquet negro songs and swing music directed by Jews were presented.

The strongly positive reaction of the American press could be dismissed as the work of "Jewish reporters whose hearts have been enraptured", while the British press "passes over with significant silence the painful impression which the not exactly tactful welcome to the Royal couple by Roosevelt and LaGuardia and others created in British circles." Clearly, the Nazis were prepared to say or invent anything to tarnish the visit's success.

What they would have made of the royal couple's final dinner with the Roosevelts is hard to imagine, since it was obviously such a happy gathering, with both the President and the King addressing each other warmly and eloquently. Before the royal couple came down, Roosevelt displayed his customary grace as far as the Canadian Prime Minister was concerned, showing him the cables that the King had seen earlier ("to the effect that Chamberlain was becoming concerned about what might happen around August 1st. Also messages regarding German submarine bases along the coast of South America near Trinidad"). The heat at Hyde Park was broken by a terrific thunderstorm that evening, and the Queen came over to where Mackenzie King stood at the window and they watched it together ("The Queen yielded to taking a mild form of cocktail, saying she was afraid she was getting into bad habits. It was the only time I have seen her take anything of the kind, but I think she needed some little stimulant after the day's exertions"). As a farewell gift, George gave FDR an inkstand much like the one he had presented to both Tweedsmuir and Mackenzie King ("I am not sure that the two others have not some gilt upon them") and paid a gracious tribute to the President's mother. The party became so spirited that the stiff upper lip of Sir Ronald Lindsay quavered, and he "did not know whether he should be shocked or join in the hilarity, did not seem to know what was happening to his sovereign that the King was enjoying the evening immensely, and the Queen was most animated in her talks with the President."

> Before the dinner was over, the President began to tell us a most amusing story about a funeral where a body had been shipped in a casket with spirits of rum. The hour was getting late. The ladies were going to their rooms to get their wraps, but they stayed at the door and watched us while we laughed until we almost cried. It was an immense relaxation—the King enjoying the whole situation immensely and joining in the most natural way in the fun of the occasion.

The thunderstorm had not stopped people from showing up in the thousands to watch the royal couple board their train at Hyde Park station. The King and Queen waved to the Roosevelts, who waved heartily back, while the crowd looked on and cheered. Eleanor later described the scene and the emotion it evoked:

> The steep little banks rising on the side of the river were covered with spectators who waited, rather silently, until our goodbyes were said. But, as the train pulled out, somebody began singing "Auld Lang Syne" and then everyone was singing, and it seemed that there was something of our friendship and our sadness and something of the uncertainty of our future in that song that could not have been said in any other words.

The Royal Train retreated up the track with the sound of singing and the President's voice calling to them as they disappeared into the darkness, "Good luck to you! All the luck in the world!"

We stood and waved, but my mother-in-law reminded us of the old superstition that one must not watch people out of sight, and so before they turned the bend we were back in our cars and on our way home.

CHAPTER ELEVEN

"Our Minds and Hearts Are Full"

Monday, June 12:

WHEN THE KING AND QUEEN AWOKE THAT MORNING, they were back in Canada. The rain and high winds that had battered New York State the previous night had come north of the border as well, and the effects could be seen in the overturned tree stumps and the barns with their roofs torn away. Gone however were the screaming motorcycle escorts, the nervous Secret Service men, and the Army sharpshooters — replaced by the familiar red coats of the Mounties. Raymond Daniell, writing in the *New York Times* and *The Globe and Mail*, described the hurricane that had preceded the Royal Train into the Eastern Townships as no more than "the rattle of all the Yankee pistols and cartridge belts". Obstreperous the G-men might have been, but they had been thorough and dedicated enough for Scotland Yard, and everyone had eventually gotten along. Still, even the British journalists admitted their relief at returning to the more placid and familiar Dominion. America had been too big, too hot, and altogether too dramatic.

Much as everyone would have denied it, there was an air of anticlimax about the next four days. The tension on all sides over how the royal couple would be received in America had vanished with their tumultuous welcome. The press had been charmed, the politicians adroitly flattered, and the President had been a delight. There was nothing more to prove. The task now would be to keep up the performance for a few days longer, and somehow to shrug off the wearing effects of the previous week's humid heat, and the almost constant dinning from the millions who had cheered them. It would not be easy. As Pallie Pascoe wrote about the slow jog through the maritime regions of the country, "the balance of the trip was and still is a kind of nightmare. We went to so many places, saw so many people and never got any place." Only the Prime Minister, his face glowing in the presence of the flash bulbs, seem to grow more invigorated day by day.

The first major stop was in the bustling textile town of Sherbrooke ("the 'bonne entente' of English-speaking and French-speaking Canadians," according to John Bassett, Jr., in the *Globe*; "here there is never a civic election, but alternate two-year terms for English and French mayors"). More than a hundred thousand people had gathered here from nearby points in Quebec and the United States (the highlight of the day, *before* the arrival of the King and Queen, had been when one of the excursion trains, while taking on water, had accidentally released a shower of soot and spray onto the well-dressed citizens on the station platform — thus raising a cheer from the bleachers). The skies were cloudy and high winds continued to blow as the royal couple emerged from their carriage. After the official welcome, they moved as usual towards the veterans massed at the station. There to greet them was Archdeacon Frederick Scott, "poet-padre" of the Canadian Army and the father of F. R. Scott. No slave to formality, Scott shook hands warmly with the royal couple, then introduced them to the daughter and widow of Colonel W. G. Barker, the much-decorated V.C. winner who had single-handedly defended an aerodrome in France against a large squadron of German planes. "At this point," wrote Bassett, "officialdom in the person of Prime Minister Mackenzie King and Mayor Marcus Armitage of Sherbrooke again took charge of the proceedings."

From Sherbrooke, the Royal Train ran along the track on the south side of the St. Lawrence, passing through communities like East Angus, where a million cords of wood had been used to construct a huge archway in the form of a castle. In spite of the cloudy and uncertain weather, people could be seen at every crossing and water tank, their horses often tethered to nearby snow fences. At one stop, the Queen came face to face with one of the anomalies of the Canadian mosaic — a group of French Canadians, all of whom proudly sported Highland names. But however routine the receptions had become for those aboard the pilot and the Royal trains, they were a novelty still for the people who farmed the seigneurial farms or worked in the bush country of the southern shore, and the welcomes were as warm and enthusiastic as Their Majesties had experienced anywhere.

By early evening, the Royal Train had reached Lévis, across from Quebec City. Homes and streets were decked out with flags and bunting from the Feast of Corpus Christi and these had been left up for the arrival of the King and Queen. Even the vivid orange and yellow trolley buses were decorated, and policemen paraded up and down like debutantes in their white gloves, carrying hat-boxes for their helmets in case it rained. There was no time to unveil the monument to the Royal Visit up on the steep cliffs, so officials had arranged for the five-ton piece of stone to be brought instead to the railway station for the ceremony. People, who had come to Lévis by bus, train, and ferry, perched on the cliffs to watch the proceedings, and sang the royal anthem in French. Maurice Duplessis was there, and he and Mackenzie King laughed and joked together in the easy and unnatural way of rival politicians. Once again, the warmth of the greeting from the crowd had the Queen in tears.

At Rivière-du-Loup, the royal couple also heard "God Save the King" sung in French, this time by an assembled choir who later serenaded the official party with a rollicking version of "Alouette". In a farewell address to the province of Quebec, George VI spoke of the attachment of French Canadians to the Crown, and his words were cheered by the assembled throng, whose size and enthusiasm surprised everyone. "There were moments," said the Prime Minister, "when it really looked as though the crowd might crush in upon the King and Queen." Here the poise learned by the royal couple in the past three weeks was apparent, particularly to reporters who had not seen them since Quebec City. "I have a feeling that the King rather enjoys having crowds surge about him," noted Mackenzie King shrewdly, having already observed how the potential danger posed by large and excitable groups of people served George VI as a kind of personal test of character. "He likes to make it apparent that he has no concern. . . ."

That evening, while the Royal Train trundled through the last few miles of the province, the Prime Minister was summoned to the royal carriages. He and the King sat together and chatted on a wide variety of topics, ranging from the discussions with Roosevelt ("What a fine fellow he is," said the King), political gossip and world affairs, to the Monroe Doctrine (which he asked Mackenzie King to explain to him), and, inevitably, the success of the tour.

> He said to me: "This trip has meant a great deal to me, and a great deal to the Queen." I said to him it ought to give him reason to feel that he could stand on his own. He asked me if I thought they had grasped a new idea of kingship. I was not exactly sure what he meant, and said: did he mean the common touch with the people, firsthand interest in their affairs? He said: yes, no more [of] the high hat business, the kind of thing that my father and those of his day regarded as essential, as the correct attitude. That certain things could not be done.

Tuesday, June 13:

In the morning, the Royal Train steamed through Campbellton, Dalhousie Junction, and Bathurst before stopping at Newcastle, where flowers were presented by Marjory Davidson, whose great-great-great-grandfather was William Davidson, the first British settler on the Miramichi in 1764. Here the King and Queen left the Royal Train for the 108-mile drive along the Miramichi to Fredericton. They did so reluctantly, for neither enjoyed long car rides, and the King's temper was not improving. But the weather at least was perfect, brilliant sunshine and a cool breeze, as they sped along the dusty roads of the old stage route.

Towards noon, they stopped for a half-hour rest in tiny Doaktown, and had tea at the home of Jimmie and Addie Gilks. Not surprisingly, the unscheduled stop took on a fabled character for the inhabitants.

The Gilkses ran a guest-house that catered to travellers on the road between Newcastle and Fredericton and to the many sportsmen who fished for salmon along the Miramichi which flowed just behind the house. For some weeks they had been aware of a flurry of activity among government officials, a number of whom had stopped and eaten at Doaktown, including RCMP Commissioner Stuart Wood and Major Randolph Crocker. None of this seemed unusual, given the elaborate preparations a Royal Visit would require. Like the other residents of the village, the Gilkses were expecting no more than a fine view of the royal couple as they swept through on their way to the city. But on June 12 a telegram was sent from the Royal Train to Major Crocker, asking him to arrange as discreetly as possible for a stop midway between Newcastle and Fredericton. And this set in motion one of the most memorable days in Addie Gilks's life. Later that same day, an Inspector Drysdale called, ordered supper, and asked the Gilkses if they could keep a secret. Their Majesties would be arriving the following afternoon with a party of twenty-five and would require some refreshment of tea and wafers. The Gilkses were to act no differently than they would for other guests and were asked to make no display. Addie Gilks, nearly overwhelmed by the news, assured Drysdale that they could be relied upon, then set about making preparations:

> Some people thought we should have had a carpet laid from the Royal car to the house and hot-house flowers for decorations; that however would not have been typical of an ordinary Canadian home. Their Majesties had never seen the inside of one, so this gave them opportunity. They had been entertained at many grand functions during the month, but the twenty-five minute visit at my house was the only stop of its kind during the whole tour.
>
> I was very glad on the morning of the thirteenth when I could see the grey dawn breaking. My husband and I had been keyed up to such a pitch that we were unable to sleep, so when the clock chimed four, I said, "Jimmie, let's get out of this as we are not sleeping!"

An advance guard of RCMP officers under an Inspector Farthing had arrived at the guest-house that night. They were up early as well, inspecting the premises "all over the place inside and out, continually on duty".

The house had to be put in order when breakfast was over. The only flowers used were purple and white lilacs which I mixed and placed in the centre of the table. We prepared tea-pots and trays, with their loads of cups and saucers, napkins, loaf-sugar, sliced lemons, milk and cream, and the little wafers. Then when we were all prepared and waiting the photographers from the Information Bureau insisted that we come outside and have our pictures taken.

We were told that the Royal Party would arrive about ten-thirty, but due to some delay they did not arrive until eleven o'clock. I cannot describe the thrill I experienced when at last we saw the Party coming through the arch, which had been erected as a welcome sign, just below our house. They approached so quickly that I thought "oh! they are not going to stop at all."

The pilot car and motor cycles came first turning speedily into our yard; the Royal car came next, and the first glimpse I had of our Sovereign almost took my breath away. I stood paralyzed for a moment, and my heart was in my mouth! After a moment I controlled myself—I was standing in the doorway — and Lieut. Colonel Piers Leigh . . . presented me to their Majesties. I bowed as they extended their hands, so I shook hands with the King and Queen. Wasn't it a wonderful experience?

We all entered the house and I presented James, my husband, to them. They shook hands with him also, and he bowing low over the Queen's hand, kissed it. He had remarked the night before, "I will kiss the Queen's hand, if it be the last thing I do on earth!"

Their Majesties chatted with us for a few minutes, then I left to superintend the serving of tea, thus I was in the dining-room directing the girls with the trays, and on glancing up there was the Queen at my side. Placing her hand on the table she said "we will have tea here."

We immediately arranged things, and our Royal Guests came to the dining-room accompanied by the Hon. Mr. Mackenzie King, Prime Minister of Canada, and one of the Ladies in Waiting to the Queen; Mr. Stafford Anderson, our local Member of Parliament, and Mrs. Anderson, his wife. They all seated themselves informally about the table. I poured tea for the King and Queen, placing their cups on a special silver tray, which I handed to one of the girls, who waited upon them.

Other girls served the remaining members of the party who scattered themselves about in the other rooms, on the verandah, and on the lawn. The King and Queen enjoyed their refreshments, and the few moments of peace and quietness, the King remarking, "this is a real pleasure."

When the meal was over I received a pleasant surprise. I was in the kitchen with my back to the door speaking to my husband, and on turning around, I saw our beloved King and Queen standing in the kitchen. They talked with us about fishing, inquiring what kind of fish were caught, when was our busiest season, and other matters of local interest. My husband was so taken back with their appearance in the kitchen that he was unable to retain his presence of mind enough to answer all the questions put to him. They chatted with us naturally and with as much interest as any other guests we have had in our home. One of the first remarks of the Queen was, "Oh! it is somewhat similar to an English Country Inn." I am sure their informal visit was enjoyed.

Their Majesties bowed to the girls assisting me, then returned through the dining-room to the front of the house. My husband and I accompanied them, and on passing the Guest Book, I summoned courage to say, "would I be asking too much for your signatures on my Guest Book?" Very graciously the King stopped and picking up the pen to write, hesitated as he inquired, "what is the date?" I promptly replied, "it is June the thirteenth, and we have been looking forward to this day for a long time." The King wrote the date and signed his name, and handing the pen to the Queen, spoke in an undertone, and she added her signature. I now treasure these signatures and have them in a frame under glass. I also treasure the cups they used, and the chairs they sat on. The chairs are now identified by inscribed brass plates marking the event, and screwed to their backs.

After signing the Guest Book the Equerry in Waiting took out his watch, and announced, "time's up." But their Majesties still lingered. . . . talked a few minutes more, then shook hands with us, and went out followed by their entourage. . . . Word had quickly circulated throughout the neighbourhood that their Majesties had stopped at the Gilks House, and what excitement the magic news gave rise to! Helter and skelter people ran in their desire to see and observe all.

When the Royal visitors appeared on the verandah steps before their departure, a hush fell on everybody. A woman told me since that she was stifled by her emotion. Another said she felt such deep reverence that she wished for complete silence; she was afraid she would miss seeing everything.

All was quiet for a brief spell, except for a robin in a near by tree singing gleefully, "Cheer up! cheer up!" Then spontaneously the crowd started to sing The National Anthem, "God Save The King." The Royal Party drove off resuming their way to Fredericton. A flood of wild cheering and singing broke out; the people's expression of loyalty and love. Never before had Doaktown given way to such emotion.

It was interesting and amusing to hear of little episodes which occurred during the Royal Visit to Doaktown and our house. Such as that of the woman who was lame for years, but when she heard of their Majesties presence in the village became so excited that she forgot her infirmity and ran as she had not done since childhood, in her eagerness to be present at the stirring event.

Another lady crawled under a wire fence in her excitement and being of portly build became wedged between the fence and the ground. This was not dignified, but who cared? Were not the King and Queen here?

My husband and I have pleasant memories of the visit of the late King, the beloved George VI, and our Queen Mother Elizabeth, to our house to cherish for the rest of our lives. Sometimes we take these memories out and talk about them as if they were rare gems. If we possessed the Hope Diamond, we could not prize it more.

It's not hard to imagine what a relief it would be for the King and Queen to exchange speeches of welcome and honour guards for the pleasures of an ordinary home and tea in "very plain cups". And there is a postscript to the story about Their Majesties' short stay in Doaktown. J. E. Michaud was Minister of Fisheries in 1939, and like every other minister in the Dominion Cabinet took his turn accompanying the royal party through his own region. According to his son, Jacques Michaud, discreet measures had been taken at the Gilkses' for the "comfort" of the Queen and her ladies-in-waiting, but for some unfathomable reason tour officials had completely forgotten about the King:

> My father, noticing the mounting royal discomfort, suggested that relief might be found at the back of the large barn next to the farmhouse. It is thus that my dad stood shoulder to shoulder with his Monarch, while relieving themselves on the side of a barn in the Miramichi (Lord Beaverbrook country) surrounded by a protective cordon of RCMP, all discreetly looking the other way.
>
> I often had the occasion to chauffeur my father around New Brunswick after he became Chief Justice of the Queen's Bench Division, and it was during our passage through Doaktown in 1955 that he told me the story, noting that he had often been sorely tempted to put up a commemorative plaque on the barn which was still standing at a sharp bend in the road. My father was a very close-mouthed individual who was not prone to small talk or gossip. He also had an immense respect for the Monarchy, as did most French Canadians at that time, and I never heard him tell this story to anyone again.

The rest of the journey to Fredericton was completed with the top of the royal limousine up because of the chill in the air and the dust that billowed up from the road. Early in the afternoon, the royal party reached the provincial capital with its pleasant streets shaded by the early June foliage. Seventy-five hundred children waited to greet them at the Parliament Buildings. Also waiting, unfortunately, was a large line-up of dignitaries — so many, in fact, that "before it was over, Their Majesties were wringing their hands with pain." The official welcome to New Brunswick came from Premier Allison Dysart in the Assembly Chamber beneath the portraits of George III and Queen Charlotte, a reminder that a great part of New Brunswick was Loyalist country. One hundred additional guests were on hand for the provincial luncheon at Beaverbrook Hall in the Lady Beaverbrook Building, where the royal party dined on lobster caught at the mouth of Saint John Harbour. As nearly everywhere else, chicken was the main course, but served in this instance with truffles, mushrooms, foie gras, and a cream sherry sauce. One of the waiters at the headtable was Leo Legere, who normally worked at the Admiral Beatty Hotel in Saint John. "Leo returned to Saint John," recalled his son Edmund, "not only with great pride in having been given the honour of serving Their Majesties, but with a celluloid tube inscribed HRH, which contained a similarly stamped cigarette (in 1945, fifteen-year-old Edmund, desperate for a smoke, opened the tube but found, after one puff, that the royal tobacco was far too strong for him).

After a final drive along Fredericton's elm-shaded streets, the royal party boarded a special train that took them on the seventy-mile run to Saint John. Late in the afternoon they again climbed into their waiting limousines at Fairvale and proceeded into the city along cobblestoned streets, past the spot where the first United Empire Loyalists had landed in 1774. There were clear skies, a tangy sea breeze from the Bay of Fundy, and a greeting from the population of fifty thousand (including ten thousand schoolchildren) so boisterous that reporters accorded it the noisiest reception since New York City. "A wonderful sight," wrote Mackenzie King, "seeing the Province as we climbed rocky hills with great crowds on the sides." Union Jacks were everywhere in Saint John, fire hydrants were painted red and silver, and, to mark this special day, a special collection had been taken up to provide food for the poor and needy. But the King, in spite of his cheerful behaviour in public, was still in a black mood from the dust-filled motor ride that morning. At the Admiral Beatty Hotel, where they had stopped for a short rest, he strode impatiently past a clutch of waiting dignitaries to where Leo Legere was standing. "Leo," the King said, "*where is it?*" — and Legere took him into the royal suite and showed him the bathroom. Before leaving Saint John, the royal couple heard "God Save the King" sung once again in French, watched a sail-past by the Saint John yacht squadron, and, as if in response to the public's ceaseless fascination with both royalty and multiple births, met Saint John's famous Mahaney Quadruplets.

Back aboard the Royal Train once more, they had a quick view of the Reversing Falls before whizzing through Sussex to Moncton, where fifteen thousand jammed into Station Square and a further ten thousand stood along the rail line. Arrangements had been made for four thousand children to march past the platform, and the King, with his fine sense of punctuality, finally suggested that the band play something more lively to keep things moving. ("H.M. has seen the importance of hurrying the events and not letting anything drag.") Then it was Dorchester, Sackville, and, finally, their destination for the night, Cape Tormentine on New Brunswick's north coast.

Wednesday, June 14:

Under grey skies and a heavy pouring rain — weather that locals obligingly told the press was the worst they could remember — thirty thousand people had arrived during the night from as far away as Amherst, Springhill, and Sackville. They stood patiently in the wet, straining for a glimpse of the King and Queen, but so much in the mood for celebration that they happily cheered everyone who poked his face out from either train: the engineers climbing down from their locomotives, the Mounties who walked about, drenched and uncomfortable, and even the photographers emerging from time to time to consider the chances of snapping a decent picture. A brief appearance by the royal couple set off wild applause, and in spite of the police the crowd scampered after the train as it moved slowly along the track to where the long grey destroyer *Skeena* lay moored at the pier. At dockside, the Queen extended a hand from beneath her black umbrella to test the weather and spoke to the King; the King, shivering in his Admiral's uniform, apparently agreed with her and said, "Let's go"; and they hurried over the track cinders and along the duckboards to the gangplank. By this time, those who had shown a fine disdain for fences and police lines had caught up to Their Majesties. They stopped of their own accord, about six feet away, and sent up a volley of cheers to which the royal couple responded with smiles and a wave of the hand.

It was the worst weather of the tour. The rain came down in cold sheets as they made the 2½-hour journey across the Northumberland Strait, and except for a brief let-up in Charlottetown, continued for the entire day. Royal enthusiasm being what it was, the crowd was large and heedless of the elements, and Charlottetown Harbour was full of speedboats, old coal and potato schooners, and fishing smacks to welcome them. The King remembered his earlier visit in 1913, and long before they arrived he was on the bridge, swathed in his slicker and gazing intently at the red cliffs ahead.

The royal convoy came into harbour in suitably dramatic fashion, with the destroyer *Saguenay* in escort, three large RCAF bombers flying overhead, and the guns thundering out from Fort Edward. A smart honour guard of P.E.I. Highlanders waited at Marine Wharf, and from there they drove up the wide and extravagantly decorated avenue to Province House and a ceremonial welcome from Premier Thane Campbell. In the Confederation Chamber, they met a number of dignitaries, including ninety-four-year-old Mrs. Aremas Lord of Souris, daughter of one of the Fathers of Confederation.

The torrential rains that had torn and scattered many of Charlottetown's elaborate decorations had not affected the crowds that day. Thirty-five thousand people were gathered along the streets of the provincial capital, including five thousand children brought in by special trains and buses from all over the Island. Shirley Jay, who lived on a farm twenty miles east of Charlottetown, remembered coming in on the train that morning, dressed in new clothes for the occasion:

> A special train was put on and there were no toilets. Being a small child, of course, I immediately needed a bathroom. I distinctly remember the chamber pots under the seats — provided for just such an emergency. It poured rain the whole time we crowded in for a glimpse of the King and Queen. Of course, our new clothes were ruined but my parents didn't seem to mind.

For most of the morning, Islanders had endured the bad weather, and stood in orderly rows along the royal route. The eventual appearance of the King and Queen on the Legislature balcony, however, was a signal for royal hysteria. For the rest of the day, people ran from place to place, wherever the royal couple were scheduled to appear — trampling lawns, invading the streets, crowding close to the procession of limousines in hopes of one more look at Their Majesties. The closest most of them got was outside the Legislative Assembly when the Queen saw a line-up of disabled veterans in worn berets and with campaign ribbons on their serge jackets, and immediately led the King over to them.

His Majesty was once again not in the best of tempers, having discovered as he came ashore in the rain that he could not even get a restorative glass of whisky. Prince Edward Island remained teetotal in 1939, and it was naturally felt that the Sovereign would set a good example. The situation was tremendously embarrassing to the Lieutenant-Governor, George des Brisay De Blois, and his wife. "I felt particularly sorry for the Governor," wrote Mackenzie King of that luncheon, which, "much too long and elaborate", had begun with the King slipping on the stairs (and uttering a mild oath), persevered through a few miscues by the servants and an awkward moment when the King groused about the noise the orchestra was making, and ended finally with the assembled guests rising to drink the royal couple's health with unfermented grape juice. And as if Prohibition, royal temperament, and social catastrophe weren't enough to deal with, there was still the weather.

Outside Government House, where the rain continued to drizzle down, more than 1,500 people had gathered for the garden party scheduled for that afternoon. While waiting for Their Majesties to make an appearance, the invited guests abandoned their dignity to crowd under umbrellas, huddle under the marquees, or, in some cases, hug the walls of the white mansion. The efforts were only partly successful, and a number of expensive gowns and morning suits had been pretty thoroughly soaked before the decision was made to cancel the event. A few people were admitted to Government House for a quick word and nod from the royal couple, and then the King and Queen emerged and briefly wandered the grounds from group to group. Through it all, the band of the Light Horse Guards played cheerfully on. At 4:30, the royal procession returned to Marine Wharf, followed every step of the way by the crowds that burst over the fences and past the guards in their enthusiasm.

Another choppy crossing on the *Skeena*, uneventful except for rumours of seasickness among the royal party — and the appearance in the royal quarters of a special cake baked by the ship's cook. "Well iced, but so large that no one would wish to break into it," according to the Prime Minister, who was sitting over a cup of tea with Their Majesties and his ailing Finance Minister, Charles Dunning. None of them could face a crumb after the elaborate spread at Government House. As usual, it was the Queen who took the initiative, cutting a slice and instructing the King to open the porthole. "It would not do," she said, "to have the cook think that the cake had not been appreciated."

They came ashore at Pictou, where Nova Scotia's Scots had landed more than 150 years earlier — and where 15,000 descendants were huddled in heavy coats against winds that sent their hats skimming crazily over the patchwork countryside. "It was pretty windy," Mackenzie King noted sourly, "and the mayor was anything but gifted in arranging matters." Never mind. There was a welcome in Gaelic, the pipers played the "Skye Boat Song", and the Queen, in a suit of periwinkle blue, accepted a bouquet of sunset roses and chatted with a group of nurses from the Great War. And, as elsewhere, the placidity of the crowd lasted only as long as the scene remained generally static. But when the royal party moved to the waiting limousines for the fifteen-minute ride to New Glasgow, the crowd shook off its trance and rushed forward for a better view. In the words of the local journalist who signed herself "Evangeline":

> We made a dash for the main street, to catch another glimpse of Their Majesties. We saw decorous matrons sprinting uphill, hair flying, clutching flags in one hand and camp stools in the other. . . . When they had passed, a heavy-set miner in his working clothes turned a shining face to his companion saying, "Isn't it wonderful, we have seen them."

In New Glasgow, the streets were lined with thousands of miners, including the draegermen of Stellarton (famous across North America for their part in the dramatic rescue attempts two years earlier at the Moose River Mine), who were there to provide first aid. Also on hand were two hundred striking miners from Sydney who had arrived, dirty, cold, and hungry, after hitchhiking along miles of muddy roads to get there. Tour officials were worried at first that these men might attempt to petition the King, but the visit was completed without incident. As one miner said to a reporter, "All this countryside has been scarred with trouble, strikes and disasters. But today differences are forgotten and wet eyes are dried."

The royal party made its way through the dense crowds to the Royal Train, which was waiting for them at the New Glasgow railway station. But, when they arrived, people thronged about the rear of the train in such numbers that the King finally told the besieged Prime Minister to climb up into the royal car — which he did to gratifying applause, nevertheless afraid that in the crush "the King and Queen might not escape uninjured." The royal couple, however, seemed once more to have recovered their spirits, and remained for a long time on the observation platform. It was as well they did, since the train had been unhitched and for the moment no one knew where the Royal Train's engine was. When the locomotive was finally located and the train moved out, it was discovered that the water had been turned off in the Married Quarters — and the King lapsed once again into a bad temper.

The last night on the Royal Train was spent on a siding east of Truro. With the King finally restored to something like good humour, he and the Queen entertained Mackenzie King to dinner as a farewell gesture. The next day they would complete the last sixty miles of the eight-thousand-mile jaunt across the continent and back; the most famous train in Canadian history would then carry Lord Tweedsmuir, the Prime Minister, and members of the Interdepartmental Committee back to Ottawa before it was broken up and its engines and carriages were put back on their normal runs. That night, the only sounds that broke the stillness of the Nova Scotia countryside were those of the twenty-six reporters who had stayed behind in New Glasgow to finish their stories, and who blundered, dripping wet and swearing mildly, into the RCMP picket that surrounded the two trains.

Thursday, June 15:

After a peaceful night's rest, Mackenzie King rose shortly after seven. His thoughts on the last day of the Royal Tour were "mostly of the service which, from now on, I would like to render to the people of Canada by way of particular attention to the problems of the poor, and, above all, the promotion of peace. . . ."

The blue and silver Royal Train shunted into Truro a little after nine in the morning, and among the twenty thousand on hand to greet them in the sunshine was the oldest pair of twins in the British Empire ("two elderly women of about 93") and Lord and Lady Tweedsmuir, who climbed aboard. Tommy Lascelles whisked them instantly away to the Married Quarters, where Mackenzie King learned later that Tweedsmuir had received a G.C.V.O. (Knight Grand Cross of the Royal Victorian Order); his Secretary, Shuldham Redfern, a knighthood; and the Government House Comptroller, Colonel Eric Mackenzie, a C.V.O. (Commander of the Royal Victorian Order). The Prime Minister pouted when he found out ("typical of exclusiveness of Englishmen in that they did not make mention of the matter to me . . . considering that I was P.M."). About eleven, the Royal Train stopped outside Halifax for an official portrait.

> The location was not a good one. The photographer had to get on top of a bathing house with his tripod. The Queen said to me: What a fortunate thing it was that the little chicken house was located there, or we would have had difficulty in getting a picture. . . . I was interested in watching how the King took charge of the arrangements themselves. Told everyone where they should stand, and how they should stand. The Queen invited me to come and stand to her left. She, the King and I each had a railway tie as a place to stand.

Just before noon, the Royal Train circled around Bedford Basin, passing by a lonely bandstand by the edge of the water, all that remained of the Duke of Kent's estate. Skirting the North End of the city (flattened with the loss of two thousand lives by the great Explosion of 1917), they reached Union Station, where Lieutenant-Governor Robert Irwin, Premier Angus L. Macdonald, and others waited to greet them. As if desperate for the last bits of formality to be completed, the King and Queen descended from their carriage so quickly that Mackenzie King was forced to break into a run to make it to the reception platform in time for the customary introductions. While this was going on, the sixty-five porters, trainmen, cooks, waiters, and police of the Royal Train lined up beside the blue and silver carriages. Then they were presented one by one to Their Majesties by Eph Coleman of the Interdepartmental Committee.

After a last cheer from the staff of the Royal Train, the King and Queen moved through the crowds to their waiting limousine for the short trip to Province House. Others in their entourage were not so fortunate. People had been massed around the station in huge numbers all morning, some standing on train carriages while others, principally children, clung perilously to the nearby power-line tower. With the royal couple leaving, they surged forward for a last look. Two ladies-in-waiting were cut off from the official cars, and the Tweedsmuirs only reached theirs with difficulty. So many people had descended on the city (perhaps as many as a hundred thousand) that hundreds had reportedly walked the streets all night looking for a place to sleep, and even ships in the harbour had been pressed into service to provide beds. Those parts of the royal route not buried in Union Jacks and bunting that morning (a little sodden from rain the day before) were covered by cheering humanity as the King in his Admiral's uniform and the Queen wearing her favourite shade of blue waved, smiled, saluted, and passed by. The crowd in turn waved, smiled, cheered, and tried desperately to get the couple into range of their view-finders.

There was the official welcome at Province House, a bouquet from the Premier's daughter, Coline, handshakes with the Members, and the official unveiling of a portrait of the late George V. At the civic reception on the Grand Parade, the Halifax sun was so hot that several councillors could be seen with their heads draped in handkerchiefs while waiting for the royal couple to arrive. The Mayor remembered the King from May of 1913, when they had both attended a tea-dance at Government House. The young Prince Bertie, attached to the *Cumberland*, had been reserved and quiet that night; it had been the young Walter Mitchell who had made a splash, having just returned from New York with the latest footwear — a pair of brightly coloured suede shoes. Now shod in conservative leather, he introduced the dignitaries, including Chief William

Paul of the Micmacs, who wore around his neck a large silver medal that had been presented to the tribe in the time of George III.

After the government luncheon at the Nova Scotian Hotel Their Majesties rose to deliver their farewell addresses to the Dominion. The speeches were be heard across North America, in Europe, and around the world, and the BBC's Richard Dimbleby was scheduled to introduce the broadcast. Unfortunately, he had arrived at the entrance to the Nova Scotian's banquet-room without his proper invitation. The sergeant at the door had strict orders regarding unauthorized persons entering the room, and was not going to make an exception for this large and over-excited Englishman. Dimbleby, growing desperate as air time approached, tried a second and a third time before finally charging in. After a few minutes of grappling with the guards, he was rescued by someone from the royal party and, dishevelled and with his press armband ripped away but in the best traditions of journalism and show business, he arrived at the microphone as the broadcast was about to begin.

The King's address was an emotional one, sincere and deeply felt. Speaking in both English and French, he told Canadians how much the tour had meant to himself and the Queen personally. And in spite of the fatigue that had descended on him in these last days, the occasional fits of temper, the apparent boredom he showed from time to time with the formal moments, what he said was the truth. It *had* been a wonderful tour, it *had* moved him deeply — sometimes to tears — to see the affection in which he was held by the ordinary people of this country. He had received a welcome of which "the memory will always be dear" — not least because of the contrast North America presented to the deteriorating situation in Europe:

> From the Atlantic to the Pacific, and from the tropics to the Arctic, lies a large part of the earth where there is no possibility of war between neighbours, whose peoples are wholly dedicated to the pursuits of peace, a pattern to all men of how civilized nations should live together.

He sat down to loud applause, adjusted his tie, sipped his drink, and watched as his wife stepped to the microphone. She confessed to Mackenzie King later that "when the King spoke it was all she could do to keep from crying," and he felt the same way now as she told the audience how touched she had been by the women and children she had met and by the miles people had come to see them.

> This wonderful tour of ours has given me memories that the passage of time will never dim. To the people of Canada and to all the kind people in the United States who welcomed us so warmly last week — to one and all on this great friendly continent, I say thank you. God be with you and God bless you. Au revoir et que Dieu vous bénisse.

To the Prime Minister, who watched her from the head table, she seemed at that moment "benignly vested with humility". When she had finished, the orchestra played "God Save the King" one last time, the luncheon guests standing silently except for "the L-G. and his wife singing the words, and myself keeping company with them pretty much by going through the motions."

In the afternoon, the King and Queen took a more extensive drive through the city. They visited Camp Hill Hospital to shake hands and chat with the veterans on the lawn, among them Jigger MacDonald, a double amputee well known on the streets of Halifax. At the Garrison sports ground, along with 75,000 others camped on the side of Citadel Hill, they watched an elaborate historical pageant on the founding of Nova Scotia. Afterwards, the Premier had a surprise in store for them. Angus L. Macdonald had pressed repeatedly to be allowed to present the Salteria triplets—Mary Elizabeth, Marion Ann, and Mary Louise — but the Interdepartmental Committee had just as steadfastly refused. The "silly fuss" seemed to have died down for good until the royal party strolled across the street from the Garrison grounds, whereupon, in Hugh Keenleyside's words, "the triplets and their parents popped out of a clump of trees and, of course, the Premier presented the sticky little monsters to the King and Queen."

Having now dealt with a representation of the country's quints, quads, and triplets, the royal couple continued on to a grassy plot where they threw four shovelfuls of earth around a tree planted on their Coronation Day. The King then got into an animated discussion with the gardener about his greatest enthusiasm, rhododendrons, before they set off for a quiet tea with Lieutenant-Governor Irwin at Government House.

What was apparent, even to those in the crowd who only saw him for a moment, was that George VI was nearing the point of exhaustion, indeed had almost reached it several times in the past few days, and that only the imminent end of the long journey and the Queen's emotional support had kept him going. As Mackenzie King later wrote about the Lieutenant-Governor's tea:

> The King was obviously tired but managed to keep the conversation going fairly well. I wished I could have assisted him a little more. We had, however, another round of exhibiting my cigarette case, and the little box I had of matches for lighting his cigarettes. Used the little box for two more cigarettes for the King.

There was one last noisy and emotion-draining scene to be played out before the King and Queen said their final goodbyes to Canada that day. All the city and half the province seemed to have found their way down to Pier 20 that evening where the 42,000-ton *Empress of Britain* was moored, waiting to carry the royal party back to England. People clung to rooftops, and nearly spilled over the top of the Nova Scotian Hotel. The thousands along the quay echoed the chants that had been heard right across the country: "We want the King! We want the Queen!" Returned soldiers, in their own special place at the dockside, sang "Tipperary" and "We'll Never Let the Old Flag Fall", and dissolved into bedlam when the royal couple arrived, and the King passed down their ranks. And, in a final gesture of farewell, Angus L. Macdonald, who had spoken earlier that day to the Queen in Gaelic, now stooped and kissed her hand in the manner of an old Highland chieftain.

Aboard the *Empress of Britain*, the royal couple were shown to their suites (the King occupying the same one Mackenzie King had used on his way to the coronation); then there was an informal farewell in the ship's library to the reporters, radiomen, and photographers who had followed them across the continent. Pallie Pascoe was there, along with his fellow postal workers Bill Ross and Lou Gignac. They had worked hard until four o'clock that afternoon; then, after a quick bath, shave, and haircut, they had presented themselves at "the Royal Boat". The proceedings by now were so relaxed that the Queen for the first time led the way around the circle of men and women. "They really shook hands," reported Pallie. "Bill Ross was presented with a cigarette case, and Lou and I received a silver pencil, all bearing the Royal coat of arms and I'll have that until I'm carried away." And there was a special goodbye to the Mounties who had guarded them on the trip across the Dominion — Sgt. Williams and Constables Coughlin, Langlois, and Portelance.

Afterwards, in a more private meeting with members of the royal party, Mackenzie King received a large volume signed by the King and Queen recording the history of the Royal Oaks planted throughout the Empire at the time of the coronation. It was, the Queen assured him, for his own personal library at Laurier House.

> I carried away in my mind of our last talk together a picture of the Queen talking to me in a very sweet and beautiful way, the King almost leaning on her right shoulder and standing, as it were, a little above her, talking to me as I held in my hand the large volume. . . .

Afterwards, he dawdled around outside the suite while the Governor General said his final goodbyes to the royal couple, aware as always of the symbolism of the moment, and determined that he and Tweedsmuir should leave the ship together after saying goodbye to the King.

The crowd at dockside meanwhile had continued to sing, chant, and grow in excitement as the minutes ticked past the scheduled seven-o'clock sailing time. At last Mackenzie King came bustling down the gangplank, followed by the Governor General, the gangplank was hauled in, hawser cables were cast off, and the ship began to move slowly, almost imperceptibly, away from the pier. The royal couple appeared on the bridge to wave (the Queen being nearly invisible until one of the ship's officers found her a chair to stand on). Like seasoned performers who tease an audience and always leave them wanting more, they appeared again and again at the railing, always brought back by the fervent shouting. The soldiers led the crowd in "Auld

Lang Syne", because at times like this old times are always the best times. "God Save the King" broke out from a dozen different places in the crowd.

Hundreds of boats, large and small, all gaily decked out in bunting, formed up around her. Slowly the tugs nosed the *Empress* into the centre of the harbour. Slowly she passed, turned, and passed the pier again with her naval escort: *Skeena, Saguenay, Glasgow,* and *Southampton,* and with an escort of smaller vessels led by the great *Bluenose,* champion of the North Atlantic fishing fleets. "Yes, it *has* to be farewell now," said the radio commentator:

> The Royal Yacht is picking up speed as she moves by us. The King and Queen are waving to all on shore. And we're waving back as hard as we can. We're sorry to see them go. The days from May 17th have gone too fast. . . .

On the Halifax breakwater, where in a few short months wives and sweethearts would gather to watch as the convoys moved out, a nine-hundred-voice choir sang "Auld Lang Syne" and "Will Ye No' Come Back Again". The ship moved out to sea on water as smooth and glossy as silk — and into the flaming glow of the sunset. Fishermen at Chebucto Head prepared to light their giant bonfire. "No farewell could have been finer," in Mackenzie King's words, "than that given by the day, the people and the country." The last glimpse he had of them was "the King standing at the side of the Queen and the Queen with hand upraised, the light shining on it. . . . "

People on shore waved long after they could be seen. And far out to sea, the figures of the King and Queen could be discerned standing on the bridge, waving, waving, waving back. The *Empress* grew steadily smaller, the sun dipped below the horizon, and darkness fell.

CHAPTER TWELVE

A Country of the Larger Air

BEFORE THE *EMPRESS OF BRITAIN* was even out of sight, there were signs that the old discords, which had been largely held in check during the Royal Visit, were reawakening. Mackenzie King could sense a sudden distancing between himself and Lord Tweedsmuir as they trotted off the *Empress of Britain*. "T. saw me standing there near the head of the stairs, but doing so, however, he turned quickly towards his wife and did not look in my direction again, but walked down the stairs as though he had been surprised I had not left the ship before him." That small incident was enough to arouse the Prime Minister's barely dormant suspicions ("Evidently, there had been in his mind that it should be of record that he was the last to leave the ship after saying goodbye to the King"). Affronted by what he took to be the Governor General's coolness, he resolved to be a little difficult himself. As the two men made their way to the CPR Building where the official party was to be seated for the Royal Yacht's final sail-past, "I allowed myself to fall considerably behind and make it rather difficult for members of his staff to try to keep me up with the others. . . . " The gesture was probably lost on the Tweedsmuirs, who, to the consternation of those present, swanned off somewhere on their own. Mackenzie King let it pass for the moment. Gathering with Sir Edward Beatty, Angus L. Macdonald, and others on the balcony, he waved the *Empress* out of sight, the scene "like a bit of grand opera and a highly triumphal note at the close".

At dinner with the Tweedsmuirs later that night, Mackenzie King congratulated "H.E." upon the honour he had received

from the King after being shown "the particular star, or whatever it was. . . . " Afterwards, he and Arnold Heeney got away
as soon was decently possible to the Nova Scotian Hotel to
shake a few hands with the press. A large dinner had been laid
on for the passengers of the pilot train ("at which I believe
some of us at least took a couple of extra trips to the Punch
Bowl," wrote Pallie) and Walter Thompson of the CNR was
being honoured for having achieved the impossible — keeping
both the reporters and the royal party happy. This was certainly a more congenial atmosphere for Mackenzie King than
the one he had just left, and he joined in the merriment. "We
did an awful lot of singing," Pallie recorded of that night, "but
from PRIME MINISTER Mackenzie King down to myself, a
grand time was had and all acted like a bunch of youngsters
who had been good too long."

The Royal Train's journey back to Ottawa was a leisurely
one for members of the Interdepartmental Committee. Eph
Coleman, Hugh Keenleyside, Stuart Wood, Frank Delaute,
Howard Measures, and many others could sit back in satisfaction over a job well done. They had attended to all the
finicky details, soothed ruffled feathers, crossed their fingers
on occasion, and generally kept everything running smoothly.
Now they caught up on their rest, met in the lounge, or simply
watched the countryside go by. The Prime Minister was enjoying the trip as well, particularly when he could look out, as he
did at Matapédia, and see a crowd of children gathered around
the blue and silver train, calling out, "We want Mackenzie
King!"—although, as he noted with a prim delight in his diary,
he was careful not to go out of the car, "or to permit any
demonstration". And he had his own reward, beyond the
praises of the King and Queen which continued to ring in his
ears. He had ordered a new suede circular collar-box with a
drawstring top, upon which he had engraved in silver:
"W.L.M.K. — Royal Visit 1939. A Present To Myself."

The Royal Train arrived back in Ottawa on Saturday, June
17, and the Prime Minister, bronzed by weeks of hot sunshine
on railway platforms and exultant in the tour's great success,
told reporters, "I am feeling 100 per cent better than when the
tour started." And it was true. In spite of the unpredictable
hours, the stiff and solemn occasions that required yet another

change of clothes, and the rich diet of banquet dishes ("particularly lobster, cucumbers, and other indigestible things"), he felt fitter than he had in years.

> When I arrived at Laurier House I took little Pat in my arms and carried him into the morning room. He seemed to know I was coming home, was feeling his way, wagging his tail, to the open door. We had an affectionate reunion. . . . He barked in the elevator and again and again in the library. I went direct to dear Mother's painting, then knelt down at the accustomed seat and thanked God for having brought the King and Queen safely through the long journey. . . .

The pressing problems of the nation could wait a few more days. Saturday afternoon, Mackenzie King set off for Kingsmere, his retreat in the Gatineau Hills, thinking it best to "get to the woods and the streams for a few days to sort out the many impressions of the trip". He read over some mail and walked around the grounds with friends, noting the generally good condition of the shrubs, the iris, and — "particularly pleasing" — the herbaceous borders. After dinner, he read aloud from "Gray's Elegy", and before retiring around 10:30 looked over the latest dispatches and their anxious news of Japan's increasingly warlike actions:

> I had a good night's sleep, very sound. Little Pat slept equally sound at my side, took him in beside me for a few minutes after waking. Before breakfast we went for our walk down the Open Road, between the trees leading from the house to the field, there I burst out into song "Holy Holy Holy" — "There is a Happy Land", and later "Oh God of Bethel". Pat and I walked to the Stone where we each gave our pledge of faith anew to each other — Pat barking at me as we stood together on the stone in the bright sun. . . .

Pallie Pascoe meanwhile had made his way back to Saskatchewan. After seeing Lou Gignac off at Lévis, and Bill Ross at Ottawa, and after a few short visits with friends along the way, he arrived in Regina on June 18:

> Ada was there to meet me with the car, and boy, I was kind of glad to see her when she walked into the station. We stayed

at Regina that night, attended a Ladies' Night at the Lions' Club with about 20 Moose Jaw Lions and their wives. Drove to Moose Jaw June 19th landing about 5.00 P.M. tired, but happy and so ended the greatest of all my experiences including the War. And now I stand just a little steadier, feel a little stronger and a little more important when and where I hear— "GOD SAVE THE KING!"

Meanwhile, the *Empress of Britain*, flagship of the Canadian Pacific fleet and fastest liner on the Atlantic run, had been steaming towards Newfoundland at a steady twenty-four knots. At twice the tonnage of the *Australia*, the ship was too large to enter St. John's Harbour, and the small convoy had made instead for Conception Bay on the east side of the island. Early in the morning of the sixteenth, off Cape Race, the cruiser *Berwick* from the America and West Indies Squadron had joined the liner and her two remaining escort vessels *Glasgow* and *Southampton*, and by evening the four ships had entered Conception Bay and, passing a huge iceberg in the distance, cast anchor off Bell Island.

Next morning in a pouring rain the royal couple welcomed the Governor of Newfoundland, Sir Humphrey Walwyn, and his wife aboard ship, and then together they embarked in the royal barge for the nine-mile voyage over heaving seas to Holyrood at the head of the bay. There, an honour guard had been formed by a double line of schooners, cutters, and small coastal boats — working ships, many of them piled high with lumber and fishing supplies, that gloried in names like *Saladin*, *McGloshen*, *Agnes*, *Shulamite*, and *Marvita*. Acknowledging the cheers of the villagers, the King and Queen stepped into the Humber car for the hour's drive to St. John's. Twenty-one archways of fir and spruce had been constructed along the route, which meandered through twelve tiny villages on the Avalon Peninsula, and all along the road shy knots of people stood, hoping for a glimpse and a wave. "Paradise greets their Majesties" read one sign — but on this day there was rain, mud, cold, and the evidence of economic conditions so desperate they had forced Newfoundland to abandon its Dominion status for the benevolent rule of a colonial administration.

The official party arrived in St. John's before noon, and was met by city and colonial officials near the spot where, according to tradition, Sir Humphrey Gilbert had raised the flag of England more than 350 years before. The capital of the Ancient Colony was a continuous blaze of bunting, and its population of 15,000, true to the pattern of Canadian cities, had doubled almost literally overnight. Here, also, houses along the royal route were swathed in Union Jacks, shops boasted patriotic displays in their windows, and the streets were lined by cheering people, including thousands of schoolchildren brought in for the day. Together, the King in his Admiral's undress uniform and the Queen bundled up in periwinkle blue mounted the pavilion inside the city entrance. A day's rest aboard the *Empress* and a few games of deck tennis had done wonders for His Majesty, and he made a good speech to the crowd, touching on the Island's hard times and expressing hope for the future.

At grey-stoned Government House, he inspected an honour guard of veterans from the Royal Newfoundland Regiment; laid a wreath during a short service at the war memorial; met with Thomas Ricketts, the youngest Victoria Cross winner in the British Empire; and, with the Queen, planted two commemorative oak trees. At the Governor's garden party that afternoon, the Guards played "Ode to Newfoundland", while the royal couple made their way through long lines of the distinguished and the deserving. Then, in what had become a familiar and popular gesture, they walked over to the iron railings that surrounded the grounds of Government House to chat with the people standing outside. There was one more event before the King and Queen left St. John's, a visit to the Feildian Grounds, where the Boy Scouts, Girl Guides, Church Lads Brigade, and Salvation Army Life Guards gave them a tumultuous greeting. Then there was the forty-mile journey to Portugal Cove, their touring car finally descending the steep hills to the fishing village where the *Empress* and her escorts waited offshore in a growing gale.

But Their Majesties' day was not yet over. The itinerary called for visits to all three escort vessels — a perilous undertaking in the choppy seas and gathering darkness. With the unreliability of some of the smaller launches, this became an authentic adventure. The royal couple were forced to brave the elements as they jumped for companion ladders and balanced on the edge of boats while transferring nine times in all between various vessels, before finally making it back to the *Empress of Britain* late that evening. They had suffered no more than a slight drenching from the spray, although a sailor aboard the liner, a twenty-three-year-old Newfoundlander, had earlier fallen to his death while tying down a lifeboat cover. By the time the convoy had rounded Cape St. Francis, the seas were running higher than ever. Three miles beyond the narrow harbour of St. John's, the powerful searchlights of the warships gave a final salute to Newfoundland, and from Signal Hill a huge bonfire sprang up in farewell.

The *Empress* made good time on the return journey. The air above the Atlantic remained cool and her passengers saw little of the sun, but the fog and ice that had halted the ships in their sea lanes on the way west just a month before did no more than slow them down from time to time. The *Empress*, with its full-size tennis courts, giant swimming-pool, and Turkish bath, seemed virtually deserted with just the small royal entourage aboard. In the panelled dining-room, decorated in pink and dotted with a grove of artificial palms, eight tables were laid by a staff used to serving a shipboard complement of four hundred. Here the King and Queen sampled the ship's fare, or dined on the bounty of the Dominion: deer and beef from Ontario, maple syrup from Quebec, buffalo from the West, shrimp, live lobster, and halibut from Nova Scotia, and Gaspé salmon from the season's first run — as well as fresh cream, milk, and eggs.

Everyone in the party was tired from the exertions of the past four weeks ("I think we must have seen everybody in Canada" was how the King put it), and yet as relieved as they were to be free of the never-ending formalities, the constant din of the crowd, and the narrow confines of the Royal Train, a melancholy could be detected among the group as day after day they rode the great empty ship on an empty sea. The royal couple made infrequent appearances on the deck, although the King showed a little of his Wimbledon form from time to time on the tennis court. People caught up on their sleep, and, in the evening, gathered to watch some of the King's efforts at filming the tour. They began to talk with longing about the first sighting of the white cliffs on England's southern coast. There was some light cricket practice.

On the final night of the voyage, the royal flotilla ran into its first bad weather. Rain and heavy winds swept over the ships, and by the early morning of June 22, they were feeling their way slowly up the English Channel in a heavy fog. The scheduled review of the Home Fleet, planned as one of the greatest naval receptions in British history, had been cancelled because of the uncertainty of the elements, but two flights from the aircraft-carrier *Ark Royal* buzzed overhead in salute. By nine that morning, however, the sun began to burn through the mists, and the *Empress* gathered speed. The King and Queen were out on deck, both looking fit and recovered.

At mid-morning off the Isle of Wight, the *Empress of Britain* was approached by the grey form of the destroyer HMS *Kempenfelt*. Fifteen minutes later, the two princesses in their camel-hair coats and tammies were scrambling up the companion ladder and rushing into their parents' arms. The King was astonished at the change in his daughters, unable to believe how much Elizabeth had grown in five weeks, or how much thinner Margaret Rose had become ("not like a football as I used to be"). The princesses themselves were full of questions about the Royal Visit, having already followed their parents' tour on the map in their schoolroom, as well as receiving letters and calls on the trans-oceanic radio-telephone (the Queen's bad-tempered Corgi, Dookie, who was fond of biting footmen and courtiers, had even been held up to the receiver once to bark down the Atlantic cable for the benefit of the royal couple). The family retreated to the royal suite for a more private reunion, before setting off on a tour of the ship.

The children seemed to provide a much-needed release from the journey's tensions, inspiring a mild hilarity at the final luncheon on board. The *Empress*'s vast dining-room had been decorated with streamers, and Lord Airlie insisted on taking down balloons and popping them with his cigarette. People laughed loudly and told jokes across the table, the orchestra launched into "The Lambeth Walk", and Crawfie, the princesses' Scottish governess, got mildly squiffy on champagne cocktails. Even the King was inspired to play the comedian, and to the delight of his children pushed balloons out the portholes at the excursion steamers that now circled around them.

England's skies were drab and grey as they docked that afternoon at Portsmouth. The two princesses clung excitedly to their father and looked down on the scene—the water about them dotted with old side-wheelers and sailboats, the constant din of sirens, guns, and circling airplanes, and the cheers from those massed along the quay. Queen Mary was the first person to stride up the gangplank, looking none the worse for her auto accident. Following in her wake came the rest of the royal family: the Duke and Duchess of Gloucester, the Duke and Duchess of Kent, the Princess Royal and the Earl of Harewood. Everyone trooped below for a few private minutes before the King and Queen appeared at the ship's rail and stepped ashore in the Old Country once again.

"London's Big Cheer Is Ready" ran the headline, and hours before the King and Queen arrived, the city's inhabitants had set out to rival the wild scenes they had read about for the past month. Spectators sporting patriotic ribbons were lined up twenty and thirty deep, waving flags and singing to pass the time. Here and there people held up signs reading "Well Done". The supreme importance of the occasion was signalled by the flocks of fashionable Londoners who lounged about the palace gates in evening dress (before drifting back to the West End, where restaurants were offering such delights as "Le Homard comme au Canada" and "La Bonbonnière des Quintuplets").

Across the river, the flags and bunting that disguised the dinginess of Waterloo Station had already provided an unintentional welcome for another group of voyagers. Two hundred and eighty-eight German Jewish refugees from the liner *St. Louis* had been allowed into England (others were admitted to France, Belgium, and the Netherlands) and had arrived the day before. For these lucky few survivors, whose desperation had taken them from Hamburg to the port of Havana and back to the Old World again, the reception in the enormous rail terminus must have seemed unreal. They were met by Jewish relief workers, hugged by relatives and friends, and had flowers thrust into their hands. Piled near by was everything they had been able to carry away from their life in Germany in the helter-skelter common to all refugees—cheap fibre suitcases, bags of costly crocodile and pigskin leather, and old cardboard boxes. Safe now after so many weeks of uncertainty, many of them wept unashamedly. "Look, Daddy," said one small child, pointing about Waterloo Station, done up in vivid colours like a birthday cake, "the English people have decorated their station for us." (Of the 937 refugees who travelled on the *St. Louis*, only 240 are known to have survived the war.)

Europe's uneasy calm was very much on the minds of Prime Minister Neville Chamberlain and other members of the large reception party who gathered at Waterloo on the evening of June 22 when the gleaming engine, *Sir Francis Drake*, decked with British, Canadian, and American flags, pulled the special royal train into the station. Events had moved swiftly on in the King's absence; Italy and Germany had signed their Pact of Steel, and Britain was busy forging alliances of her own. The mood of crisis had by now been communicated to the British public, and lay behind the emotional outpouring on the streets of London that night. There was the wild exuberance of Coronation Day, a continuous full-throated cheer which ran ahead of the King and Queen for the two-mile journey to Buckingham Palace, dying away only when the landau carrying the royal couple and their daughters passed the Cenotaph. In increasingly anxious times, the British had looked about for a rallying-symbol to lift their morale — and found it unexpectedly in the family of the "small, shy, unprepossessing man" who was their king. Fresh from their triumphs in America, George VI and Queen Elizabeth had returned to England with the aura of national heroes.

Perhaps the most extraordinary scene took place at Parliament Square, where M.P.s and members of the House of Lords had lined the sidewalks in front of Westminster. The bells of St. Margaret's began to ring as the landau with its mounted escort of Lifeguards turned the corner slowly to where, wedged among the cabbies, schoolboys, and bankers, the likes of Winston Churchill, David Lloyd George, and others yelled and waved top hats under the enthusiastic cheerleading of the Archbishop of Canterbury. The moment was memorably described by Harold Nicolson in his diary:

We lost all dignity and yelled and yelled. The King wore a happy schoolboy grin. The Queen was superb. She really does manage to convey to each individual in the crowd that he or she has had a personal greeting. It is due, I think, to the brilliance of her eyes. But she is in truth one of the most amazing Queens since Cleopatra. We returned to the House with lumps in our throats.

More than a million people had come out to greet the royal party along the route. A further fifty thousand milled about in front of Buckingham Palace after the royal carriage had disappeared behind the gates and the royal standard once again fluttered from the flagpole. The insistent chanting continued, and the King and Queen came out on to the balcony to wave to the crowd. Still nobody left, and, while the royal family sat down to dinner, Londoners kept up the noise and cheering in front of the palace gates, singing "Under the Spreading Chestnut Tree" (one of the King's favourites) and "The Lambeth Walk". Their efforts were finally rewarded just before nine when the King in tails and the Queen in a flowing heliotrope gown again stepped onto the balcony, this time with the princesses in tow. The King raised his arm, smiling, the Queen blew the crowd a kiss, and little Margaret Rose, in a pink party dress, waved till her arm ached. The spirit of celebration among Londoners continued for some hours more, and it was midnight before the Mall had completely emptied.

It was the end of the "high-hat" era and the beginning of what George VI described to Mackenzie King as his role as a "people's king". Certainly, to those who watched the Sovereign speak next day at the Guildhall, it was apparent that something had changed. The speech to members of the Corporation of London and other distinguished guests was little more than a summing up of the Royal Visit. But the confidence with which the King carried himself, and the ease with which he addressed his audience, were entirely new.

In Canada, I saw everywhere not only the mere symbol of the British Crown; I saw also, flourishing as strongly as they do here, the institutions which have developed, century after century, beneath the aegis of that Crown; institutions, British in origin, British in their slow and almost casual growth, which, because they are grounded root and branch on British faith in liberty and justice, mean more to us even than the splendour of our history or the glories of our English tongue.

From his seat in the Guildhall, Tommy Lascelles looked on approvingly:

I have never heard the King — or indeed few other people — speak so effectively, or so movingly. One or two passages obviously stirred him so deeply that I feared he might break down. This spontaneous feeling heightened the force of the speech considerably. . . . It was very interesting to watch the effect of his words on such hardnosed experts as Winston Churchill, Baldwin and the Archbishop of Canterbury; it was patent that each of them and indeed everybody else in that historic place, was deeply moved.

"That tour made us!" the Queen was later to tell Mackenzie King. "It came at just the right time, particularly for us." She and the King had introduced a new note of informality in their roles, had allowed themselves to be seen as ordinary people, and had permitted daylight in upon the magic of monarchy. It had not happened in any carefully thought-out way; it had just happened, as the Queen was to tell her friends, and she and the King had seized upon it — with overwhelming success.

Naturally there was criticism. Alaric Jacob, the Reuters reporter who had watched as "huzzaing crowds succeeded one another at every whistle-stop across Canada", and had suffered (as the King had) through every playing of "God Save the King" ("the dull Hanoverian tune"), felt the Royal Visit had been little more than a circus. And, while the King was "obviously a worthy man, the Queen a woman of spirit as well as charm", he felt they had been thrust into unconvincing roles:

They were like a pair of film actors making a cheap and nasty popular appearance tour. The uniforms were pretty, the pageantry well-arranged, but what stood out above all else was the surpassing vulgarity of the kingly office. What low, what trivial people are attracted to royal personages in the modern world! As race-horses attract varlets, so kings allure social parasites. To exhibit oneself like a primitive totem, a primitive father-image — this seemed the attribute of a childish office which an adult society would long since have discarded.

The occasional critical comment in the British newspapers was duly noted by Lester B. Pearson as second in command at the High Commission in London, where he had been busy scrutinizing hundreds of adulatory press clippings (his favourite headline was "MONARCH INVOKES BLESSING OF GOD UPON THIS REALM: Assents To Nine Bills"). He couldn't, for instance, resist passing on an article from *Reynolds News* which poured scorn on the Queen's claim to be "a real Scots lass", and which observed that "the Queen's mother was a Cavendish-Bentinck, her grandmother a Miss Smith of Kent, her great-grandmother a Miss Carpenter of Herts., and so on. Her father [the Earl of Strathmore] certainly owns Glamis Castle, but he also owns a lot of Stepney, where the slums are."

Others more than made up for the rude comments of a few British journalists by the extravagant praise they showered on the royal couple's performance during the Royal Visit — and especially that of Queen Elizabeth. Americans were particularly generous, even if it didn't make a great deal of difference in their isolationist policies at the time. The attitude of those who had been afraid the King and Queen "might go south with the silverware" was replaced by the warm sentiments of one politician who told reporters that "if America can keep Queen Elizabeth, Congress will regard Britain's war debt as settled." Dixon of the *Daily News* had gone from hard-boiled to soft-centred in the first days on the tour, and became similarly smitten with the Queen's charms:

> That gracious lady — and you'll have to bear with us if we seem to grow lyrical about her — can take any city faster than Grant took Richmond! Your Correspondent is still walking around in a trance from having chatted with Their Majesties and shaken the royal hands.

Dixie Tighe of the *New York Post* summed up her own encounter with royalty with an exultant phrase, "The Queen clasped my dirty paw."

"The King's Tour Is The Queen's Triumph" stated the *New York Times* flatly. And there could be little denying the effect her personal charm had on the public — or the extraordinary effort she put into her royal role. In photo after photo, it is the Queen who turns to the camera and smiles while the King, his face unable to conceal the weariness he feels, can be seen in the background, plodding on to the next function. Time after time, it was the Queen who directed the King's attention to what he should be noticing, persuading him to bear up one moment longer, to talk with one more person. And George VI, as vulnerable to her charm (and her stern command) as anyone else, took great satisfaction in his wife's success. Once, twelve years earlier, during their tour of New Zealand when they were still the Duke and Duchess of York, he had jumped from the royal train as it pulled into a town, and run along the station platform for the pure delight of seeing how the crowds greeted his wife.

The King himself had not been forgotten, despite the avalanche of stories about the Queen's charm, her wardrobe, and (especially) her smile. In spite of his chronic ill health and his shyness, he had forced himself as never before to become a truly public figure. This was recognized in a cartoon of the day which shows the American "little man" standing on sheaves of papers labelled "parades", "speeches", "receptions", etc. In his hand is a bubbling champagne glass which he holds up in a toast, saying, "Gentlemen, the King — a guy who can take it."

Meanwhile, back in Canada, everything was settling back into its routine. The party was over. Across the country, flags and bunting had been taken down and stored away; morning suits and silk toppers had been cleaned and returned to the costume rental. Thousands of Royal Visit scrapbooks were shoved into drawers, with the last newspaper photos of the King and Queen waving goodbye from the ship hastily stuffed into the back pages (to be properly glued in at some later time). Shoved even farther back on high shelves of Canadian cupboards were tiny Union Jacks, cardboard periscopes, flattened pennies, and commemorative candy bowls. People slipped back into their normal routines.

Interest had remained at a high level as long as the royal couple were in the country. When the farewell addresses of the King and Queen were broadcast from Halifax, Canadians had clustered around their radios, and the streets in some parts of the country had been almost empty. In London, Ontario, the Public Utilities Commission had reported a 10-per-cent rise in consumption over the previous day — indicating more than 17,000 radios tuned to the special broadcast. But now, with the King and Queen on their way home aboard the *Empress of Britain*, press dispatches concerning the Royal Visit dwindled from a daily average of 9,000 to just 7,650 — many of the stories coming from a fresh wave of reporters launched into the streets to try to make some sense of what had just happened.

Some businesses reported spectacular sales increases — such as one manufacturer of corn plasters and arch supports, or the Toronto businessman who had sold two million flags by the end of the tour, against an average of 150,000 a year. Sales of men's and women's clothing had risen by 20 to 25 per cent in some places, while storekeepers reported that purchases of china and jewellery were away up. Quebec tourism was up 65 per cent, and every week of the tour major department stores had reported sales totals that topped those of 1938 — with many of the increases in goods having no discernible connection to royalty or patriotism. And, while the stock market was not significantly affected, traders loyally claimed that the visit of the King and Queen had helped to beat a defeatist attitude — and could lead to many new jobs being created. About the only business reporting any loss (other than the occasional bleacher concessionaire) was the Liquor Board in Toronto, which had of course closed down during the royal visit to the city — a fact that caused Ralph Allen of *The Globe and Mail* to conclude that, "with or without coercion, Toronto regarded the advent of Their Majesties as an ideal occasion to show itself how to be happy though sober."

If business was up, crime was down. Several communities, like Winnipeg, reported unlawful activities at a low ebb. Typically the crime rate "swooped" just before the visit to a particular city and remained low for two or three days afterwards — whether from the increased vigilance of the police or, as one official suggested, because "crooks, even pickpockets, were enthralled" with the occasion. One Ottawa judge, attempting to explain the decline in juvenile delinquencies, stated that "the hearts of our children are so filled with love and affection for

King George and Queen Elizabeth that they have had no time for wrong-doing."

Everyone seemed to agree as well that the tour had given the monarchy a new lustre in Canada, reinvigorated the links with the Mother Country, and (the hope as wistfully common then as now) strengthened national unity. Washington and New York had been public-relations triumphs. As Violet Markham wrote from England to her friend Lord Tweedsmuir on the nineteenth of June: "But of course the three days in the U.S. is of more value than the three weeks in Canada — you know that as well as I do, and though you may look down your official nose as you read this, you will send me a trans-Atlantic wink at the same time."

The jibes about the royal tour's success from certain quarters in Europe could be treated with a snap of the fingers. "If Germany is in any doubt about the warmth of the reception here and in the United States," said Ontario Conservative leader George Drew, flinging out a challenge before an appreciative audience at Peterborough's Empress Hotel, "may we suggest that Herr Hitler write and suggest that he pay a State visit to New York." And in a flight of rhetoric, nicely judged to milk the applause, he thundered, "Will the American people play and sing 'Horst Wessel' and 'Deutschland Über Alles' as they did 'God Save the King' and 'Rule Britannia' last Saturday?!"

Not that a stake had been driven through the isolationist heart of America. On the surface, little if anything had changed; and it can only be guessed what the effect of the American people's warm feeling towards the royal couple may have been on subsequent events. Nor was talk of neutrality entirely silenced in Canada — not in Quebec at least. *Le Devoir* had conjured up a prophetic image as the *Empress of Britain* sailed from Halifax: "Canadian land fades in the eyes of the royal passengers. At this distance, it seems like a vague line of yellowish brown, and that resembles waves of assault of an army in khaki." On the other hand, there had been a new rush to the recruiting-offices in the wake of the tour, and one regiment, the de Maisonneuves, was reported to be swamped with volunteers and unable to take on more men for the time being.

Of course, other criticisms of the Royal Visit fell closer to home. Alongside the pile of congratulatory letters and telegrams that awaited the Prime Minister's return to Ottawa were other, less complimentary ones. The newspapers bristled with indignation. "Loyalist", of Pictou County in Nova Scotia, wrote of heart-broken children watching a car rushing along the highway in the dusk of evening at twenty-five miles per hour, and of tour organizers who functioned along "German lines of officialdom". Similarly, thousands of children in Bruce and Huron counties in Ontario had waited for hours in the hot sun to see little more than a whirl of action as the Royal Train swept by. In Sudbury, there were bitter complaints about how company executives had monopolized the royal party to the exclusion of ordinary people. "The King and Queen did not come to Canada to be bored by selfish politicians and curtseying social climbers," *The Globe and Mail* chided, "but to see and be seen by unprivileged masses."

And, of course, it was fair to ask exactly what the royal couple *had* seen on their first whirlwind tour of the Dominion. "What are the principal physical features of Canada?" queried Harris Turner of the *Western Producer*, who had set his own exam on the subject. Answer: "Flags, aldermen, children and dining-rooms."

Q. Has public speaking been developed to a high art in Canada?
A. No.
Q. What is the common food of the people?
A. Chicken and ice cream.
Q. Are the professions overcrowded in Canada?
A. The aldermanic profession — which is the only one they appear to go in for — seems to be a little overdone.
Q. Are the people well-dressed?
A. You'd be amazed.

Judith Robinson, not surprisingly, had her own ideas on the subject — in this case a small dose of 1939 social realism. "A few choice views of freight car dormitories, some interiors of jails and lockups," she wrote, "close-ups of street-corner arrests for soliciting alms, glimpses of one-night stands in hostels; ours would be another sort of official picture gallery."

Finger-pointing continued at the local level. Guelph City

Council held an "alibi" meeting to discuss who was to blame for the Royal Visit "fizzle", and decided after much discussion to blame the Prime Minister ("Let us put the onus where it belongs — on Mackenzie King"). He had acted "like an officious office boy", harrumphed one alderman, himself livid at having been "chased" from the station platform ("not nearly as far as the whole selfish caboodle of them will be chased at the next civic election," replied one dissenting citizen — a sign that City Council's views on the Royal Visit, and the Prime Minister's part in it, were not universally shared).

But whatever its effect on social and foreign policy, national unity, or local politics, the experience of the 1939 royal tour was largely a personal one for Canadians. For them, the overriding impression of the visit by the King and Queen had been "the charm and gentility and beauty of this little woman," as the Opposition leader Robert Manion had expressed it, "and the common sense and democratic attitude of her husband." For four weeks, while the Royal Train had travelled from one end of the country to the other, people had drunk in every detail of the royal couple's personal lives — from detailed reports of the Queen's forty costume changes (her taste for pastel blues, off-the-face hats, and parasols having an instant effect on the fashion industry), to the King's fondness for cheese and the fact that he seldom ate soup. For those who managed to see them face to face (8.5 million people according to Vincent Massey's optimistic figures), it was the couple's apparent youthfulness, the Queen's flawless complexion, the King's firm grip. But most of all, people were astonished — as Canadians always are — that such a startling event could have happened *here*. "Fancy," an old man in New Brunswick had said, tears running down his face, "the King and Queen have passed my very door."

But what made the 1939 Royal Visit uniquely memorable were the extraordinary times in which it took place: at the end of a depression, at the onset of a terrible war, at a time when monarchy and the British connection still had a powerful hold on the imagination of Canadians.

In 1939, Joyce Musson's family was living in the small town of Melita, Manitoba, where her father worked as a butcher. The Mussons had originally come out from England in 1908 to homestead in Saskatchewan; but their ties to the Old Country remained strong, and they were determined to see the Royal Train when it came through on its way west. So, one evening in May, everyone piled into the old half-ton truck, the parents in the cab and the three kids — including Joyce — in the back, and drove some ninety miles to a spot near Brandon on the main line. They had arrived well ahead of time, and had several hours to wait.

> People were lined up all along the tracks, out in the open on the bald prairie, patiently waiting. My mother and father started to sing some of the old songs — "Drink To Me Only With Thine Eyes", "Keep the Home Fires Burning" — things of that sort, and all along the tracks, people joined in, with alto and tenor and bass voices here and there adding to the harmony. As one song died away, someone would start another, and it would catch on and spread along the crowd, and the hours passed with a great welling-up of friendly spirit, although we were all strangers from all points of the compass.
>
> Finally, the great moment arrived, and the Royal Train came rumbling slowly along the tracks. Everyone cheered, and when the end of the train came in sight, we could see that their Majesties were standing there, waving and smiling at the crowd assembled in their honour. We all stood at attention and sang God Save The King with our chests fairly bursting with emotion, and even as I write these words 50 years later, the tears come to my eyes as I think of it. How can one explain it? One of those unforgettable moments — for it was no longer than that really. I suppose it was another era, 100 years behind the times even then, and in the middle of a hopeless existence, we reached out to all that seemed noble and worthwhile.

Notes

The following abbreviations are used in the notes:

Black — see bibliography, C. Black; Bradley — Lorraine Bradley, letter/interview; Burns — see bibliography, J.M. Burns; CBC — CBC Radio Archives; Coughlin — Const. J. Coughlin materials from RCMP Centennial Museum; ER — see bibliography, Eleanor Roosevelt; Elliott Roosevelt — see bibliography E. Roosevelt and J. Brough; GM — *The Globe & Mail*; GLENBOW — Glenbow Institute; Howarth — see bibliography, P. Howarth; Ickes — see bibliography, H.L. Ickes; Jacob — see bibliography, A. Jacob; Jay — Shirley Jay, letter/interview; Keenleyside — see bibliography, H. Keenleyside; Lascelles — see bibliography, D. Hart-Davis; Lash — see bibliography, J.P. Lash; Lefebvre — K. Lefebvre, letter/interview; Legere — E. Legere, Sr., letter/interview; Leonard — R. Leonard, letter/interview; Macartney — B. Macartney, letter/interview; MAN ARCH — Manitoba Archives; Manchester — see bibliography, W. Manchester; Martin — see bibliography, P. Martin; Michaud — J.P. Michaud, letter/interview; MK — William Lyon Mackenzie King Diaries; Moose Jaw — Moose Jaw Royal Visit Booklet; Morgan — see bibliography, T. Morgan; Mortimer — see bibliography, P. Mortimer; NAC — National Archives of Canada; NBC — National Broadcasting Corporation; Nicolson — see bibliography, H. Nicolson; NS ARCH — Nova Scotia Archives; NYDN — New York Daily News; NYT — New York Times; NYWT — New York World-Telegram; Pascoe — Pallie Pascoe memoir of the Royal Tour; PRO/DO — Public Records Office (Kew) Dominions Office; PRO/FO — Public Records Office (Kew) Foreign Office; Putnam — J. Putnam, letter/interview; Readwin — unpublished material supplied by Loys Readwin; Redfern — S. Redfern to V. Wilcox; Scott — see bibliography, F.R. Scott and A.J.M. Smith; Sinclair — see bibliography, D. Sinclair; Stone — C. Stone, letter/interview; Stover — M. Stover, letter; Taylor — M. Taylor, letter/interview; USC Archives — Library of the University of Southern California Archives; VAN ARCH — Vancouver Archives; Vcr Sun — Vancouver Sun; Wheeler-Bennett — see bibliography, J. Wheeler-Bennett; Wilcox — see bibliography; Willis-O'Connor — see bibliography, H. Willis-O'Connor; Yaegar — T.R. Yaeger, letter/interview; Zolf — see bibliography, L. Zolf

Chapter One: Below Quebec City

5. "affection for you", MK 13/11/38 (quoted in Stacey, 188); 7. "touches Canadian soil", CBC 17/5/39

Chapter Two: Preparations

8. "shower-bath", Wheeler-Bennett 380; 8. "When the King and the Queen came to Stratford", Scott, 25; 9. "a religious experience", Ibid.; 10. "to my dying day", Scott, 25; 11. "First time in history", MK 7/8/39; 12. "I need not assure you", PRO/FO 371/21548; 12. "demands of the Protocol people", Ibid.; 12. "The American people", Ibid.; 12. "struck popular imagination", Wilcox 120; 13. "such boyish enthusiasm", PRO/FO 371/2158; 14. "unpopularity for somebody", Wilcox 120; 15. "And as for the Canadas!", Scott, 23; 16 "In

short they have followed him", Ibid.; 16."How he looked when he danced", Ibid.; 18. "such puckish pranks", Willis-O'Connor; 19. "another and violent outburst", PRO/DO 121/65; 20. "flabby sentimentality" Redfern, letter to Victoria Wilcox; 21. "he is functionless", Wilcox 138; 21. "reversal to colonial status", Ibid.; 22. "through Destiny", MK 5/12/38; 22. "you and I are out of business", Redfern; 22. "itching to be in the foreground", MK 25/11/39; 23. "was slightly perturbed", PRO/DO 121/65; 23. "Tweedsmuir has still to see", MK 25/11/38; 24. "even a Canadian one", PRO/DO 121/65; 25. "another Court manoeuvre", MK 28/2/39; 26. "they *are* a very fine people", Lascelles, 72; 26. "There might be riots", MK 25/11/38; 26. "like an old boot", PRO/DO 121/65; 26. "sensitive balance of his mind", Wilcox 137; 27. "a little squirming tonight", MK 2/3/39; 27. "He is tired", PRO/DO 121/65; 27. "spike the guns of intrigue", MK 2/3/39; 27. "the same old game", MK 4/3/39; 28. "Do you wonder", MK 11/3/39; 28. "did not propose to be tramped on", Ibid.; 29. "trained in India", Ibid.; 29. "the tragic part", Ibid.; 29. "making a personal matter", PRO/FO 371/21548; 29. "a dangerously foolish manner", PRO/DO 121/65; 29. "already lost South Africa", MK 11/3/39; 30. "We had no shape", Scott, 36; 32. "a brass farthing", PRO/FO 371/21548; 32. "who never travels west of Toronto", PRO/DO 121/65; 33. "Trying official functions", Readwin; 33. "royal torture", *Time* 15/5/39; 34. "the gasworks, the tannery", Readwin; 34. "No Great Lakes", Ibid.; 34. "must wear trousers", NAC TM3472FJ; 35. "his illuminated soul", NAC RG6D2 Vol 414; 35. "excrescence of a tree", Ibid.; 35. "I do not care", NAC RG6 D2 Vol 419; 35. "I am very loath", Ibid.; 35. "Is there anything", Ibid.; 35. "Being a goldfish", NAC RG6 D2 Vol 413; 36. "The enclosed memorandum", NAC RG6 D2 Vol 419; 37. "an aggressive campaign", NAC RG6 D2 Vol 417; 37. "no untoward incident", Ibid.; 37. "imaginary conversations", Ibid.; 37. "Their Majesties' pictures", *Financial Post*, undated, NS ARCH R51/vol 3/1319; 38. "right-thinking Canadian people", Oxford (Ontario) *Journal*, undated, Readwin; 38. "preference for a light Sherry", VAN ARCH; 38. "I hereby offer", Ibid.; 39. "should be made a plasterer", NAC RG6 D2 Vol. 419; 39. "no end of disappointment", MK 5/12/38; 41. "built in Glasgow", *Time* 8/5/39

Chapter Three: Fog and Ice

43. "anxiety and broken hopes", *Time* 22/5/39; 45. "some old admiral", Sinclair 235; 45. "like a white cloud", Wheeler-Bennett 377; 46. "surrounded by dense fog", Wheeler-Bennett 378; 49. "hierar-

chical, universal, and continuous", Black 196; 49. "loyalty of French Canadians", *La Presse* 27/4/39; 50. "cheer in French", Ibid.; 53. "Decked in bunting", *Time* 22/5/39; 53. "all very simple", MK 16/5/39; 54. "Can only trust in Providence", Ibid.; 54. "two extra days", Wheeler-Bennett 379

Chapter Four: Into the Heart of French Canada

56. "Canadian crowds", NYT 18/5/39; 57. "Every person seemed stunned", Pascoe; 57. "smile matches the sunshine", CBC 17/5/39; 60. "A Quebec sun beamed", GM 18/5/39; 61. "An old woman", Vcr Sun 18/5/39; 61. "No Canadian can hear", Ibid.; 61. "That's French they're singing", Ibid.; 63. "thunderstruck spectators", *La Presse* 18/5/39; 63. "Strangely, no one was thinking", *Le Devoir* 18/5/39; 63. "most thoughtfully decorated", Couglin; 65. "If a bridge fails", *Time* 29/5/39; 67. "a country uncle", Scott, 41; 67. "he took care to take", MK 18/5/39; 68. "normally unemotional breasts", *Le Devoir* 29/5/39; 69. "the little cubs", MK 18/5/39; 70. "Debutantes", MK 18/5/39; 70. "Tonight, after dressing", Ibid.; 73. "loyalty and patriotism", *Le Canada* 19/5/39; 74. "Had it not been", MK 18/15/39

Chapter Five: Daylight Upon Magic

75. "quaint, Arcadian stuff", *Time* 29/5/39; 76. "the crowd was rather good", Coughlin; 76. "the entire route was lined with people", MK 19/5/39; 77. "full flowering of our nationhood", Ibid.; 78. "a genius for the right kind of publicity", Wheeler-Bennett 380; 78. "The only gangsters", *Le Devoir* 31/5/39; 78. "not yet very civilized", *Le Devoir* 23/5/39; 78. "terrified of the press", MK 30/5/39; 79. "pink-cheeked, 22 year old Bruno Seymours", *Time* 29/5/39; 79. "painted fingernails", Mortimer 81; 81. "pull up chairs and shoot olive pits", *Time* 29/5/39; 81. "the young couple next door", Readwin; 82. "Reporter Gabs With King", *Time* 29/5/39; 83. "photograph so badly", Mortimer 174; 85. "wished I could tell them", MK 20/5/39; 85. "acted like sweethearts", Coughlin; 85. "They groan, 'Oh, dear!'", Willis-O'Connor; 87. "raised my hand", Ibid.; 87. "Whatever it was", *L'Actualité*; 88. "red, red trail", GM 22/5/39; 88. "a deep hush", Ibid.; 88. "worshipped and their unknown places", Ibid.; 89. "faces of the Scotland Yard detectives", Wheeler-Bennett 380; 89. "Where in hell", Willis-O'Connor; 89. "A blind veteran", GM 21/5/39; 89-91. Sinclair; 91. "glad to get out of here", Coughlin; 92. "extend as a concertina", MK 21/5/39; 92. "dust in the balance", Ibid.; 93. "just

as natural with him", Ibid.; 94. "will never grow up", Readwin; 94. "stools, lunches and umbrellas", Ibid.; 95. "There rose a mighty cheer", Ibid.; 95. "gathered the lunch remainders", Ibid.; 98. "enjoyed this part of the trip", MK 22/5/39; 100. "diamond sculls stroke", GM 23/5/39; 100. "the Queen wearing", CBC 22/5/39; 101. "makes friends", MK 22/5/39; 101. "McCullagh's horse", Ibid.; 102. "bloody horrors", GM 22/5/39; 102. "hands were slightly grubby", GM 23/5/39; 158. "Disappointment", Readwin; 103. "heartless to rush by", MK 22/5/39

Chapter Six: Where the West Begins

106. "I need very much", MK 23/5/39; 108. "stuttered for miles and miles", GM 24/5/39; 108. "Wide-winged gulls", Ibid.; 108. "where the west begins", Readwin; 109. "band has stopped", CBC 23/5/39; 110. "banquet for myself", MK 24/5/39; 110. "waves and dips", MAN ARCH; 111. "Would you call that a real canadien home [?]", Ibid.; 111. "seven foot high and very broad", Ibid.; 111. "Queen in Hertfordshire", Ibid.; 112. "names, racial origins", Ibid.; 112. "Indians have been placed on my doorstep", Ibid.; 112. "no danger of the crowd", Ibid.; 112. "a magnificent fern", Ibid.; 112. "please help me", Ibid.; 113. "my advent in Canada", Ibid.; 113. "not fond of cocktails", Ibid.; 113. "husband should precede the wife", Ibid.; 113. "high-stepping baton-twirling", Ibid.; 113. "hordes didn't come", Stover; 114. "SOBBING WET!", Stover; 114. "a devout Jewish nationalist", Zolf; 115. "The King, the Queen and Mr. King", GM 24/5/39; 116. "valiant heroes of the French race", GM 24/5/39; 117. "carefully cultivated anachronism", Time 5/6/39; 118. "big sticker on his car", Pascoe; 118. "For some unknown reason", VAN ARCH; 119. "glimpse of the prairies", MK 24/5/39; 119. "planned for the gentlemen", MAN ARCH; 119. "full evening dress", Ibid.; 120. "Nothing more stirring", MK 24/5/39; 120. "moved about freely", Ibid.; 121. "full of life and charm", Ibid.; 121. "plenty of sunshine", Readwin; 123. "kept waving one hand", MK 25/5/39; 125. "dressed up like a Christmas tree", Pascoe; 125. "Main Street was a picture", Ibid.; 126 "Be happy though a bit uncomfortable", Moose Jaw; 126. "The sight of the streets", MK 25/5/39; 127. "Sweetest face. Grand hands.", GM 26/5/39; 127. "the little lad first smiled", MK 25/5/39; 128. "A German has been shot by a Pole", Ibid.; 129. "Our isolated settlement", Stone; 130. "Old and young", GLENBOW; 130. "no feather-legged Clydes", Ibid.; 131. "By all means", Ibid.; 132. "hard times", MK 26/5/39; 132. "took the eye of the press", GLENBOW; 133. "to rescue Her M.", MK 26/5/39

Chapter Seven: Washday in Savona

135. "effect of the hills", MK 27/5/39; 136. "clap of thunder", Pascoe; 139. "importance of royal patronage", Jacob 238; 141. "Swellest Little Woman", Ibid.; 141. "Soon afterwards the correspondent", Ibid.; 141. "held her in my arms", MK 28/5/39; 142. "never laughed harder in my life", Ibid.; 143. "Field or Heaven", GM 29/5/39; 144. "scenery is perfectly exquisite", MK 28/5/39; 146. "Monday was not observed", *Kamloops Sentinal* 26/5/39; 147. "Faith in Darkness", MK 29/5/39; 148. "Chinese in their costumes", Ibid.; 149. "Everything is on a grand scale", Ibid.; 149. "old sweats, old fragments", GM 30/5/39; 150. "our Scottish Queen", MK 29/5/39; 151. "the doors were thrown open", Ibid.; 151. "The night in the hotel", Pascoe; 151. "garlands in their hair", MK 30/5/39; 152. "Lascelles went for Patullo pretty hard", MK 30/5/39; 154. "a triumphal climax", Ibid.; 155. "the question of Munich", Ibid.; 156. "When he last saw the reporters", Ibid.; 156. "our premier peeking over their shoulders", Readwin; 157. "legislative members, their cousins and their aunts", Ibid.; 157. "Mackenzie King and his satellites", Ibid.; 157. "curtailing the speech", Ibid.; 157. "far from the theatre of war" Ibid.; 157. "fulsome devotion to the Throne", Ibid.; 158. "they screamed", Ibid.; 159. "brought out a stretcher", MK 31/5/39; 160. "The King and Queen", Pascoe

Chapter Eight: "Lost Children, Fainting Women, Bewildered Visitors . . ."

163. "One of the greatest surprises", MK 2/6/39; 164. "modern Cars and Buggies", GLENBOW; 165. "Then the Drive", Ibid.; 166. "they are liable to say", GLENBOW; 166. "very beautiful", MK 2/6/39; 167. "his amour-propre", Ibid.; 168. "movies were taken of Aberhart and myself", Ibid.; 168. "terrible lack of organization", Ibid.; 168. "literally to throw Aberhart", Ibid.; 169. "a good trip home", GLENBOW; 169. "lost a little of the constant smile", MK 2/6/39; 170. "Edmonton left a wonderful picture", Ibid.; 170. "a lovely sight", MK 3/6/39; 171. "Curtseying isn't a very common practice", CBC 3/6/39; 171. "waved his silk hat", MK 3/6/39; 172. "almost a miracle", Ibid.; 172. "two little girls", Ibid.; 173. "huge cloud of dust", Pascoe; 173. "never saw a more radiant look", MK 3/6/39; 174. "The King and Queen", Pascoe; 174. "until you've seen 40,000", GM 4/6/39; 176. "never wash that handkerchief", Taylor; 176. "old man of 98", MK 4/6/39; 176. "The silver and blue", CBC 4/6/39; 177. "Lorna Doone" MK 4/6/39; 177. "the Queen's blue eyes", Bradley; 178. "sweating and covered with mosquitoes", Leonard;

179. "An anonymous keynoter", GM 7/6/39; 179. "Jenny waving", MK 6/6/39; 179. "playing out the string", GM 7/6/39; 180. "a continuous stream of people", MK 6/6/39; 180. "why civic employees", Readwin; 180. "Is it the intention", Ibid.; 181. "used to load and unload coal", Ibid.; 181. "Windsor Excited", GM 6/39; 182. "easily the finest display", MK 6/6/39; 182. "Word was passed", Martin, 208; 183. "Curtsey? Who, me?", Tor Star 7/6/39; 183. "another huge crowd", MK 6/6/39; 185. "I slipped behind", Lefebvre; 185. "As the Royal Train was departing", Ibid.; 185. "guns were too old", Macartney; 186. "Regina Musical Ride", MK 7/6/39; 187. "Rome with a first night show", Readwin; 188. "beautiful sunny warm day", Yaegar; 189. "I said to the King", MK 7/6/39; 190. "Half way across the plain iron bridge", NBC 7/6/39; 190. "fresh as a debutante", NYT 8/6/39

Chapter Nine: "That Honeychile Missus Queen"

191. "Canada, the Empire", Wilcox 120; 192. "so many guns", Pascoe; 192. "In the loveliest way", MK 6/6/39; 193. "Officials", Ibid.; 193. "life and death struggle", ER 184; 195. "sinister secret diplomacy", Manchester 177; 195. "mislead the innocent", Howarth 91; 195. "American public opinion", Wilcox 135; 196. "Selling George VI", Scribner's 7/2/39; 197. "You must remember", Ibid.; 198. "It must be borne in mind", Ibid.; 198. "At some point", Ibid.; 198. "The little Queen", Morgan 510; 199. "he listed the furniture" ER 185; 199. "a linen blanket", Ibid.; 200. "Franklin always behaved", Ibid.; 200. "Oh dear, oh dear" NYWT 25/5/39; 307. "I should not be at all surprised", Lash, Eleanor and Franklin 753; 307. "I told Franklin", ER 186; 202. "boasting about the reception", Higham Papers, USC Archives; 203. "the King and Queen after all", NYT 8/6/39; 203. "I can hardly bear to read it", Lash, Love, Eleanor, 267; 204. "As a mark of gratitude", GM 8/6/39; 204. "Received this morning", MK 8/6/39; 205. "never have I seen a crowd", NYWT 9/6/39; 205. "almost like the top of a stove", MK 8/6/39; 206. "I said nothing", Ibid.; 207. "It's like heaven", Wilcox 144; 207. "Everyone presentable", Scott 25; 207. "Canada's National Debt", GM 9/6/39; 208. "biggest and snootiest", NYDN 9/6/39; 209. "We had just reached", Wheeler-Bennett, 63; 210. "the type of democrat", Ickes 645; 210. "lived down to its reputation", Elliott Roosevelt 234; 211. "Garner monopolized the King", Ickes 646; 211. "As beautiful a voice", MK 8/6/39; 212. "reminds me of Queen Victoria", Lash, Love, Eleanor, 267; 213. "calculated government dragooning", Wheeler-Bennett 383; 213. "the people of England", NYT 6/39; 216.

"I feel great embarrassment", MK 9/7/39; 217. "According to the press headlines", NYT 6/39; 217. "Mrs. Roosevelt did not kneel", NYT 14/6/39; 218. "the illusion was so perfect", NYWT 10/6/39; 219. "I broke out in goose pimples", Pascoe; 220. "Even FDR is content", Lash, *Love, Eleanor,* 268

Chapter Ten: "New York Goes King Crazy"

221. "known as Coca-Cola", Keenleyside 497; 222. "danced up the stairs", Readwin; 222. "drop telephone directories", PRO/FO 371/21548; 223. "Avoid letting such entrepreneurs", *Scribner's* 7/2/39; 224. "I hesitate to push myself forward", MK 10/6/39; 225. "doesn't approve of cocktails", Wheeler-Bennett 387; 226. "definitely anti-Russian", PRO/FO 371/22801; 226. "Why don't my Ministers", Wheeler-Bennett 389; 227. "spoke very frankly", MK 10/6/39; 227. "told the King repeatedly", Ibid.; 228. "Young man", Burns 393; 228. "a door between us", MK 10/6/39; 228. "pickpockets in New York", Pascoe; 229. "three hayseeds", Ibid.; 230. "a new designation for Mackenzie", MK 11/6/39; 231. "dashing about in a little brown gingham dress", Lash, *Eleanor and Franklin* 754; 232. "little bigger than midgets", Elliott Roosevelt 235; 232. "much disappointed", MK 11/6/39; 232. "FDR was satisfied", Lash, *Love, Eleanor,* 269; 233. Chamberlain was becoming concerned", MK 11/6/39; 234. "Before the dinner was over", Ibid.; 234. "steep little banks", ER 198; 235. "We stood and waved", Lash, *Love, Eleanor,* 268

Chapter Eleven: Our Minds and Hearts Are Full

236. "Yankee pistols and cartridge belts", GM 11/6/39; 237. "a kind of nightmare", Pascoe; 237. "bonne entente", GM 11/6/39; 237. "took charge of the proceedings", GM 11/6/39; 238. "there were moments", MK 12/6/39; 238. "the King rather enjoys", Ibid.; 239. "a fine fellow", Ibid.; 240-244. Gilks memoir; 244. "mounting royal discomfort", Michaud; 244. "wringing their hands", MK 13/6/39; 245. "Leo returned", Legere; 246. "hurrying the events", MK 13/6/39; 247. "A special train", Jay; 249. "Well iced, but so large", MK 14/6/39; 249. "It was pretty windy", Ibid.; 249. "matrons sprinting uphill", Readwin; 250. "All this countryside", Ibid.; 251. "exclusiveness of Englishmen", MK 15/6/39; 251. "top of a bathing house", Ibid.; 254. "sticky little monsters", Keenleyside 495; 255. "The King was obviously", MK 15/6/39; 256. "they really shook hands", Pascoe; 256. "I carried away", MK 15/6/39; 257. "The Royal Yacht", CBC 15/6/39; 257. "No farewell could have been finer", MK 15/6/39

Chapter Twelve: A Country of the Larger Air

258. "T saw me", MK 15/6/39; 259. "extra trips to the Punch Bowl", Pascoe; 260. "When I arrived at Laurier House", MK 17/6/39; 260. "I had a good night's sleep", MK 18/6/39; 260. "Ada was there to meet me", Pascoe; 266. "Look Daddy", Readwin; 267. "We lost all dignity", Nicolson 405; 268. "I have never heard the King", Mackenzie King Papers 227335; 268. "pair of film actors", Jacob 239; 269. "a real Scots lass", NAC RG6 D2 vol 417; 271. "happy, though sober", Readwin; 271. "crooks, even pickpockets", Readwin; 272. "trans-Atlantic wink", Wilcox 120; 273. "selfish politicians", Readwin; 273. "flags, aldermen, children", Ibid.; 273. "jails and lockups", Ibid.; 274. "where it belongs", Ibid.; 275. "lined up along the tracks", Putnam

Bibliography

Abella, Irving, and Harold Troper, *None is too Many*, (Toronto, 1982).

Berton, Pierre, *The Dionne Years* (Toronto, 1977).

Black, Conrad, *Duplessis* (Toronto, 1977).

Boorman, H.R.P., *Merry America*, (Maidstone, 1939).

Burns, James MacGregor, *Roosevelt: The Lion and the Fox* (New York, 1956).

Carter, Carolle J., *The Shamrock and the Swastika* (Palo Alto, 1977).

Carnegie, R.K., *And the People Cheered* (Toronto, 1940).

Crawford, Marion, *The Little Princesses* (London, 1950).

Gordon, Keith, *North America Sees Our King and Queen*, (London, 1939).

Hart-Davis, Duff, ed., *In Royal Service: Letters and Journals of Sir Alan Lascelles: 1920-1936*, (London, 1989)

Higham, Charles, *American Swastika* (Garden City, 1985).

Howarth, Patrick, *George VI* (London, 1987).

Hutchison, Bruce, *The Incredible Canadian* (Toronto, 1952).

Ickes, Harold L., *The Secret Diaries of Harold Ickes* (New York, 1954).

Jacob, Alaric, *Scenes From A Bourgeois Life* (London, 1949).

Keenleyside, Hugh L., *Hammer the Golden Day* (Toronto, 1981).

Lanctot, Gustave, *The Royal Tour of King George VI and Queen Elizabeth in Canada and the United States* (Toronto, 1964).

Lash, Joseph P., *Eleanor and Franklin* (New York, 1971).

Lash, Joseph P., *Love, Eleanor* (New York, 1982).

Manchester, William, *The Glory and the Dream* (Boston, 1974).

Martin, Paul, *A Very Public Life* (Ottawa, 1983).

Morgan, Ted, *FDR* (New York, 1985).

Mortimer, Penelope, *Queen Elizabeth: A Portrait of the Queen Mother* (London, 1986).

Nicolson, Harold, *Diaries, 1930-1964*, edited by Stanley Olson (London, 1980).

Raddall, Thomas H., *Halifax: Warden of the North* (Toronto, 1971).

Roosevelt, Eleanor, *This I Remember* (New York, 1949).

Roosevelt, Elliott, and James Brough, *A Rendezvous With Destiny* (New York, 1975).

Scott, F.R., A.J.M. Smith, (eds.), *The Blasted Pine* (Toronto, 1967).
Sinclair, David, *Two Georges* (London, 1988).
Stacey, C.P., *A Very Double Life* (Toronto, 1977).
Thomas, Gordon, *Voyage of the Damned*, (New York, 1974).
Thompson, John Herd with Allen Seager, *Canada 1922-1939: Decades of Discord* (Toronto, 1985).
Wheeler-Bennett, John, *King George VI* (London, 1958).
Wheeler-Bennett, John, *Special Relationships*
Willis-O'Connor, H., Madge Macbeth, *Inside Government House* (Toronto, 1954).

ARTICLES

Zolf, Larry, "I want my redtime Tory", *Weekend Magazine*, 3rd April 1976, p. 3.

UNPUBLISHED MATERIALS

Constable James Coughlin (RCMP Centennial Museum)
Addie Gilks memoir of the royal visit to Doaktown
William Lyon Mackenzie King Diaries (National Archives)
Moose Jaw Royal Visit Booklet
Pallie Pascoe memoir of the Royal Tour
Shuldham Redfern, letter to Victoria Wilcox
Deane Russell, "Rule By the Hands of the Clock"
Villiers memoir of the royal visit to Savona
Victoria Wilcox, "Prime Minister and Governor General: Mackenzie King and Lord Tweedsmuir, 1935-1940"

NEWSPAPERS AND PERIODICALS

Guelph Beacon-Herald	*Le Canada*	*New York World-Telegram*
The Globe and Mail	*Le Devoir*	Oxford (Ontario) *Journal*
Kamloops Sentinel	*Le Soleil*	*Toronto Daily Star*
L'Actualité	*Maple Ridge Gazette*	*Vancouver Sun*
La Presse	*New York Times*	

RADIO MATERIALS

CBC Radio Archives

INTERVIEWS AND PRIVATE LETTERS

Thérèse Belanger	Bresn LaPierre	Joyce Putnam
Lorraine Bradley	Kenneth Lefebvre	Carl Stone
Mathilde Ganzini	Edmund Legere, Sr.	Mel Stover, letter
Jean Louis Gouin	Roy Leonard	Margaret (Murray) Taylor
Laurent Hardy	Bill Macartney	T.R. Yaeger
Shirley Jay	Jacques P. Michaud	

Index